T0211284

Lecture Notes
in Business Information Processing   **298**

Series Editors

Wil M.P. van der Aalst
  Eindhoven Technical University, Eindhoven, The Netherlands
John Mylopoulos
  University of Trento, Trento, Italy
Michael Rosemann
  Queensland University of Technology, Brisbane, QLD, Australia
Michael J. Shaw
  University of Illinois, Urbana-Champaign, IL, USA
Clemens Szyperski
  Microsoft Research, Redmond, WA, USA

More information about this series at http://www.springer.com/series/7911

Robert Pergl · Russell Lock
Eduard Babkin · Martin Molhanec (Eds.)

Enterprise and Organizational Modeling and Simulation

13th International Workshop, EOMAS 2017, Held at CAiSE 2017
Essen, Germany, June 12–13, 2017
Selected Papers

 Springer

Editors
Robert Pergl (iD)
Czech Technical University in Prague
Prague
Czech Republic

Russell Lock (iD)
Loughborough University
Loughborough
UK

Eduard Babkin (iD)
Higher School of Economics
National Research University
Nizhny Novgorod
Russia

Martin Molhanec (iD)
Czech Technical University in Prague
Prague
Czech Republic

ISSN 1865-1348   ISSN 1865-1356 (electronic)
Lecture Notes in Business Information Processing
ISBN 978-3-319-68184-9   ISBN 978-3-319-68185-6 (eBook)
DOI 10.1007/978-3-319-68185-6

Library of Congress Control Number: 2017955232

Printed on acid-free paper

This Springer imprint is published by Springer Nature
The registered company is Springer International Publishing AG
The registered company address is: Gewerbestrasse 11, 6330 Cham, Switzerland

Preface

Enterprises are sometimes called "socio-technical systems." They are heterogenous systems consisting of humans, material and immaterial artefacts working together. Their development is arguably the greatest challenge of contemporary enterprise. We can observe attempts to make technical systems become more "human" and humans more technical (i.e., structured and predictable). These factors come alongside fast technical development and evolving views of social sciences as well as neurological and cognitive disciplines. Enterprise engineering is thus arguably the broadest contemporary discipline for both academics and industry of human endeavour. This makes enterprise engineering a demanding discipline to master.

The International Workshop on Enterprise and Organizational Modeling and Simulation (EOMAS) was founded with the intention of helping enterprise engineers with their challenging job. Similarly to other engineering disciplines, modeling and simulation have proven to be a highly helpful tool. The EOMAS community has been working hard on various topics spanning from formalisms and methods through software and tooling up to coordination and organizational domains to put together pieces resulting in effective ways of modeling and simulation.

This year, we met for the 13th anniversary in Essen, Germany, during June 12–13, as a traditional workshop of CAiSE. Out of 26 submitted papers, 12 were accepted for publication as full papers and for oral presentation, each paper carefully selected, reviewed, and revised.

This year, we also had two novel formats: a hands-on session on the OpenPonk conceptual modeling platform and "show us your project" session for sharing interesting projects and work in progress of the participants.

I would like to cordially thank the whole EOMAS community, namely, the authors, the Program Committee, and the chairs for their commitment, enthusiasm, and diligent work, which resulted in a high-quality event that was satisfying both professionally and personally. I am looking forward to the next, 14th edition, which is already being prepared with the same goal: to make it even better!

June 2017   Robert Pergl

Organization

EOMAS 2017 was organized by the Department of Software Engineering, Czech Technical University in Prague, in cooperation with CAISE 2017 and CIAO! Enterprise Engineering Network.

Executive Committee

General Chair

Robert Pergl   Czech Technical University in Prague, Czech Republic

Program Chairs

Russell Lock   Loughborough University, UK
Eduard Babkin   National Research University – Higher School of Economics, Russia
Martin Molhanec   Czech Technical University in Prague, Czech Republic

Program Committee

D. Aveiro
E. Babkin
J. Barjis
A. Bobkowska
M. Boufaida
P. de Bruyn
S. Colucci
F. Donini
S. Fosso Wamba
S. Guerreiro
F. Hunka
P. Kroha

R. Lock
P. Malyzhenkov
V. Merunka
M. Molhanec
M. Ntaliani
J. Pavlek
R. Pergl
S. Ramaswamy
V. Romanov
G. Rossi
A. Rutle
S. van Kervel

Sponsoring Institutions

Czech Technical University in Prague, Czech Republic
AIS-SIGMAS
CIAO! Enterprise Engineering Network

Contents

Enterprise Engineering

Formal Methods

Simulation of Alliance Networks Composition in Knowledge Economy

Daria Novototskih$^{(\boxtimes)}$ and Victor Romanov

Department of Informatics, Russian Plekhanov University,
117997 Moscow, Russia
dnovototskih@mail.com, victorromanovl@gmail.com

Abstract. Knowledge generation and diffusion in the modern digital economy as well as innovation process implying novelty technologies, products and services promotion on the market are considered. Production function included R&D or knowledge term regarded as moving force in the self-organizing process of network alliances composition. The model of the networks alliances composition based on the knowledge profile of the firms and measures their similarity or dissimilarity and quadratic programming with binary variables is proposed. Results of the modeling with genetic programming algorithm for partner selection are presented. In paper, we used quadratic methods of programming method as possible way for partner selection. Genetic algorithm and multi-valued logic (Lukasiewicz logic) were applied for these aims. The results of genetic algorithm are discussed in conclusion as possible way for including increment of production function due to new partner's attraction.

Keywords: Alliance network · Simulation · Partner selection · Algorithms · Production function increment

1 Introduction

Modern economy is increasingly based on knowledge and information. Knowledge is now recognized as the driver of productivity and economic growth, leading to a new focus on the role of information, technology and learning in economic performance. The term "knowledge-based economy" stems from this fuller recognition of the place of knowledge and technology in modern economy. The knowledge-based economy is reflected in "new growth theory" term. The growing codification of knowledge and its transmission through communications and computer networks has led to the emerging "information society". The importance of knowledge and technology diffusion requires better understanding of knowledge networks and "national innovation systems".

"Knowledge-based economy" is economy that directly based on the creation, distribution and application of knowledge and information. Although knowledge has long been an important factor in economic growth, economists are now exploring ways to incorporate more directly knowledge and technology in their theories and models. "New growth theory" reflects the attempt to understand the role of knowledge and technology in driving productivity and economic growth [1].

© Springer International Publishing AG 2017
R. Pergl et al. (Eds.): EOMAS 2017, LNBIP 298, pp. 3–19, 2017.
DOI: 10.1007/978-3-319-68185-6_1

In such conditions, the sense of production function definition is changing. Incorporating knowledge into standard economic production functions is not an easy task, as this factor defies some fundamental economic principles, such as scarcity.

The most significant increment of production function is determined by innovation process and novelty of the production. An innovation process is very complex one it consists from several stages and at each stage it demands large amount of energy and different resources from innovator that is from authors, startups or small or medium enterprises (SME). Innovation begins with new scientific research, progresses sequentially through stages of product development, production and marketing, and terminates with the successful sale of new products, processes and services. It is recognized now that ideas for innovation can stem from many sources, including new manufacturing capabilities and recognition of market needs. Innovation can assume many forms, including incremental improvements to existing products, applications of technology to new markets and uses of new technology to serve an existing market [2].

Inter organizational alliances thus accord advantages to startups that are usually associated with the privilege of advanced age, including access to strategic and operational knowhow, possession of stable exchange relationships and innovative capabilities, external endorsement of its operations and the perceived quality and reliability of its products and services among potential customers, suppliers, employees, collaborators and investors.

The remainder of this paper is organized as follows. Section 2 describes the main components of knowledge economy; the problems of partner's selection are described in Sect. 3. Section 4 explains criteria of partner selection and models. Section 5 presents of application of multi-valued logic. Finally, we present our performance results, related work and conclusion.

2 The Main Components of Knowledge Economy

2.1 Knowledge Transfer and Dissemination

The knowledge-based economy places great importance on the diffusion and use of information and knowledge as well as its creation. Strategic know-how and competence are being developed interactively and shared within sub-groups and networks, where know-who is significant. The economy becomes a hierarchy of networks, driven by the acceleration in the rate of change and the rate of learning. What is created is a network society, where the opportunity and capability to get access to and join knowledge- and learning-intensive relations determines the socio-economic position of individuals.

Knowledge is increasingly being codified and transmitted through computer and communications networks in the emerging information society. Also required is tacit knowledge, including the skills to use and adapt codified knowledge. Government policies will need more stress on enhancing the knowledge distribution power of the economy through collaborative networks and the diffusion of technology and providing the enabling conditions for organizational change at the firm level to maximize the benefits of technology for productivity.

The science system, essentially public research laboratories and institutes of higher education, carries out key functions in the knowledge-based economy, including knowledge production, transmission and transfer. Traditional production functions focus on labor, capital, materials and energy; knowledge and technology are external influences on production. Now analytical approaches are being developed so that knowledge can be included more directly in production functions. Investments in knowledge can increase the productive capacity of the other factors of production as well as transform them into new products and processes. In addition, since these knowledge investments are characterized by increasing (rather than decreasing) returns, they are the key to long-term economic growth.

The network characteristic of the knowledge-based economy has emerged with changes to the linear model of innovation. The traditional theory held that innovation is a process of discovery which proceeds via a fixed and linear sequence of phases. Innovation requires considerable communication among different actors – firms, laboratories, academic institutions – as well as feedback between science, product development, manufacturing, which are presented on Fig. 1.

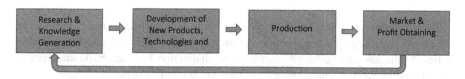

Fig. 1. The main stages of knowledge movement from generation to market

In the knowledge-based economy, firms search for linkages to promote inter-firm interactive communication and for outside partners and networks to provide complementary assets. These relationships help firms to spread the costs and risk associated with innovation among a greater number of organizations, to gain access to new research results, to acquire key technological components of a new product or process, and to share assets in manufacturing, marketing and distribution. As they develop new products and processes, firms determine which activities they will undertake individually, in collaboration with other firms, in collaboration with universities or research institutions, and with the support of government.

All this activity is frequently lumped together as research and development, but it represents premarket activity by a variety of agents, including public scientific institutions, universities, lone inventors, and firms. It is only when stage production is reached, at the point where there is a marketable product or new process, that innovation is achieved. This phase of commercialization triggers the start of another chain of events, broadly characterized as diffusion, which covers the widespread adoption of the new product or process by the market. It is also vital to understand that there is feedback between the various stages: innovation is rarely a linear progression through the stages shown. There is also feedback between the diffusion and innovation stages. As consumers, or other firms, start using the innovations, they often adapt or improve them, or relay information on how to do so back to the innovating firms.

2.2   Innovation and Novelty Production Implementation

Innovation is thus the result of numerous interactions by a community of actors and institutions, which together form what are termed national innovation systems. Increasingly, these innovations systems are extending beyond national boundaries to become international. They consist of the flows and relationships which exist among industry, government and academia in the development of science and technology. The interactions within this system influence the innovative performance of firms and economies. In the knowledge-based economy, the science system contributes to the key functions of:

- knowledge production – developing and providing new knowledge;
- knowledge transmission – educating and developing human resources;
- knowledge transfer – disseminating knowledge and providing inputs to problem solving.

The science system has traditionally been considered as the primary producer of new knowledge, largely through basic research at universities and government laboratories. In the knowledge-based economy, the distinction between basic and applied research and between science and technology has become somewhat blurred.

There exists essential distinction between an innovation from an invention or discovery. An invention or discovery enhances the stock of knowledge, but it does not instantaneously arrive in the market place as a full-fledged novel product or process. Innovation occurs at the point of bringing to the commercial market new products and processes arising from applications of both existing and new knowledge.

We have already seen that there are two main types of innovation: process innovation, the introduction of new techniques for production, and product innovation, the offer for sale of a new type or design of a good or service product. The essential effect of process innovation is one of cost reduction in production. If the market is perfectly competitive, all knowledge about production is assumed to be known by all firms. Hence, as soon as the process innovation occurs we assume that all firms immediately start to use it. In such a case, there is no financial incentive to undertake R&D targeted toward creating the process innovation. This means that there are no economic profits to reward the innovator.

The innovator could produce and sell the good for a rising price and for this reason get additional profit. Even if the innovator did not want to produce all the market demand, in principle it could license its process innovation to all other firms and receive royalties equal to these profits. Introducing patents certainly increases the financial incentive to innovate.

If the product has a broader and more favorable set of characteristics than an earlier variety, then, even with a higher price, it can still be good value for money. Further analysis of these alternative situations is given below. If the product innovation creates a new variety or improves the quality of an existing product, then drawing a new demand curve is not the best way to conceptualize the change. Suppose the market is imperfectly competitive before this product innovation, hence the firm already faces a downward-sloping demand curve.

By introducing a new product, the firm aims to achieve an outward shift and steeper slope to the demand for its product (analogous to the effect of advertising, increasing product loyalty to the firm). Note that even though consumers are charged a higher price, they buy more and have more consumer surplus. Of course, over time the market may become more competitive as more product innovation occurs and this may reduce prices. A general way of describing this situation is to say that consumers benefit from the increase in product variety and/or the rise in the quality of the products on offer. Even if a new product is more expensive than existing ones, if it has exactly the right set of characteristics to match the customers' tastes, they may be happier to buy this item. If the product has a broader and more favorable set of characteristics than an earlier variety, then, even with a higher price, it can still be good value for money.

2.3 Knowledge Capital Production Function

Traditional *"production functions"* focus on labor, capital, materials and energy; knowledge and technology are external influences on production. Now analytical approaches are being developed so that knowledge can be included more directly in production functions. Investments in knowledge can increase the productive capacity of the other factors of production as well as transform them into new products and processes. And since these knowledge investments are characterized by increasing (rather than decreasing) returns, they are the key to long-term economic growth.

Some kinds of knowledge can be easily reproduced and distributed at low cost to a broad set of users, which tends to undermine relationships or investing substantial resources in the codification and transformation into information private ownership. Investment in knowledge is a primary source of productivity growth. Firms invest in R&D and related activities to develop and introduce process and product innovations that enhance their productivity.

Knowledge capital is considered to by innovation output measured as the percentage of innovation sales to total sales. We will then try to establish the existence of a relationship between innovation and productivity by applying econometric methods that correct for estimation problems inherent to the statistical features of the data. The theoretical framework for the study is Codd-Douglas production function with two variables expressed as [3]:

$$Q_{jt} = Ae^{\alpha t}X^{\beta}K^{\gamma}e^{jt} \tag{1}$$

Where Q_{it} rate of productivity of the firm j at moment t. X is a vector of input variable and K is research and development (R&D). The parameter α is a measure of the rate of disembodied technical change, β is the elasticity of production about a vector of standard inputs such as labor, human capital, physical capital, and so forth, γ is the elasticity of production with respect to change R&D, ε is the error term, and A is a constant measuring firm efficiency. It is quite common to express the above relation in logarithmically or the first difference of the variable.

The focus is whether innovation contributes to the explanation of differences in productivity growth among firms, when controlling for physical capital, human capital, firm size, types of output and other characteristic factors relevant to the firm's performance. It should be noted that *a priori* we expect a positive relationship between innovation and productivity growth. Hence, the key variables in this study are value added per employee, the share in the firm's total sales that is related to innovative products partly or totally developed by the firm, innovation investment as a share of total sales, human capital, a proxy for physical capital and firm size defined by employment.

In the paper [4] the authors assume the regional of firms' production function including knowledge capital as an input follows:

$$Y_{jt} = A(K_{jt}) K_{jt}^{\alpha_K} L_{jt}^{\alpha_L} e^{u_j + v_j + \varepsilon_{jt}} \tag{2}$$

where j represents the cross-section (the region or firm) and t the period Y_{jt} indicates the output. $A()$ is the function of knowledge capital KN_{jt}, K_{jt} and L_{jt} represent the capital stock and labour input at time t in region j respectively, α_K and α_L represent the coefficients of elasticity and labour input at the provincial level, respectively, u_i and v_i indicate the cross-section and time dimension on economic growth, ε_{it} is random error term.

In the paper [5] the authors see the first goal of the paper thus to relax the assumptions on the R&D process that are at the center of the knowledge capital model. They are recognizing the uncertainties in the R&D process in the form of shocks to productivity. They model the interactions between current and past investments in knowledge in a flexible fashion. This allows to better assess the impact of the investment in knowledge on the productivity of firms. A firm carries out two types of investments, one in physical capital and another in knowledge through R&D expenditures. The investment decisions are made in a discrete time setting with the goal of maximizing the expected net present value of future cash flows. The firm has the Cobb-Douglas production function:

$$y_{jt} = \beta_0 + \beta_l l_{jt} + \beta_k k_{jt} + \omega_{jt} + \varepsilon_{jt}, \tag{3}$$

where y_{jt} is the log of output of firm j in period t, l_{jt} the log of labor, and k_{jt} the log of capital. Capital is the only fixed (or "dynamic") input among the conventional factors of production, and accumulates according to

$$K_{jt} = (1 - \delta) K_{jt-1} + I_{jt-1} \tag{4}$$

This law of motion implies that investment I_{jt-1} chosen in period $t - 1$ becomes productive in period t.

The productivity of firm j in period t is ω_{jt} as "unobserved productivity" since it is unobserved from the point of view of the econometrician (but known to the firm). Productivity is presumably highly correlated over time and perhaps also across firms. In contrast, ε_{jt} is a mean zero random shock that is uncorrelated over time and across firms. The firm does not know the value of ε_{jt} at the time it makes its decisions for period t.

3   The Problem of Selecting Partners and Key Stages of the Process

By attracting new partners or to join the alliance company launches a new product, improves the competitive quality of the existing product, thereby increasing profits, attracting new technologies, new knowledge and competencies, reduce costs.

Partner selection is one of the most critical alliance capabilities in the establishment of alliances. The right choice of partner has been identified in numerous studies as a precondition for alliance success. Designing a partner selection process including steps, criteria, tools and success factors, appears to be vital for alliance success. The application of analytic and systematic methods in partner selection could increase the success rate of partnerships. This study suggests that partner selection process is an important alliance capability and has a significant influence on alliance performance.

Firms undertake strategic alliances for many reasons: to enhance their productive capacities, to reduce uncertainties in their internal structures and external environments, to acquire competitive advantages that enables them to increase profits, or to gain future business opportunities that will allow them to command higher market values for their outputs. Partners choose a specific alliance form not only to achieve greater control, but also for more operational flexibility and realization of market potential. The main steps in partner selection process are listed on Fig. 2.

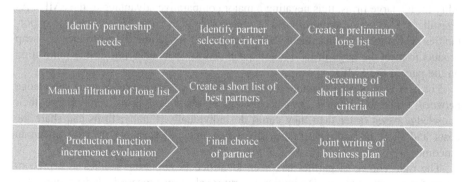

Fig. 2. The main steps in partner selection process

Their expectation is that flexibility will result from reaching out for new skills, knowledge, and markets through shared investment risks. The generic needs of firms seeking alliance as cash, scale, skills, access, or their combinations, then by their strategic intentions. A decision to cooperate is not a responsive action, but is fundamentally a strategic intent, which aims at improving the future circumstances for each individual firm and their partnership as a whole [6].

The Main Motives to Enter a Strategic Alliance:

- Knowledge exchange
- Gaining access to new technology, and converging technology
- Learning & internalization of tacit, collective and embedded skills
- Cost sharing, pooling of resources
- Developing products, technologies, resources
- Complementarity of goods and services to markets.

It is only when stage is reached, where there is a marketable product or new process, that innovation is achieved. This phase of commercialization triggers the start of another chain of events, broadly characterized as diffusion, which covers the widespread adoption of the new product or process by the market. It is also vital to understand that there is feedback between the various stages: innovation is rarely a linear progression through the stages shown. There is also feedback between the diffusion and innovation stages.

What is concerning SMEs, within their limited resources, SMEs must find ways to achieve production economies of scale, to market their products effectively, and to provide satisfactory support services. Collaborating with other organizations is one method. SMEs are flexible and more innovative in new areas, but can lack resources and capabilities. But strong ties with larger firms can limit opportunities and alternatives for SMEs, and innovative SMEs are more likely to make external networks with other SMEs or institutions such as universities and private research establishments.

Based on these modes, we will in this research a number of collaboration models using various combinations of actors, their roles, and the strength of their ties. While alliances with large firms have often benefited SMEs, they can also oblige SMEs to share their technological competence with the large firms, leading to increased flexibility for the large firms, thus negating a major comparative advantage of the SMEs. As a result, as SMEs gain opportunities to collaborate with large firms, they lose opportunities to compete against them. SMEs may also be required to produce a cheap product to meet the large firms' lowest specifications, thus delaying further innovation on the part of the SMEs.

For us it is important to underline that, alliances foster the exchange of knowledge between firms: by joining their technological resources, firms can enlarge their knowledge bases faster than they could do individually. Finally, firms can share the costs and risks of a project, especially when this is expensive or with uncertain outcome.

The right choice of partner has been identified in numerous studies as a precondition for alliance success. Designing a partner selection process including steps, criteria, tools and success factors, appears to be vital for alliance success. The application of analytic and systematic methods in partner selection could increase the success rate of partnerships.

Based on these modes, we can design a number of collaboration models using various combinations of actors, their roles, and the strength of their ties: the dominant models involving SMEs. At the exploration stage, SMEs are most likely to use external partnerships so they can concentrate on retaining high levels of internal competence in a limited number of technology areas though they show a preference for networking with public research institutes and universities because of the fear of giving away their technology to competitors. But at the exploitation stage, SMEs attempt to create value by entering supplier–customer relations with large firms, outsourcing agreements or strategic alliances with other SMEs [7].

While alliances with large firms have often benefited SMEs, they can also oblige SMEs to share their technological competence with the large firms, leading to increased flexibility for the large firms, thus negating a major comparative advantage of the SMEs. Thus, as SMEs gain opportunities to collaborate with large firms, they lose opportunities to compete against them. SMEs may also be required to produce a cheap product to meet the large firms' lowest specifications, thus delaying further innovation on the part of the SMEs.

4   Partners Selection Criteria, Strategy and Optimization Model

Model and multi-objective genetic algorithm for member selection of R&D teams was described in paper [8]. We have used the idea and have modified it for our aims.

We can differ enterprises' profile or by specification (nomenclature) of product produced or by set of patent used in the production process per the International Classification of Patents (ICP) [9]. The set of patents, used in the production process is forming knowledge base of the enterprise and its knowledge profile. So, we can assume that every firm F_j, $j = 1, 2 \dots N$ may be associated with a vector Z_j consisting of M components $(z_{j1}, z_{j2}, \dots z_{jM})$ (each of which represents role of the knowledge or patent category (technological classes) i, $i = 1, 2, \dots M$ in the production function. As we explain below, these vectors can in turn be associated with a metric knowledge space in which the collaborations occur. Thus, we define the knowledge profile of a firm in the knowledge space as:

$$Z_j = \left(z_{j1}, z_{j2}, \dots, z_{lM}\right), j, r = \{1, 2, \dots N\}; i = \{1, 2, \dots M\} \qquad (5)$$

In order to evaluate difference between two enterprises' profiles in the knowledge space we use the Euclidean metric:

$$d_{jr} = |Z_j - Z_r| = \sqrt{\sum_{i=1}^{M} \left(z_{ji} - z_{ri}\right)^2} = \sqrt{\sum_{i=1}^{M} \left(\Delta_{jri}\right)^2} \qquad (6)$$

Consider formal description of the problem of alliance team formation We will define an alliance as network or a set of nodes, (the firms), and links between them. We assume that algorithm of partner's selection for decision making about joining the pair of the firms uses the Δ_{jri} value. Let us accept expression (3) as starting formula for production function definition. If every patent technological class add some value, the products output we will modify production function as:

$$y_j = \beta_0 + \beta_l l_j + \beta_k k_j + \sum_i^M \lambda_i \xi_{ji}, \ where \ 0 \leq \lambda_i \leq 1, \xi_{ji} = ln \ z_{ji} \qquad (7)$$

$y_{jt} = \beta_0 + \beta_l l_{jt} + \beta_k k_{jt} + \omega_{jt} + \varepsilon_{jt} + \sum_i^M \lambda_i \xi_{jit}$ – production function of the firm F_j at moment t.

$y_{rt+1} = \beta_0 + \beta_l l_{rt+1} + \beta_k k_{rt+1} + \omega_{rt+1} + \varepsilon_{rt+1} + \sum_i^M \lambda_i \xi_{rit+1}$ production function of the firm F_j at moment t + 1 after substitution firm F_r patent technological class values. Then, if

$$\beta_l l_{jt} = \beta_l l_{rt+1}, \beta_k k_{jt} = \beta_k k_{rt+1}, \omega_{jt} = \omega_{rt+1}, \varepsilon_{jt} = \varepsilon_{rt+1}, \qquad (8)$$

we get:

$$y_{rt+1} - y_{jt} = \Delta y_{jrt} = \sum_i^M \lambda_i \xi_{rit+1} - \sum_i^M \lambda_i \xi_{jit} = \sum_i^M \lambda_i \left(\xi_{rit+1} - \xi_{jit} \right)$$
$$= \sum_i^M \lambda_i \left(\Delta \xi_{jri} \right) \qquad (9)$$

We accept this value as measure of utility of the (F_j, F_r) partners pair.

Suppose that including one additional partner F_j into alliance costs for logistics and communication v_i unit and exist restriction of total Q units for including expense. The decision maker selects members from N candidate members to form a team so that to satisfy the constraints: $\sum_r^M v_r^M x_r \leq Q$ and at the same time to ensure maximum of total production function increment due to new partners attraction. Let us consider the task more formally.

For each partners pair (F_j, F_r); $r, j = 1, 2, ..., N$.

Then we can define Ψ_{ij} just as

$$\psi_{jr} = \Delta y_{jr}^M \qquad (10)$$

We suppose that greater ψ_{jr} is, and then the new candidate member utility is higher. According to the overall values of alliance productions, function increment the following optimization model is built to select the most preferred members from N alternatives, satisfying constraints:

Maximize $\Phi = \sum_j^N \sum_r^N {}_{r \neq j} \psi_{jr} x_j x_r$ subject to $\sum_r^M v_r^M x_r \leq Q$, where $x_j, x_r \in \{0, 1\}$, $j, r = (1, 2, ..., N)$.

The described model was realized by genetic algorithm. Below is presented the algorithm of the program on Python language. Total algorithm-schema contains 4 steps.

This model is a 0-1 quadratic programming problem. It is presented step-by-step as follows:

Step 1 Initializing. Input the necessary parameters which contain the number of genetic generations, population size, crossover and mutation probability, and generate the initial parent population. Then calculate the corresponding fitness values of the individuals.

Step 2 Selecting, crossover and mutating. Apply binary tournament selection strategy to the current population, and generate the offspring population with the predetermined crossover and mutation probabilities.

Step 3 Combination. Combine initial population and current, and select population size optimal individuals to generate the next population, per the fitness values of the individual in the frontiers.

Step 4 Stopping. If number of genetic generations is reached, return the individuals (solutions) in population of the next generation and their corresponding objective values as the Pareto-(approximate) optimal solutions and Pareto-(approximate) optimal fronts.

Otherwise, go to **Step 2.**

It is well-known that there exists a lot of software packages and programs for genetic programming.

The specific of our approach is that this program is assumed a part of program complex that including programs for production function increment estimate when new partners are added. For convenience, we decided to make small simple unit for execution of this project.

The program contains the next components:

(a) Input data entering.

Input data incudes:

1. Initial graph of main point connection with potential partners
2. Increments of production function data for every partner in the initial graph
3. Values of costs connected with log
4. Selection for attentional partner's incorporation into the alliance

The input interface is presented on Fig. 3:

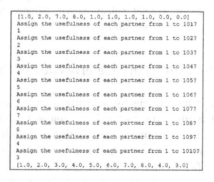

Fig. 3. Interface of input data entering

(b) The algorithm of data processing includes initial population creation and testing it for utility value computing, initial population modification by application mutation of components and crossover. The next population estimation by utility calculating. Selection and including the best string in population. And repeating the cycle for the selection the best population.

(c) The resulting data are represented as graph connecting main point with partner selected total estimate of utility of partners' combination selection and expenses.

Different representations of the partner selection are presented on Fig. 4:

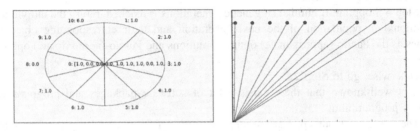

Fig. 4. Graph of pairs selection by algorithm

The correction of authorism is checked on test data. The program is selecting the best partners satisfying constraints.

The research presents a new method to solve the alliance formation problem using the individual and collaborative information. A 0-1 programming model is built to select optimum set of members. The derived solution set of the model can be used to support the decision of the alliance formation. The proposed method considers not only the individual information of members but also the collaborative information between members. It reflects comprehensive information of candidate members in member selection. It also helps to reduce uncertainty regarding cooperation among the potential members. The model can be embedded in the decision support system and process the complex decision problem of partner selection for alliance teams using both the individual and the collaborative information.

5   Partner Selection with Many Heterogeneous Criteria

Unfortunately, not always the criteria for selecting partners are homogeneous. The criteria can be measured in different scales and represented by different types of data. In this case, it is advisable to use, scaling, normalization and multi-valued logic [10].

Let D be set of selection variants and there is a set of criteria D → R, R - the set of real numbers. Estimate $\varphi_i(x)$ of variant x on the criterion φ_i, we will denote $x_{(i)}$, and a set of estimates of the same variant according to different criteria $\tilde{x} = (x_{(1)}, \ldots, x_{(k)})$ will be called the vector estimation of variant x. Vector evaluations of variants y, z, we denote respectively as $\tilde{y}, \tilde{z}$.

Record $\tilde{x} \geq \tilde{y}$ means that $x_{(1)} \geq y_{(1)}, \cdots, x_{(k)} \geq y_{(k)}$, and the entry $\tilde{x} > \tilde{y}$ - that $\tilde{x} \geq \tilde{y}$ and $\tilde{x} \neq \tilde{y}$. We say that R is represented by a set of criteria $\varphi_1, \ldots, \varphi_k$, is a partial order if and only if $xRy \equiv \tilde{x} > \tilde{y}$.

Examples of Selection Functions:

1. Scalar optimization mechanism - the best choice for a given scalar quality criterion $\varphi(x)$ variant $x \in X$:
   $$C_0(x) = \{x \in X | x = \arg\max \varphi(x)\}.$$
2. Conditionally - extreme gear - selection, defined scheme of mathematical programming with the objective function $f_0(x)$ and restrictions $f_i(x)$, $i = 1, \ldots, m$:
   $$C_{M\Pi}(x) = \{x \in X | x = \arg[\max f_0(x), f_i(x) \leq 0, i = 1, \ldots, k].\}$$
3. Optimization mechanism of dominance, defined by a binary relation R:
   $$C_R(x) = \{x \in X | \forall y \in X, xRy\}.$$
4. The locking mechanism: choice non-improvable by R elements x:
   $$C_{\bar{R}}(x) = \{x \in X | \forall y \in X, y \bar{R} x\}.$$
5. The mechanism of restrictions defined by a binary relation R and a given element u $\in$ G and choice of $x \in X$, better by R than $u \in G$:
   $$C_u(x) = \{x \in X | xRu\}.$$
6. Selection based on Pareto criterion $C^\pi(x)$ can be regarded selection rule as:
   $$C^\pi(x) = \{x \in X | \neg(\exists y \in X)(\tilde{y} > \tilde{x})\} \text{ or as relation:}$$

$$x R^\pi y \equiv (\forall i)(\varphi i(x) \geq \varphi i(y)) \wedge (\exists i)(\varphi i(x) > \varphi i(y)), (i = 1, \ldots k).$$

The estimation of variant x_j, $j = 1, 2, \ldots n$ according criterion φ_i, $i = 1, \ldots, k$ designate $x_{ij} = \varphi_i(x_j)$. Let us designate this matrix Φ. Let C_i be normalized matrix of estimates comparison variants pairs (x_j, x_l) $j, l = 1, 2, \ldots n$ under specific criterion i. Depending on the problem formulation, the elements of the matrix of pairwise comparisons c_{jl} and c_{lj} and must meet certain normalization relation. If the options are equivalent (as well as if the options are incomparable), we denote them $x_i \sim x_j$. If the version x_j is preferable than x_l, $x_j \succ x_l$, the condition $c_{jl} > c_{lj}$ it should be satisfied. Consider the different possible normalization ways.

1. Simple normalization.
$$\forall j, l, j \neq l, \quad c_{jl} = \begin{cases} 1; & x_j \succ x_l \\ 0; & x_j \prec x_l \\ 0,5; & x_j \sim x_l. \end{cases}$$
2. Tournament normalization
   $$\forall j, l, \ c_{jl} \geq 0, \quad c_{jl} + c_{lj} = N, \text{ where}$$
   c_{jl} – points score, N – Total games number
3. Skew-normalization
   $$\forall j, l, \quad c_{jl} + c_{lj} = 0$$
4. Probabilistic normalization
   $$\forall j, l, \ 0 \leq c_{jl} \leq 1, \quad c_{jl} + c_{lj} = 1, \quad \sum_l c_{jl} = 1$$
5. Signature normalization
$$c_{jl} = \begin{cases} 1; & x_j \succ x_l \\ 0; & x_j \sim x_l \\ -1; & x_j \prec x_l. \end{cases}$$

For example, consider five options to choose partners, in the presence of the four criteria (Table 1):

Table 1. Criteria matrix Φ

Variants	Criteria			
	φ_1	φ_2	φ_3	φ_4
x_1	133	600	999	90
x_2	125	300	940	60
x_3	166	600	999	90
x_4	30	200	998	70
x_5	140	400	950	80

In the three-valued logic of Lukasiewicz the following truth table of basic Boolean functions takes place (Table 2).

Table 2. Three-valued truth table for logic of Lukasiewicz

A	B	A∧B	A∨B	¬ A	$J_{-1}(A)$	$J_0(A)$	$J_1(A)$	$A^* = \max(J_1(A), J_0(A))$
1	1	1	1	−1	−1	−1	1	1
1	0	0	1	−1	−1	−1	1	1
1	−1	−1	1	−1	−1	−1	1	1
0	1	0	1	0	−1	1	−1	1
0	0	0	0	0	−1	1	−1	1
0	−1	−1	0	0	−1	1	−1	1
−1	1	−1	1	1	1	−1	−1	−1
−1	0	−1	0	1	1	−1	−1	−1
−1	−1	−1	−1	1	1	−1	−1	−1

The next designation are used at the table:

$$j_{-1}(x) = \begin{cases} 1; & x = -1 \\ -1; & x \neq -1, \end{cases}$$

$$j_0(x) = \begin{cases} 1; & x = 0 \\ -1; & x \neq 0, \end{cases}$$

$$j_1(x) = \begin{cases} 1; & x = 1 \\ -1; & x \neq 1. \end{cases}$$

Let us form the matrices C_i, i = 1, 2, 3, 4 pairwise comparison of options for each criterion $\varphi_i(x)$ and perform a signature normalization:

$C_{jli} = \text{sgn}(\varphi_i(x_j) - \varphi_i(x_1))$, where i – the criterion number, j, 1 – version number. Using the criterion of Pareto selection and the truth table of logical functions in three-valued logic and applying matrices C_i (k = 1, 2, 3, 4) we write (Fig. 5).

	C^1			
0	1	1	1	-1
1	0	-1	1	-1
1	1	0	1	1
-1	-1	-1	0	-1
1	1	-1	1	0

	C^2			
0	1	0	1	1
-1	0	-1	1	-1
0	1	0	1	1
-1	-1	-1	0	-1
-1	1	-1	1	0

	C^3			
0	1	0	1	1
-1	0	-1	-1	-1
0	1	0	1	1
-1	1	-1	0	1
-1	1	-1	-1	0

	C^4			
0	1	0	1	1
-1	0	-1	-1	-1
0	1	0	1	1
-1	1	-1	0	-1
-1	1	-1	1	0

Fig. 5. Pairwise comparison matrices

Pareto-optimal solutions in the form of a logical function of the following form:

$$R_\pi(x_j, x_l) \equiv \bigwedge_{i=1}^{4} (C^{(i)})^* \wedge \bigvee_{i=1}^{4} C^{(i)} \text{ or } R_\pi(x_j, x_l) = R_\pi^1(x_j, x_l) \wedge R_\pi^2(x_j, x_l), \text{ where } R_\pi^1 -$$

conjunction of matrices $(C_i)^*$ and R_π^2 – disjunction of C_i matrices.

$$\text{Then } R_\pi^2 = \begin{matrix} 0 & 1 & 0 & 1 & 1 \\ -1 & 0 & -1 & 1 & -1 \\ 1 & 1 & 0 & 1 & 1 \\ -1 & 1 & -1 & 0 & 1 \\ -1 & 1 & -1 & 1 & 0 \end{matrix}$$

R_π^2, as we have seen, contains the element 1 and only if the variant x_j x_l at least one of the criteria.

Let us apply operator * to the all matrices Ci:

	C^1*			
1	1	-1	1	-1
-1	1	-1	1	-1
1	1	1	1	1
-1	-1	-1	1	-1
1	1	-1	1	1

	C^2*			
1	1	1	1	1
-1	1	-1	1	-1
1	1	1	1	1
-1	-1	-1	1	-1
-1	1	-1	1	1

	C^3*			
1	1	1	1	1
-1	1	-1	-1	-1
1	1	1	1	1
-1	1	-1	1	1
-1	1	-1	-1	1

	C^4*			
1	1	1	1	1
-1	1	-1	-1	-1
1	1	1	1	1
-1	1	-1	1	-1
-1	1	-1	1	1

$$\text{Then } R_\pi^1 = \begin{matrix} 1 & 1 & -1 & 1 & -1 \\ -1 & -1 & 1 & -1 & -1 \\ 1 & 1 & 1 & 1 & 1 \\ -1 & 1 & -1 & 1 & -1 \\ -1 & 1 & -1 & -1 & 1 \end{matrix} \text{ and } R_\pi = R_\pi^1 \wedge R_\pi^2 = \begin{matrix} 0 & 1 & -1 & 1 & -1 \\ -1 & 0 & -1 & -1 & -1 \\ 1 & 1 & 0 & 1 & 1 \\ -1 & -1 & -1 & 0 & -1 \\ -1 & 1 & -1 & -1 & 0 \end{matrix}$$

The matrix R_π^1 has ones if for a given pair x_j, x_l x_j on any of the criteria is not inferior to x_l. So number 3 is the best variant and the graph of preferences have the next view (Fig. 6):

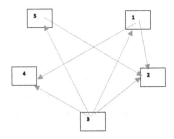

Fig. 6. Variance dominance graph

6 Conclusions

In this article, as far as we know, for the first time we proposed to use as a criterion for the choice of a partner increment of a production function and to determine this task as a task of binary square programming. It is important to note that we tried to consider in an increment of a production function process of receipt of new knowledge by alliance due to joining of new partners.[1]

We have developed only two components from the general program complex – the genetic algorithm for the choice of the best partner and a multi-criteria algorithm of the partner choice based on Lukasiewicz's logic. We plan to develop an algorithm and to enhance it regarding assessment of an increment of a production function, but it will demand validation and verification of model on real examples.

References

1. The Knowledge-Based Economy: Organisation for Economic Co-operation and Development, Paris (1996). https://www.oecd.org/sti/sci-tech/1913021.pdf
2. Chobanova, R. (ed.): Demand for Knowledge in the Process of European Economic Integration. Bulgarian Academy of Sciences (2008). http://www.iki.bas.bg/RePEc/BAS/ecbook/B_demand_for_knowledge.pdf
3. Lööf, H., Heshmati, A.: Knowledge capital and performance heterogeneity: a firm level innovation study. Int. J. Prod. Econ. **76**(1), 61–85 (2002)
4. Fu, X., Zhu, S., Gong, Y.: Knowledge capital, endogenous growth and regional disparities in productivity: multi-level evidences from China (2009). http://publications.aston.ac.uk/18462/
5. Doraszelski, U., Jaumandreu, J.: R&D and Productivity: The Knowledge Capital Model Revisited. Universidad Carlos III, September 2006. http://www.ieb.ub.edu/aplicacio/fitxers/2007/7/Jaumandreu.pdf
6. Strategic Alliances & Models of Collaboration. School of Management, University of Surrey. http://epubs.surrey.ac.uk/1967/1/fulltext.pdf

[1] This research was conducted in the framework of the basic part of the scientific research state task in the field of scientific activity of the Ministry of science and education of the Russian Federation, project no. 2.9577.2017.

7. Twardy, D., Duisters, M.: Partner Selection: A Source of Alliance Success (2009). https://www.zuyd.nl/onderzoek/lectoraten/innovatief-ondernemen/~/media/Files/Onderzoek/Kenniskring%20Innovatief%20Ondernemen/Partner%20Selection%20-%20a%20source%20of%20alliance%20succes%20Duisters.pdf
8. Fan, Z.P., Feng, B., Jiang, Z.Z., Fu, N.: A method for member selection of R&D teams using the individual and collaborative information. https://www.researchgate.net/publication/223445297_A_method_for_member_selection_of_RD_teams_using_the_individual_and_collaborative_information
9. Overview of the U.S. Patent Classification System (USPC). https://www.uspto.gov/sites/default/files/patents/resources/classification/overview.pdf
10. Romanov, V.: Intellectual Information Systems in Economics, Moscow (2003)

A Modified Model of Cooperative Innovation Based on Numerical P Systems - The CI-NP System: An Empirical Study of Shandong, China

Ping Chen and Xiyu Liu[✉]

School of Management Science and Engineering,
Shandong Normal University, Jinan 250014, China
hxscp444@163.com, sdxyliu@163.com

Abstract. Innovative firms attribute a greater role to their financing strategy in explaining their success and they have a different financial make-up for different departments. And different financial make-up reflects different cooperative innovation strategy. Traditional models of cooperative innovation are always streamlined or annular where the relationship of overlapping or inclusion among elements ignored. In this paper, based on the idea of numerical P systems, we modify the traditional model to improve the indivisibility and visualization into the shape of the membrane which is named CI-NP systems. We process the financial data of firms' development and have found the correlation among various elements and express it based on the case of Shandong, China.

Keywords: Cooperative innovation · CI-NP systems · Finance · Numerical P systems

1 Introduction

Innovation is broadly seen as an essential component of competitiveness, embedded in the organizational structures, processes, products, and services within a firm [1]. And the relationship between cooperation and innovation has been observed for many countries. By the combination of cooperation and innovation, they can get the necessary, various sources to create value [2] the impact of cooperation on firms' innovation propensity in emerging economies. Cooperative innovation is regarded as an interesting alternative for a firm that is trying to improve its innovation performance in the market [3]. Meanwhile, a firm must finance its activities, deploy physical and human resources, market its products and services, and coordinate all of these activities [4]. It is as important to understand the supporting role of these elements as it is to investigate the breadth of the cooperative activities in innovation of a firm [5].

There are some studies classify different cooperative innovation on the view of various processes in the business. For example, some studies are carried out to verify market orientation, internal cooperation practice, and process formality on product innovation performance and business performance in product innovation [6]. It is found that market orientation, internal cooperation practice, process formality and product

R. Pergl et al. (Eds.): EOMAS 2017, LNBIP 298, pp. 20–33, 2017.
DOI: 10.1007/978-3-319-68185-6_2

innovation performance have positive effects on the product innovation performance [7]. In maintained that efficient communications and information exchange in the research and development and marketing sector have a positive effect on research and development and cooperate performances and state that communications and information exchange between functional departments, which can draw cooperation between them are necessary for an efficient progression. Because priority is different on various elements to be considered in new product development due to difference in characteristics of marketing function and R&D function meets a high level of new product development resources, new product effect increases [8]. Furthermore, marketing and R&D cooperation improves development capability and has a positive effect on product innovation performance [9]. Many studies have explored the differences in the element affecting the firm probability to establish different types of cooperation. However, elements which influence cooperative innovation sometimes do not clearly define the scope whether it belongs to the internal or the external [10]. It also ignored the correlation among various elements.

For it is now acknowledged as a result of the cooperation between a wide variety of actors both inside and outside the firm [11]. Innovative firms attribute a greater role to their financing strategy in explaining their success and they have a different financial make-up. Financial point of view of the company, including the innovation of the company's cooperation and research institute with financiers, can take advantage of the public and private funds more effectively and improve the innovation and accelerate the commercialization and diffusion process [12]. In this paper, we process the financial data of firms' development, analyze the correlation among different financial inputs and outputs due to both internal- and external-firm heterogeneity. To coordinate complementary assets and activities is important in financial view [13]. It is a sensible way to conceptualize capabilities as the efficiency with which a firm transforms available inputs into outputs in financial view [14]. Meanwhile, based on the idea of Numerical P Systems, we modify the traditional. In the process of financial data, we have found the correlation among various elements, and try to express the modified model based on the case study of Shandong in China.

The financial data used for the present study corresponds to the survey face to 2000 high-tech firms in Shandong Province, China. And the remainder of this paper is organized as follows. In Sect. 2, we review the basic notions of innovation and demonstrate the model we modified based on Numerical P Systems. Section 3 demonstrates the case study and uses the case to visualize the modified model. In Sect. 4, we analyze the data in the case and use it to certify our model. Section 5 concludes.

2 Basic Notions and the Model

A 2013 survey of previous works on innovation found definitions which are more than 40. In an industrial survey of how the software industry defined innovation, the definition given by Crossan and Apaydin was regarded as the most complete [15], and it is said that innovation is production or adoption, assimilation, and exploitation of a value-added novelty in economic and social spheres, and renewal and enlargement of products, services, and markets, and also development of new methods of production and establishment of new management systems. It is a process and also an outcome. For innovation, cooperation becomes more and more important. Several studies have examined some of the necessary and hot cooperative complements to innovation. It is shown that 11 subjects are always the central issues in last 15 years. The study hot spot areas vary in different stages, but the combination of high-frequent key words are denser. Cooperative innovation management discipline represents the tendency from dispersion to fusion. Hot spots are closely related to firm environment at all stages. The study subject from 2000 to 2002 is strategic alliance and innovation, from 2003 to 2005 is alliance and knowledge innovation, from 2006 to 2008 is social network and innovations, and from 2012 to 2014 is dynamic network organization and innovation according the study of bibliometric analysis from SCI in 15 years (2000–2014). There are also other studies of hot spots at different time points [16] and we can get that none of them ignores cooperation and innovation though they have different names at different times.

Many other studies of the hot spot on cooperative innovation mentioned above have been researched where it is found that exploration of knowledge plays an critical part on innovation performance [17]. Firms pay attention not only to the amount of knowledge they can gain from their potential partner but also to the partner's absorptive capacity. The performance of cooperative innovation for firms' development depends on its absorptive capacity of combination [18]. These elements were combined in a static model where cognitive distance between cooperation partners is set exogenously [19]. Under different knowledge regimes, the structure of networks that emerge and how firms perform within the network has been examined when the study combines the innovation networks with endogenous absorptive capacity [20]. For example, there is a traditional structural model like in Fig. 1 in order to identify the effect of different elements based on the previous studies. The structural model has been designed to be streamlined, suggests that the firms' performance of cooperative innovation make a positive effect on the development, except to the streamlined model, for example, as shown in Fig. 2 [21]. However, both of them lack the interaction or overlapping effect among elements for cooperative innovation.

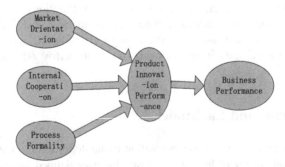

Fig. 1. This is a streamlined model of cooperative innovation which identify the effect of different elements, such as market orientation, internal cooperation practice, and process formality, on the performance of cooperative innovation.

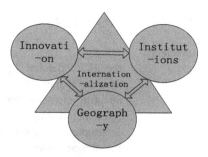

Fig. 2. A annular model where provide a glimpse into the interconnections between the constructs of institutions, innovation, geography, and internationalization.

The integration of the firm into a group has a positive influence on cooperation as it indicates access to a substantial pool of resources, which are complementary to different elements. In order to express the effect of each element on the cooperative innovation more clearly, different from the original model is designed, based on numerical P systems, we improved a new cooperative innovation model, which is called as the CI-NP system (the cooperative innovation based on NP systems).

Membrane computing is a bio-inspired branch of natural computing, abstracting computing models from the structure and functioning of living cells and from the organization of cells in tissues or other higher order structures. In short, in cell-like membrane system (which is usually called P system), multisets of abstract objects are associated with the compartments defined by membranes [22]. Numerical P systems are branches of P systems and motivated by the cell structure and the economic reality. Numerical variables are placed in the regions of a membrane structure [23]. These variables can evolve by means of programs, which are composed of two components, a production and a repartition function. A numerical P system is conceived as a dynamical system.

Formally, the form of numerical P systems is considered as follows:

$$\Pi = (m, H, \mu, (Var_1, Pr_1, Var_1(0)), \ldots, (Var_m, Pr_m, Var_m(0))) \qquad (1)$$

Where $m \geq 1$ is the number of membranes used in the system (also called the degree of $\prod$), H is an alphabet with m membranes, labeled in a one-to-one manner with the elements of H, Var_i is the set of variables from compartment i, Pr_i is the set of programs from compartment i of μ, $1 \leq i \leq m$ (all sets Var_i, Pr_i, $1 \leq i \leq m$, are finite).

Regarding firm development as the cell life, what the element does influence the performance of cooperative innovation for firms. So, we put forward the modified model which is called cooperative innovation numerical P systems and its abbreviation is CI-NP systems. Based on NP systems, we denote the CI-NP system as follows:

$$CI = (m, H, \mu, (El_1, Pe_1, El_1(0)), \ldots, (El_{1m}, Pe_m, El_{1m}(0))) \qquad (2)$$

And in order to make it easier to understand, we illustrate it by the example as follows.

$$CI = (3, H, \mu, (El_1, Pe_1, El_1(0)), (El_2, Pe_2, El_2(0)), (El_3, Pe_3, El_3(0)))\quad(3)$$

With the following components:

$H = \{1, 2, 3\}$,

the H is defined by m which means the number of membranes consisting of different affecting elements and here the system holds three membranes.

$\mu = [[\ ]_2[\ ]_3]_1$,

$El_1 = \{El_2, El_3\}$,

μ demonstrates the membrane structure.

membrane 1 means the performance of cooperative innovation, it depends on element 2 (El_2) and element 3(El_3). In order to express clearly, we write it as El_1.

$Pe_1 = (F_1|El_2, El_3), (W_2|El_2, W_3|El_3)$,

consider the performance of an elementary membrane can be estimate by the function among its affecting elements and the weight of every element also matters.

$El_1(0)$,

the initial value of the element.

$El_2 = \{El_{1,2}, El_{2,2}, El_{3,2}\}$,

the elementary membrane 2 represents one main element that affects El_1, it contains three sub-elements which are $El_{1,2}$, $El_{2,2}$ and $El_{3,2}$.

The follow is consistent with mentioned above, the expression is given only.

$$Pe_2 = (F_2|El_{1,2}, El_{2,2}, El_{3,2}), (W_{1,2}|El_{1,2}, W_{2,2}|El_{2,2}, W_{3,2}|El_{3,2}),$$

$$El_2(0),$$

$$El_3 = \{El_{1,3}, El_{2,3}\},$$

$$Pe_3 = (F_3|El_{1,3}, El_{2,3}), (W_{1,3}|El_{1,3}, W_{2,3}|El_{2,3}),$$

$$El_3(0).$$

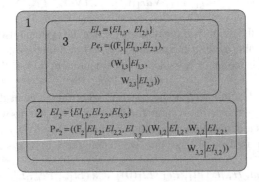

Fig. 3. An model of CI-NP systems. The model consists of three membranes where one of them is the skin membrane and represents the performance of cooperative innovation here. And other two are elementary membranes, which are representative of the number 2 and 3 and represent two main elements (El_2, El_3). And other specific meanings are mentioned above.

For an easier understanding, the system is given in Fig. 3 in a graphical representation, with the initial values specified in square brackets for each element, and with the programs given in the form production function to repartition procedure.

3   Case Study and Model Specification

Shandong Province is the third largest province in China's economy, and its GDP ranks the third which takes the 1/9 of China's GDP. Shandong was named China's one of the most comprehensive competitiveness of provinces and autonomous regions in 2013. With the continuous development of economic integration and knowledge economy, the regional economy is closely related to high-tech firms development.

High-tech firm has gradually become a leader to promote the development of regional economy. No matter taking a new road to industrialization, realizing the coordinated development of regional economy, adjusting and optimizing economic structure, or changing the pattern of economic development, it relies on the independent innovation and technological progress. That means transforming and upgrading traditional industries, and developing high-tech industry. In Shandong, high-tech firms reflect obviously the effect on the economy growth. Increasing capital formation, improving the level of technology and developing human capital are key elements to promote regional economic development. High-tech firms make an effect on the production structure through influencing the above elements to promote regional economic development.

Firms in Shandong play a critical role on the economic development, while high-tech firms matter. The study on cooperative innovation of high-tech firms in Shandong, China is important. And it is also important to research its model of cooperative innovation.

We have denoted the CI-NP system and a CI-NP system is conceived as a dynamical system. Based on the analysis we have done to the financial data of Shandong's high-tech firms, we illustrates the model specifically as follows.

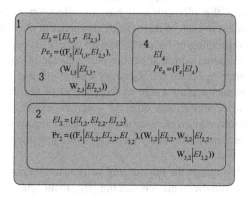

Fig. 4. In the rough expression of CI-NP systems based on Shandong's case, there are three main elements (*El*) for the performance of cooperative innovation (PCI) and each element holds some sub-elements.

$$CI = (4, H, \mu, (El_1, Pe_1, El_1(0)), (El_2, Pe_2, El_2(0)), (El_3, Pe_3, El_3(0)),$$
$$(El_4, Pe_4, El_4(0))) \tag{4}$$

For an easier understanding, the system is given in Fig. 4 in a graphical representation, with the initial values specified in square brackets for each element, and with the programs given in the form production function to repartition procedure. In order to see the difference between the modified model and original model more clearly and demonstrate the relationship between the cooperative innovation elements more visually, we put the model specification as Fig. 5 shown.

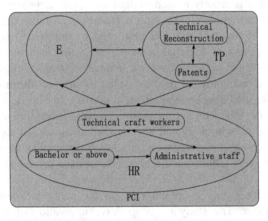

Fig. 5. The model specification based on Shandong's real study. there are three main elements which affect the performance of cooperative innovation (PCI) and they are human resources (HR), energy sources (E) and the fund for technical project (TP). And some main elements have sub-elements.

It reveals that there are different elements which all affect the performance of cooperative innovation, the element also has an effect on each other and some sub-elements are included in each of them. Each sub-element plays a role on each other and they may have overlapping or cooperation with others. In our model specification, there are three main elements which affect the performance of cooperative innovation (PCI) and they are human resources (HR), energy sources (E) and the fund for technical project (TP). These elements play a role in the process of the development of cooperative innovation and promote each other to a certain extent. Meanwhile, we take performance of cooperative innovation as the skin membrane which can include other elements in the development but their roles are not prominent as the three main element.

Most original models ignore the relationship demonstration among sub-elements. In the modified model, sub-elements containing by main elements is represented. Specifically, the fund for technical project contains the fund for technical reconstruction and patents, while human resources consists of three main sub-elements and they are technical craft workers, administrative staff and the staff who has bachelor or above. What calls for special attention is that not all the sub-element has strict independent relation with each other. They may have overlapping and also dependence with each other in the same elementary membrane.

On the whole, the model modified by numerical P systems based on the financial data regards the development in firms as cell lives. It demonstrates various elements and their relationships for cooperative innovation of high-tech firms in Shandong, China.

4   Data and Certification

The data used for the present study corresponds to the survey made by Technology Office of Shandong Province. The data is collected on high-tech firms about their financial input and output on innovation and development during the three-year period 2011 to 2013.

The total number of firms participating to the survey is 2000, 60.7% (1214 firms) of which operates in the new and high technology transformed by traditional industry. And the traditional industry transformed by new and high technology accounts for a large proportion. Electronic information technology industry and new medicine industry occupy the proportion of 11.4% (228 firms) and 13% (260 firms) respectively. The proportions occupied by the industry of new material technology, new energy and energy efficiency technology and resource and environment technology are less than 10%. They are 6.7% (134 firms), 3.1% (62 firms) and 4.3% (86 firms) respectively. There are only 4 firms (0.2%) of aerospace technology and 12 firms (0.6%) of high-tech service industry. The firm comes from different industries, and their competitiveness mainly relies on innovation and development according to the standard of high-tech industry and the development data. It is demonstrated by Fig. 6.

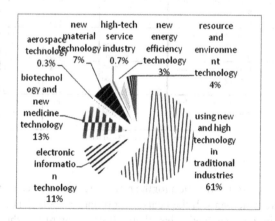

Fig. 6. The industry distribution.

We selected 30% of the data as test set, and conducted an analysis of the other 70% (1500 firms) of the data at first. By using the principal component analysis, we found three main aspects which include some inferior attributes that make effect on the development of cooperative innovation in the firms according to the financial data, as shown in Fig. 7.

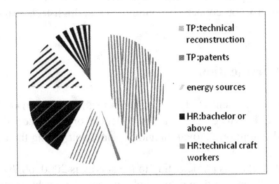

Fig. 7. The element distribution of cooperative innovation.

The dependent variable of the model is the gross industrial output value, which is dummy variable equal to one in the firm, during the three years 2011 to 2013. As we have seen in Tables 1, 2 and 3, independent variables correlation with the dependent variables have been shown clearly.

Table 1. Correlation analysis among main elements.

Correlations		Gross Industrial Output Value	Energy Sources	HR	TP
Gross Industrial Output Value	Pearson Correlation	1	.236**	.719**	.808**
	Sig. (2-tailed)		.000	.000	.000
	N	1509	1509	1509	1509
Energy Sources	Pearson Correlation	.236**	1	.258**	.244**
	Sig. (2-tailed)	.000		.000	.000
	N	1509	1509	1509	1509
HR	Pearson Correlation	.719**	.258**	1	.677**
	Sig. (2-tailed)	.000	.000		.000
	N	1509	1509	1509	1509
TP	Pearson Correlation	.808**	.244**	.677**	1
	Sig. (2-tailed)	.000	.000	.000	
	N	1509	1509	1509	1509

**. Correlation is significant at the 0.01 level (2-tailed).

By conducting Pearson correlation for the rest of the data, we verified the relationship among all or different elements. If the Pearson Correlation coefficient is less than 0.5, in other words, the significance level is less than 0.05, we regard that the overall trend for the two variables as be in consistency, but not dramatically. For example, the cost of energy sources is not correlated dramatically with any other elements, even for the value

Table 2. Correlation analysis among HR and its components.

Correlations

		HR	Bachelor or above	Technical Craft Workers	Administrative Staff
HR	Pearson Correlation	1	.858**	.782**	.514**
	Sig. (2-tailed)		.000	.000	.000
	N	1509	1509	1509	1509
Bachelor or above	Pearson Correlation	.858**	1	.689**	.467**
	Sig. (2-tailed)	.000		.000	.000
	N	1509	1509	1509	1509
Technical Craft Workers	Pearson Correlation	.782**	.689**	1	.478**
	Sig. (2-tailed)	.000	.000		.000
	N	1509	1509	1509	1509
Administrative Staff	Pearson Correlation	.514**	.467**	.478**	1
	Sig. (2-tailed)	.000	.000	.000	
	N	1509	1509	1509	1509

**. Correlation is significant at the 0.01 level (2-tailed).

Table 3. Correlation analysis among TP and its components.

Correlations

		TP	Technical Reconstruction	Patents
TP	Pearson Correlation	1	.372**	.035
	Sig. (2-tailed)		.000	.179
	N	1509	1509	1509
Technical Reconstruction	Pearson Correlation	.372**	1	.058*
	Sig. (2-tailed)	.000		.024
	N	1509	1509	1509
Patents	Pearson Correlation	.035	.058*	1
	Sig. (2-tailed)	.179	.024	
	N	1509	1509	1509

**. Correlation is significant at the 0.01 level (2-tailed).
*. Correlation is significant at the 0.05 level (2-tailed).

of Gross Industrial Output. But we can not ignore its influence on the development, though it only takes a small perception in innovative firms and its influence is going smaller and smaller faced with other cooperative elements.

Table 1 reports the three main complements of firms for innovation through comparing to gross industrial output value, namely the consumption of energy sources, human resources and the fund for technical project. The table shows that three elements exhibit a higher correlation of cooperative innovation. Additionally, the three elements include different secondary attributes which contribute to the gross industrial output value.

Tables 2 and 3 reports the secondary attributes belonged to different main elements respectively. To be specific, HR is composed of the staff who are bachelors or above, technical craft workers and administrative staff. And technical craft workers have the strongest correlation with human resource. The cost of patents and technical reconstruction attributes most to the fund for technical project. But the cost of technical reconstruction takes more proportion than the cost of patents. Tables 4 and 5 report the correlation coefficient using standard deviation, mean value, maximum value and minimum value.

Table 4. Summary statistic 1.

E1	Gross Industrial Output Value	E	HR	Bachelor or above
Gross Industrial Output Value	×	Min:0.042;Max:0.257;Mean:0.178;SD:0.097	Min:0.719;Max:0.853;Mean:0.771;SD:0.059	×
E	Min:0.042;Max:0.257;Mean:0.178;SD:0.097	×	Min:0.03;Max:0.266;Mean:0.185;SD:0.109	×
HR	Min:0.719;Max:0.853;Mean:0.771;SD:0.059	Min:0.030;Max:0.266;Mean:0.185;SD:0.109	×	Min:0.717;Max:0.905;Mean:0.827;SD:0.080
Bachelor or above	×	×	Min:0.717;Max:0.905;Mean:0.827;SD:0.080	×
Technical Craft Workers	×	×	Min:0.782;Max:0.875;Mean:0.821;SD:0.039	Min:0.595;Max:0.776;Mean:0.687;SD:0.074
Administrative Staff	×	×	Min:0.514;Max:0.783;Mean:0.648;SD:0.110	Min:0.467;Max:0.687;Mean:0.586;SD:0.074
TP	Min:0.808;Max:0.877;Mean:0.853;SD:0.032	Min:0.035;Max:0.351;Mean:0.21;SD:0.017	Min:0.677;Max:0.920;Mean:0.784;SD:0.101	×
Patents	×	×	×	×
Technical Reconstruction	×	×	×	×

Cooperation networks can be distinguished in different types of cooperative behavior and most of them consider cooperating with elements external firm. For example, as known as horizontal R&D cooperation tends to form matches between competing firms that might have similar needs in terms of product or process development, looking for resources of the same type (technological, human and so on). We tend to analyze the correlation to the gross industrial output value internal firms but on the view of finance. And as shown on Tables 4 and 5, summary statistics of their correlation among various elements also classify their mutual cooperation.

Table 5. Summary statistic 2.

E1	Technical Craft Workers	Administrative Staff	TP	Patents	Technical Reconstruction
Gross Industrial Output Value	×	×	Min:0.808;Max:0.877;Mean:0.853;SD:0.032	×	×
E	×	×	Min:0.035;Max:0.351;Mean:0.21;SD:0.017	×	×
HR	Min:0.782;Max:0.875;Mean:0.821;SD:0.039	Min:0.514;Max:0.783;Mean:0.648;SD:0.110	Min:0.677;Max:0.92;Mean:0.784;SD:0.101	×	×
Bachelor or above	Min:0.595;Max:0.776;Mean:0.687;SD:0.074	Min:0.467;Max:0.687;Mean:0.586;SD:0.074	×	×	×
Technical Craft Workers	×	Min:0.478;Max:0.811;Mean:0.633;SD:0.137	×	×	×
Administrative Staff	Min:0.478;Max:0.811;Mean:0.633;SD:0.137	×	×	×	×
TP	×	×	×	Min:0.362;Max:0.503;Mean:0.412;SD:0.064	Min:0.034;Max:0.383;Mean:0.151;SD:0.164
Patents	×	×	Min:0.362;Max:0.503;Mean:0.412;SD:0.064	×	Min:0.058;Max:0.315;Mean:0.171;SD:0.107
Technical Reconstruction	×	×	Min:0.034;Max:0.383;Mean:0.151;SD:0.164	Min:0.058;Max:0.315;Mean:0.171;SD:0.107	×

5 Conclusions

There are many previous works to explore the elements which have impact on the cooperative innovation. Previous works can be roughly divided into studying the internal element, the external element and elements on the view of process in business. However, most of them ignore the correlation among various elements.

This paper analyze the element that affecting performance of cooperative innovation in firms from the perspective of financial data. Networks are considered an economic reality. From this perspective, our model shows the relationship of inclusion which usually ignored in original model and correlation among various elements. Meanwhile, our model is constructed according to the instance data, validated the economic development of most high-tech firms in Shandong, China. At the same time, we change the original model and propose CI-NP system model based on numerical P systems, making joint among elements which play a role on the performance for cooperative innovation at the same time. It conforms to the characteristics of firms with development vitality and demonstrates the relationship between each element more fully.

However, elements in different types of firms play different roles. Meanwhile, various firms in multiple development periods emphasize on different aspects. In changing and increasingly competitive environments, successful innovations must provide a competitive edge in changing the relative position of a firm within an industry. Though based on NP systems, we have just give the model demonstrating the relationship among various elements and we haven't given the concrete expression of the production function. To do that, the next step for our work is to classify firms in different scale and its value of each element in order to find the function relation among them.

Acknowledgments. This work was supported by the Natural Science Foundation of China (No. 61472231), Humanities and Social Sciences Project of Ministry of Education, China (No. 12YJA630152), Social Science Fund of Shandong Province, China (No. 11CGLJ22), Social Science Fund of Shandong Province, China (No. 16BGLJ06), Natural Science Foundation of China (No. 61502283), Natural Science Foundation of China(No. 61640201).

References

1. Gunday, G., Ulusoy, G., Kilic, K., Alpkan, L.: Effects of innovation types on firm performance. Int. J. Prod. Econ. **133**(2), 662–676 (2011)
2. Zhang, X., Song, W.: Structure, evolution and hot spots of cooperation innovation knowledge network. Open J. Appl. Sci. **5**(4), 121–134 (2015)
3. Weiers, G.: Cooperative Innovation. Innovation Through Cooperation (2014)
4. Van de Ven, A.H.: Central Problems in the Management of Innovation. In: INFORMS (1986)
5. Chung, H.F.L.: Market orientation, guanxi, and business performance. Ind. Mark. Manage. **40**(4), 522–533 (2011)
6. Zhang, J., Zhu, M.: Market orientation, product innovation and export performance: evidence from Chinese manufacturers. J. Strateg. Mark. **2015**(1), 1–21 (2015)
7. Gil, H.C., You, Y.Y.: Effects of market orientation, internal cooperation practice and process formality on product innovation performance and business performance **9**(41) (2016)
8. Anzoategui, D., Comin, D., Gertler, M., Martinez, J., Anzoategui, D., Comin, D., et al.: Endogenous technology adoption and R&D as sources of business cycle persistence. Nber Working Papers (2016)
9. Grimpe, C., Sofka, W., Bhargava, M., Chatterjee, R.: R&D, marketing innovation, and new product performance: a mixed methods study. J. Prod. Innov. Manage. **34**(3), 360–383 (2017)
10. Gu, Q., Jiang, W., Wang, G.G.: Effects of external and internal sources on innovation performance in chinese high-tech SMES: a resource-based perspective. J. Eng. Technol. Manage. **40**(C), 76–86 (2016)
11. Corredor, S., Forero, C., Somaya, D.: How external and internal sources of knowledge impact novel and imitative innovation in emerging markets: evidence from Colombia. Adv. Int. Manage. **28**, 161–199 (2015)

12. Polzin, F., Flotow, P.V., Klerkx, L.: Addressing barriers to eco-innovation: exploring the finance mobilisation functions of institutional innovation intermediaries. Technol. Forecast. Soc. Chang. **103**, 34–46 (2016)
13. Stieglitz, N., Heine, K.: Innovations and the role of complementarities in a strategic theory of the firm. Strateg. Manag. J. **28**(1), 1–15 (2007)
14. Dutta, S., Narasimhan, O., Rajiv, S.: Conceptualizing and measuring capabilities: methodology and empirical application. Strateg. Manag. J. **26**(3), 277–285 (2005)
15. Edison, H., Ali, N.B., Torkar, R.: Towards innovation measurement in the software industry. J. Syst. Softw. **86**(5), 1390–1407 (2013)
16. Wu, A.H., Wang, Z., Chen, S.: Impact of specific investments, governance mechanisms and behaviors on the performance of cooperative innovation projects. Int. J. Project Manage. **35** (3), 504–515 (2016)
17. Xiong, J., Li, L.: Knowledge fusion for cooperative innovation from strategic alliances perspective. In: International Conference on Enterprise Information Systems, pp. 498–503 (2016)
18. Rangus, K., Slavec, A.: The interplay of decentralization, employee involvement and absorptive capacity on firms' innovation and business performance. Technological Forecasting & Social Change (2017)
19. Lichtenthaler, U.: Absorptive capacity and firm performance: an integrative framework of benefits and downsides. Technol. Anal. Strateg. Manage. 1–13 (2016)
20. Savin, I., Egbetokun, A.: Emergence of innovation networks from R&D cooperation with endogenous absorptive capacity. SSRN Electron. J. **64**, 82–103 (2016)
21. Newburry, W., McIntyre, J.R., Xavier, W.: Exploring the interconnections between institutions, innovation, geography, and internationalization in emerging markets. Int. J. Emerg. Markets **11**(2), 1 (2016)
22. Un, G., Un, R.: Membrane Computing and Economics: Numerical P Systems. IOS Press, Amsterdam (2006)
23. Zhang, Z., Wu, T., Păun, A., Pan, L.: Numerical P Systems with Migrating Variables. Elsevier Science Publishers Ltd. (2016)

Conceptual Modelling

The Design of a Modeling Technique to Analyze the Impact of Process Simulation Throughout the Business Architecture

Ben Roelens[✉] and Geert Poels

Department of Business Informatics and Operations Management,
Faculty of Economics and Business Administration, Ghent University, Ghent, Belgium
{Ben.Roelens,Geert.Poels}@UGent.be

Abstract. Simulation techniques offer a cost-effective solution to support the experimental analysis of possible business process improvements. However, the performance indicators that are used for this analysis exclusively focus on operational aspects. Consequently, the impact of process changes on the overall business performance is not taken into account. This problem can be solved by the development of a modeling technique that combines the provision of a coherent view on both the organizational strategy and business processes with a mechanism to analyze the impact of the simulated operational performance on indicators that reflect the overall business performance. This paper presents the proof-of-concept design of such a technique, which is the result of a first cycle of Design Science Research. This also includes the demonstration of the modeling technique by the bakery case example.

Keywords: Modeling technique · Process simulation · Performance indicators · Business architecture

1 Introduction

Since two decades, simulation techniques have proven their relevance for the continuous improvement of business processes [9]. Traditionally, these techniques support a cost-effective and experimental analysis of the redesign of processes by visualizing alternative configurations and testing the impact of these alternatives on relevant performance indicators [23, 24]. This analysis can subsequently be employed to determine whether an alternative should effectively be implemented. Although performance indicators that are used within business process simulation focus on the correctness, effectiveness, and efficiency of processes [24], the actual impact on the overall business performance is neglected [11]. Consequently, the redesign of processes can lead to sub-optimization as operational excellence may not lead to a better realization of the objectives that a company wants to achieve.

A possible solution for this problem is offered by Enterprise Architecture, which is a holistic approach offering an integrative view on the company. This includes the use of a coherent whole of principles, methods, and models to design and realize the business

© Springer International Publishing AG 2017
R. Pergl et al. (Eds.): EOMAS 2017, LNBIP 298, pp. 37–52, 2017.
DOI: 10.1007/978-3-319-68185-6_3

architecture, information systems (i.e., data and applications) architecture and technology architecture [10, 22].

The business architecture is an important aspect of a company as it supports the organizational vision and as it is an important prerequisite for the development of the other architecture domains [22]. More particular, a business architecture model could be useful to solve the formulated problem as it provides a multi-perspective blueprint of the enterprise [15] that connects operational process decisions (i.e., the process perspective) with the formulation of organizational objectives (i.e., the strategy perspective) via the implementation of a strategy (i.e., the infrastructure/organization perspective) [12, 22]. Subsequently, this model needs to be extended with a mechanism to assess the impact of process simulation results on the other business architecture perspectives. More specifically, the following elements are needed for the development of the intended modeling technique: (i) a model that provides a coherent view on the different business architecture elements, and (ii) a mechanism that is able to assess the impact of the simulated operational performance on indicators that reflect the overall business performance.

This paper focuses on the development of such a modeling technique. Therefore, we make use of previous research [18, 19] that presented the PGA (i.e., Process-Goal Alignment) modeling technique, which is able to provide a coherent view on the business architecture as it integrates modeling constructs of the strategy, infrastructure, and process perspectives. This business architecture model is also extended by a mechanism for setting and measuring performance goals throughout the business architecture (see Sect. 2). Furthermore, the PGA technique was evaluated and refined through several applications in a real-life organizational context [19]. As such, it provides an appropriate starting point for the development of the intended technique. The contribution of this paper is the extension of the PGA technique with a mechanism to assess the impact of simulated process configurations on the overall business performance.

The modeling technique is built according to the Design Science Research (DSR) methodology [6, 16], which guides the creation of IT artifacts through iterative cycles of the build-and-evaluate loop. More specifically, this research presents four different types of IT artifacts: (i) a modeling language that uses different (ii) constructs to provide a representation of the business architecture, (iii) an algorithm to assess the impact of process simulation results on the overall business performance, and (iv) an instantiation of the proposed technique by means of the bakery case example to demonstrate the implemented system. This case example is an extension of a previous version [18], which describes the business architecture of a fictitious bakery. This paper communicates about a first iteration of the DSR build-and-evaluate loop, which includes problem identification and motivation (Sect. 1), definition of solution objectives (Sect. 1), design and development (Sects. 2 and 3), demonstration (Sects. 2 and 3), and evaluation (as part of future research in Sect. 5).

The paper is structured as follows. Section 2 gives more details about the PGA technique, which provides the starting point for the development of the proposed modeling technique. The actual design of this modeling technique is presented in Sect. 3, as well as a demonstration by means of a case example. Related literature is reviewed in Sect. 4 to further show the need for the development of the modeling technique. Finally, Sect. 5 summarizes conclusions and identifies future research opportunities.

2   PGA Modeling Technique

The PGA modeling technique is originally presented as an approach to realize strategic fit, which entails the alignment between the strategy of a company and appropriate supporting processes [12]. To assess and improve the level of strategic fit, PGA employs different mechanisms that lead to the creation of business architecture heat maps: (i) a modeling language that offers a holistic view on value creation within the business architecture hierarchy (Sect. 2.1), (ii) the Analytic Hierarchy Process (AHP) [20] to determine the strategic priorities of elements within the business architecture (Sect. 2.2), (iii) a performance measurement system that guides process outcomes towards the intended strategic objectives by setting clear performance targets and by keeping track of the actual performance (Sect. 2.3), (iv) a strategic fit improvement analysis for the stakeholders about how improvements can be realized within the business architecture (Sect. 2.4).

2.1   Business Architecture Hierarchy

PGA [19] uses different modeling constructs to provide a holistic view on the business architecture, which include: goals (i.e., financial, customer, and internal), financial structure, value proposition, competence, process, and activity. By reviewing relevant frameworks in the Management and Information Systems literature [17], we also identified how these elements are hierarchically structured to support the creation of value in the business architecture. This resulted in the identification of valueStream relations between different business architecture elements (see meta-model fragment of Fig. 1 [19]). The definition and notation of the PGA modeling constructs are provided in Table 1 [19].

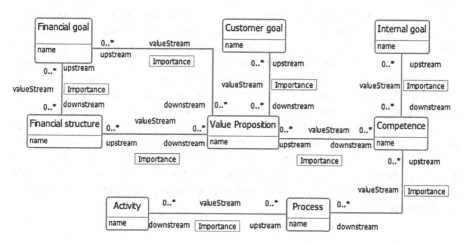

Fig. 1. PGA meta-model fragment (adapted from [19])

Table 1. Definition and notation of the PGA modeling constructs [19]

Hierarchy level	Modeling construct	Definition	Notation
6	Goal	Strategic objective that describes a desired state or development of the company. Relevant categories are financial (left), customer (middle), and internal objectives (right notation).	
5	Financial Structure	Representation of the costs resulting from acquiring resources, and the revenues in return for the offered value proposition.	
4	Value Proposition	Offered set of products and/or services that provides value to the customers and other partners, and competes in the overall value network.	
3	Competence	An integrated and holistic set of knowledge, skills, and abilities, related to a specific set of resources, which is coordinated through processes to realize the intended value proposition.	
2	Process	A structured set of activities that uses and/or consumes resources to create the organizational competences.	
1	Activity	Work that is performed in a process by one or more actors, which are engaged in changing the state of one or more input resources or enterprise objects to create a single desired output.	
-	valueStream	Representation of the hierarchical structure, through which value is created at distinct levels in the business architecture.	

This meta-model can be instantiated by means of the bakery case example. The manager of this bakery has to *improve the short-term solvency* as some of the suppliers threat to stop the delivery of goods due to late payments. This financial goal can be attained by *increasing the current assets* and/or *decreasing the current liabilities*, which reflect the financial structure of the bakery. On a lower level in the hierarchy, this will have an impact on the offered set of products and/or services to the customers (i.e., value proposition elements). Increasing current assets can be realized by *selling additional products,* as this will generate extra cash, while decreasing current liabilities is possible by using cheap raw materials to *offer low-cost products*. The following competences are crucial for the bakery to offer its products to customers: *resource sourcing*, *operational excellence*, and *marketing*. *Resource sourcing* is further sustained by the *buying* and subsequent *quality check* processes. During the *quality check*, employees execute three main activities: *taking a sample* of the raw material, *performing* the *quality procedure, and filling in the evaluation forms. Operational excellence* is supported by the processes of *kneading* the dough and *baking* the bread. This *baking* process includes the activities of *setting up the oven, preheating*, and *getting the bread out of the oven*. The *advertisement* and *sales process* are fundamental to the *marketing* competence. To sell breads on a long-term basis, it is crucial for the bakery to both *attract new customers* and to *obtain customer references*. This description results in the business architecture hierarchy that can be found in Fig. 2.

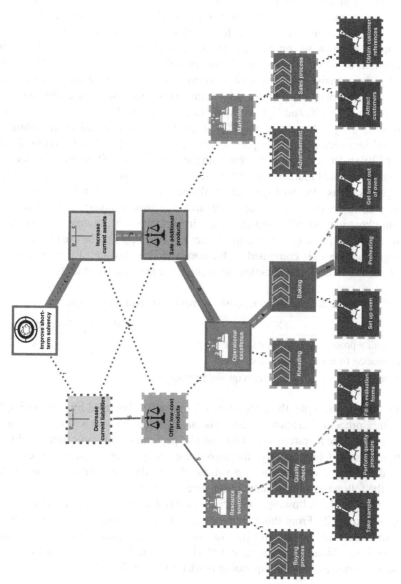

Fig. 2. Business architecture heat map for the running example (Color figure online)

2.2 Analytic Hierarchy Process

The AHP mechanism [20] is used in the PGA technique to enable the end-users to prioritize between elements, based on the extent to which value creation is supported on a higher hierarchy level in the business architecture. The hierarchy level of the business architecture elements can be consulted in Table 1. To capture the prioritization by end-users, each value stream relation is characterized by an importance attribute (see Fig. 1). To calculate this attribute, it is first needed to construct a comparison matrix, which consists of pairwise comparison values for all elements that are related by value stream relations to the same higher-level element in the business architecture [19]. More specifically, the pairwise comparison of two business architecture elements (i.e., X_i and X_j in Table 2) is implemented by the AHP comparison scale, which enables to choose values between 1 (i.e., X_i and X_j have equal importance) and 9 (X_i has extreme importance over X_j) [17]. Afterwards, the PGA Eigenvector is obtained by rescaling the normalized Eigenvector of the comparison matrix (i.e., as proposed in the original AHP procedure [20]) relatively to the element with the lowest value. This rescaling does not affect the mathematical foundations of the original AHP, as any nonzero scalar multiple of an Eigenvector is also an Eigenvector. Based on the corresponding value of the importance attribute, the color of the value stream relation is changed in the business architecture heat map to either red (i.e., high importance: ≥ 5), orange (i.e., moderate importance: ≥ 3), or green (i.e., low importance: <3) (see Fig. 2). The use of colors (i.e., red, orange, and green) is combined with a corresponding texture of the value stream relation (i.e., solid, dashed, and dotted) to account for printing constraints.

Table 2. Pairwise comparison values for the running example

X_i	X_j	AHP comparison value
Perform quality procedure	Take sample	4
Fill in evaluation forms	Take sample	3
Fill in evaluation forms	Perform quality procedure	1/2

In the running example, the AHP mechanism can be illustrated by considering the *quality check* process. This process depends on three activities on a lower level in the business architecture hierarchy (i.e., take sample, perform quality procedure, and fill in evaluation forms). Consequently, three pairwise comparisons have to be executed between these activities by choosing values of the AHP comparison scale. In this example, the following values were chosen (see Table 2).

This results in the following comparison matrix (see formula 1) and PGA Eigenvector (see formula 2). From this Eigenvector, it can be concluded that the importance attribute of *take sample* is equal to 1 (i.e., low importance), of *perform quality procedure* is equal to 5 (i.e., high importance), and of *fill in evaluation forms* is equal to 3 (i.e., moderate importance) (see corresponding border colors in Fig. 2).

$$\text{Comparison matrix:} \begin{bmatrix} 1 & 1/4 & 1/3 \\ 4 & 1 & 2 \\ 3 & 1/2 & 1 \end{bmatrix} \quad (1)$$

$$\text{PGA Eigenvector:} \begin{bmatrix} 1 \\ 5 \\ 3 \end{bmatrix} \quad (2)$$

2.3 Performance Measurement System

To execute the performance measurement, it is important to collect the relevant perform-ance data. These data include the choice of a measure type (i.e., positive, negative, or qualitative), a measure description, a performance goal, an allowed deviation percentage, and the actual performance. While a higher actual performance reflects a better performance for a positive measure (e.g., profit), it is worse in case of a negative measure (e.g., cost). Qualitative measures are used to express whether a certain criterion is actually met (e.g., preheating temperature $= 175\,°C$). Based on the actual performance, it can be determined for each of the measure types whether this performance is *excellent* (i.e., above the upper acceptance level), *as expected* (i.e., above the lower acceptance level and below the upper acceptance level), or *bad* (i.e., below lower acceptance level) (see Fig. 3). The results of this analysis are also visualized in the business architecture heat map by changing the border of the elements to the respective texture and color (i.e., dotted green, dashed orange or solid red) (see Fig. 2).

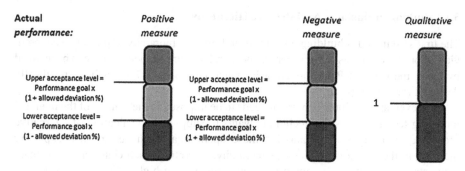

Fig. 3. Performance measurement system

For the running example, the performance measurement mechanism is applied for the activity of *filling in the evaluation forms*. This activity is measured by the *daily number of faulty forms*, which is a negative measure. As the performance goal for this activity is 4 and the allowed deviation is 12.5%, the actual performance is *bad* if it is above 4.5, *as expected* if it is between 3.5 and 4.5, and *excellent* if it is below 3.5. In this case, the actual performance of the activity is 3.8, which means that the border of the element is changed to an orange color in the business architecture heat map (see Fig. 2).

2.4 Strategic Fit Improvement Analysis

The last mechanism can be used to identify operational improvements in the business architecture heat map for a better support of the organizational strategy. This includes the identification of a critical path, which is a chain of value stream relations that starts from a goal with a bad performance. From this goal, a critical path further consists of downstream value stream relations (i.e., going from an element on a higher hierarchy level to an element on a lower hierarchy level (see Table 1)) that mostly have a high or medium importance and that connect business architecture elements of which the performance can be improved.

For the running example, the critical path (see gray color in Fig. 2) starts from *Improve short-term solvency* as a financial goal and ends at the *preheating* activity. Consequently, this activity can be considered as the main starting point to improve the strategic fit within the bakery.

3 Modeling Technique

Four steps need to be executed to apply the proposed modeling technique: (i) building a business architecture hierarchy (Sect. 3.1), (ii) executing the operational performance simulation (Sect. 3.2), (iii) determining how performance indicators can be propagated throughout the business architecture hierarchy (Sect. 3.3), and (iv) analyzing how strategic fit can be improved (Sect. 3.4). In the next paragraphs, it will be clearly indicated whether elements are new or reused from the original PGA modeling technique.

3.1 Building a Business Architecture Hierarchy

The first step includes building a business architecture hierarchy to provide a coherent view of process changes on the other business architecture elements. This can be realized by using the original PGA modeling language (see Sect. 2.1), which is specifically designed for this purpose.

However, an additional constraint needs to be imposed in the context of the intended modeling technique. As this technique wants to support the evaluation of alternative process designs, it is important that these operational elements are also explicitly included in the business architecture hierarchy. Therefore, each chain of downstream value stream relations (i.e., going from an element on a higher hierarchy level to an element on a lower hierarchy level) should at least end at a process or an activity element in the business architecture heat map. For the running example (see Fig. 2), this condition is met as the ends of the downstream value stream chains are either processes (i.e., *buying process, kneading*, and *advertisement*) or activities (i.e., *take sample, perform quality procedure, fill in evaluation forms, set up oven, preheating, get bread out of oven, attract customers*, and *obtain customer references*).

3.2 Operational Performance Simulation

The second step includes the execution of the performance simulation on the operational level (i.e., for process and activity elements) in the business architecture. On this operational level, appropriate performance indicators can reflect (i) effectiveness, (ii) efficiency, and (iii) productivity by relating to respectively (i) output factors (e.g., number of defects), (ii) the ratio of input to output (e.g., material usage/product), and (iii) the ratio of output to input (e.g., production/man-hour). Similar to the PGA technique (see Sect. 2.3), a performance goal and an allowed deviation percentage need to be specified once a performance indicator is chosen. Besides this, it is also important to discriminate between indicators that are formulated positively or negatively as this has consequences during the propagation of measures (see Sect. 3.3). An extension that is needed to support the creation of simulated performance results is the choice of a probability distribution with according parameters. In this respect, parameters can be estimated based on historical data of the organization.

For the running example, the appropriate indicator that was identified for the *take sample* activity is *the number of samples per hour*. For this indicator, the performance goal is set at the value of 50, while the allowed deviation is 5%. By analyzing the past performance of this activity, it could be decided that *the number of samples per hour* is uniformly distributed between 47 (i.e., minimum included) and 57 (i.e., maximum

Table 3. Operational performance measurement data for the running example

Element type	Name	Performance indicator				
		Description	Goal	Allowed deviation	Average performance	Standard deviation performance
Process	Buying process	% cases in which origin = supplier x	95%	2.5%	99%	0.2%
Process: Quality check						
Activity	Perform quality procedure	% cases in which procedure = correct	92%	1%	98.5%	0.5%
Activity	Fill in evaluation forms	# completed forms / hour	3	5%	3	0.1
Process	Kneading	% cases in which # minutes = 5	99%	0.2%	99%	0.175
Process: Baking						
Activity	Set up oven	# minutes	1	20%	1	0.25
Activity	Preheating	% of cases in which temperature = 175°C	95%	2%	85%	0.5%
Activity	Get bread out of oven	# collapsed breads / day	5	10%	9	1.25
Process	Advertisement	weekly advertisement budget	30.000	3%	31.000	3.000
Process: Sales						
Activity	Attract customers	# yearly new customers	100	5%	97	5
Activity	Obtain customer references	# yearly recurring customers	150	5%	162	7

excluded). In other words, each discrete value between these two boundaries (i.e., maximum excluded) has an equal probability of 0.1 to occur. To preserve simplicity, we assume that the other performance indicators in the running example are normally distributed. Consequently, it is sufficient to determine an estimated average and standard deviation. An overview of the operational performance data for the running example can be found in Table 3. These data are finally used for the production of a simulated performance for each of the indicators, taking into account their stochastical distribution and the specific values of their parameters.

3.3   Measure Propagation

In this step, it is determined how the simulated operational performance can be propagated throughout the business architecture hierarchy. This mechanism, which is not a part of the original PGA technique, is implemented by (i) rescaling the operational performance, (ii) aggregating the rescaled operational performance to all higher hierarchy levels, and (iii) adapting the border color of the business architecture elements based on the performance results.

Rescaling the operational performance. First, it is needed to rescale the simulated operational performance such that it can be interpreted independently of specific measurement details (i.e., measure type, performance goal, and allowed deviation). To enable a distinction between three performance levels (i.e., excellent, as expected, and bad), it is needed to rescale the performance with respect to their upper and lower acceptance level (see formulae 3 and 4 for positive measures).

$$performance\ upper\ acceptance\ level_{PM} = \frac{Simulated\ performance}{Perf.\ goal\ x(1 + Allowed\ deviation\%)} \quad (3)$$

$$performance\ lower\ acceptance\ level_{PM} = \frac{Simulated\ performance}{Perf.\ goal\ x(1 - Allowed\ deviation\%)} \quad (4)$$

These formulae can be illustrated for the activity of *preheating* in the running example. This activity is measured by the *percentage of cases, in which the correct temperature is obtained*. If the performance goal is 95%, the allowed deviation 2%, and the actual performance 85% (see Table 3), the rescaled performance is calculated as follows (see formulae 5 and 6).

$$performance\ upper\ acceptance\ level_{PM} = \frac{85\%}{95\%\ x(1 + 0.02)} = 0.877 \quad (5)$$

$$performance\ lower\ acceptance\ level_{PM} = \frac{85\%}{95\%x(1 - 0.02)} = 0.913 \quad (6)$$

Formula 7 and 8 are developed to cope with the rescaling of negative measures (see Fig. 3).

$$performance\ upper\ acceptance\ level_{NM} = \frac{Perf.\ goal\ x(1 - Allowed\ deviation\%)}{Simulated\ performance} \quad (7)$$

$$performance\ lower\ acceptance\ level_{NM} = \frac{Perf.\ goal\ x(1 + Allowed\ deviation\%)}{Simulated\ performance} \quad (8)$$

Rescaling negative measures is applied in the running example when considering the activity of *getting the bread out of the oven*. If the actual performance of *the number of collapsed breads per day* is equal to 9 (i.e., with respect to the performance goal of 5 and the allowed deviation of 10% of Table 3), the rescaled performance will yield the following results (see formulae 9 and 10).

$$performance\ upper\ acceptance\ level_{NM} = \frac{5x(1 - 0.1)}{9} = 0.5 \quad (9)$$

$$performance\ lower\ acceptance\ level_{NM} = \frac{5x(1 + 0.1)}{9} = 0.611 \quad (10)$$

Based on the resulting values, it can be determined whether the rescaled performance is *excellent* (i.e., the result of the rescaled performance upper acceptance level and lower acceptance level >1), *as expected* (the result of the rescaled performance upper acceptance level <1 and lower acceptance level >1), or *bad* (the result of rescaled performance upper acceptance level and lower acceptance level <1).

Aggregation to higher hierarchy level. In this phase, the relation between the performance indicators on the different hierarchical levels in the business architecture needs to be determined. Depending on the level of available information, two distinct procedures can be relevant: (i) business formulae [7] and (ii) a subjective judgment of the strategic importance by the AHP mechanism [7, 20]. This aggregation is repeated in the business architecture until the simulated operational performance is propagated to all higher hierarchy levels.

Business formulae. If there is a clear mathematical relation between the performance indicators that are used on two successive layers in the business architecture, this relation can be expressed by using business formulae. In some cases, conversion factors are needed in the mathematical equation [7].

The application of business formulae without conversion factors can be illustrated by the running example, in which the *short-term solvency* (i.e., the indicator that measures the financial goal of *improving the short-term solvency*) can be calculated as the ratio of the *current assets* to the *current liabilities* (see formula 11). These indicators measure respectively *increase current assets* and *decrease current liabilities* as two financial structure elements on the lower hierarchical level. Conversion factors are needed in the formula of the *total yearly sales*, which is the relevant performance indicator for the *sales process*. More specifically, the *total yearly sales* is based on the *number of yearly new and recurring customers* (i.e., operational measures on the lower hierarchical level). In this case, the conversion factors express the average yearly consumption for each type of customer (see formula 12).

$$Short - term\ solvency = \frac{current\ assets}{current\ liabilities} \tag{11}$$

$$Total\ yearly\ sales = \#\ yearly\ new\ customers\ x\ average\ yearly\ consumption\ by\ a\ new\ customer + \\ \#\ yearly\ recurring\ customers\ x\ average\ yearly\ consumption\ by\ a\ recurring\ customers \tag{12}$$

AHP mechanism. This procedure is relevant if there is no mathematical relation between the performance indicators on two successive business architecture hierarchy layers. AHP is a suited mechanism as it enables to determine the strategic importance of elements that are arranged in a hierarchical structure [5] and to measure the inconsistency that is inherent to these subjective judgments [20]. More specifically, the strategic importance of a lower-level element is determined by calculating the importance attribute of the value stream relations that connect this lower-lever architecture element with higher-level elements (see Sect. 2.2). These importance attributes are subsequently used to calculate the rescaled performance of the higher-level element as a weighted average of the lower-level elements.

For the running example, the rescaled performance of the *baking process* (i.e., the higher-level element) depends on three activities: *set up oven, preheating,* and *get bread out of oven.* For the last two activities, the rescaled performance was already calculated in this paragraph. For *setting up the oven,* we assume that the rescaled values are equal to 0.833 (i.e., upper acceptance level) and 1.25 (i.e., lower acceptance level). Based on the values of the importance attributes of its lower-level activities (i.e., respectively 1, 5, and 3 in Fig. 2), the rescaled performance of the *baking process* can be calculated as shown is formulae 13 and 14. As the results of both formulae are smaller than 1, it can be concluded that the rescaled performance of the *baking process* is currently *bad.*

$$performance\ upper\ acc.\ level = \frac{1x0.833 + 5x0.877 + 3x0.5}{9} = 0.746 \tag{13}$$

$$performance\ lower\ acc.\ level = \frac{1x1.25 + 5x0.913 + 3x0.611}{9} = 0.850 \tag{14}$$

Adopt border color. Based on the rescaled performance results, the color and texture of the element borders should be accordingly adapted (i.e., dotted green for an excellent performance, dashed orange for an as expected performance, and solid red for a bad performance in Fig. 2). This color-coding corresponds with the original proposal of the PGA modeling technique. For the sake of completeness, the rescaled performance figures and according color can also be found in Table 4 (see column as-is model).

3.4 Strategic Fit Improvement Analysis

The strategic fit improvement analysis is performed based on the visualized results of the measure propagation (Sect. 3.3) and the AHP mechanism (see Sect. 2.2 and 3.3). In this respect, no adaptations are needed to the identification of the critical path, as proposed by the original PGA modeling technique (see Sect. 2.4). This helps to reveal operational adaptations in the business architecture heat map, of which the impact can be assessed by repeating the operational performance simulation and measure propagation, based on the expected change in performance data (i.e., the to-be model). Based on the resulting performance levels, it can be determined whether the operational changes also lead to a better realization of the organizational goals.

For the running example, the critical path (see gray color in Fig. 2) starts from *Improve short-term solvency* as a financial goal and ends at the *preheating* activity. This can be explained as too much time is needed to put the dough in the oven due to the bakery layout. This results in a temperature that gets too high in 15% of the time, which is significantly above the performance goal of 5% (see Table 3). Furthermore, the faulty temperature also has an important impact on the *number of collapsing breads*, which is used as the performance indicator for the activity of getting the bread out of the oven.

Based on this analysis, the manager of the bakery wants to assess the impact of a new training about handling the oven on the overall business performance (i.e., the to-be model). More specifically, the manager believes that he can reduce the *percentage of cases with an excessive oven temperature* to 5%. Besides this, it is assumed that the *daily number of breads that collapse* when *getting the bread out of the oven* can be changed from 9 to 5. If we assess the impact of these operational adaptations (see to-be model in Table 4), it can be seen that the rescaled performance results of *improving the short-term solvency* increase to 1.074 (i.e., lower acceptance level) and 0.985 (i.e., upper acceptance level). Consequently, it can be expected that the operational change can improve the performance of this financial goal from *bad* to *as expected*.

4 Related Work

The importance of extending process simulation models to support the strategic planning activities of an organization was already acknowledged by past research [1, 11]. These efforts focus on the use of the REA (i.e., Resource-Event-Agent) ontology [13] to include financial parameters as the most important factor of the overall business performance. A similar idea was adopted by the e3-value ontology [3], which aims to analyze the profitability of the business model of a company. The developed modeling technique is different from these approaches as a broader view on business performance is adopted. In accordance with [8], we propose that other aspects (i.e., customer and internal goals) should be taken into account when considering the overall performance in an existing business architecture.

The Business Intelligence Model (BIM) [7] presents a modeling language that connects business processes with strategic objectives. Furthermore, BIM employs operational measures to analyze to which extent the organizational goals are sustained by appropriate business processes. In this respect, probabilistic information can be used for the evaluation of alternative strategies, which is closely related to the statistical distributions that are employed by this research (see Table 3). However, a clear difference with the proposed modeling technique includes that BIM does not discriminate between different types of goals. However, this difference is important to enable an easy understanding of the organizational strategy by business stakeholders [8]. Furthermore, BIM limits the application of the performance measurement to the process layer within the business architecture. This is fundamentally different in the proposed modeling technique, which employs measures at six different hierarchy levels (i.e., goal, financial structure, value proposition, competence, process, and activity). This is in line with other performance management frameworks, which stress the importance of measuring other organizational aspects in combination with business processes [14].

Table 4. Performance results for the running example

Element type	Name	As-is model		To-be model	
		Rescaled performance w.r.t. lower acceptance level	Rescaled performance w.r.t. upper acceptance level	Rescaled performance w.r.t. lower acceptance level	Rescaled performance w.r.t. upper acceptance level
Process	Quality check	1,072	1,010	1,071	1,010
Process	Baking	0,850	0,746	1,102	0,961
Process	Sales process	1,064	0,962	1,066	0,964
Competence	Resource sourcing	1,025	1,012	1,024	1,011
Competence	Operational excellence	0,882	0,800	1,081	0,964
Competence	Marketing	1,063	0,976	1,065	0,977
Value Proposition	Offer high-quality products	1,002	0,977	1,034	1,003
Value Proposition	Sale additional products	0,908	0,826	1,085	0,973
Financial Structure	Increase current assets	0,923	0,859	1,062	0,975
Financial Structure	Decrease current liabilities	1,028	1,036	1,008	1,010
Financial Goal	Improve short-term solvency	0,947	0,889	1,074	0,985

5   Conclusion and Discussion

This paper presents the proof-of-concept design of a modeling technique that explicitly takes into account the overall business performance to overcome the problem of strategic sub-optimization of existing process simulation techniques. More specifically, the proposed technique includes a model that provides a coherent view on the impact of alternative process configurations on other business architecture elements. This is realized by using the PGA modeling technique as a starting point, which is subsequently extended by a mechanism to analyze the impact of the simulated operational performance on the overall business performance. The different steps of the modeling procedure are also demonstrated by means of the bakery case example.

The main concern that needs to be addressed by future research is improving the relevance of the modeling technique by its evaluation in a real-life case-study context. Indeed, handling the complexity of a real-life context will provide more evidence that is conclusive about the contributions of the proposed modeling technique. This can be realized by performing Action Research [21, 25], which will enable to compare the use of the proposed technique with similar approaches (e.g., e3-value, BIM, etc.).

Furthermore, in-depth case studies can help to refine the different steps (e.g., the choice of probability distributions during the operational performance measurement, the use of the AHP mechanism or possible alternative approaches such as the conjoint analysis technique [4], etc.) of the modeling procedure based on reflection and learning about iterative cycles of building, intervention and evaluation in the organizational context. As such, we will combine the rigorous design of the modeling technique with demonstrated utility for business practitioners. In this respect, it will also be necessary to include the new mechanism in the existing PGA tool support, which is currently implemented through the ADOxx meta-modeling platform [2].

References

1. Church, K., Smith, R.: REA ontology-based simulation models for enterprise strategic planning. JIS **22**(2), 301–329 (2008)
2. Fill, H., Karagiannis, D.: On the conceptualisation of modelling methods using the ADOxx meta modelling platform. EMISA **1**(8), 4–25 (2013)
3. Gordijn, J., Akkermans, H.: Value-based requirements engineering: exploring innovative e-Commerce ideas. Requir. Eng. **8**(2), 114–134 (2003)
4. Green, P., Rao, V.: Conjoint measurement for quantifying judgemental data. J. Mark. Res. **8**(3), 355–363 (1971)
5. Hafeez, K., Zhang, Y., Malak, N.: Determining key capabilities of a firm using analytic hierarchy process. Int. J. Prod. Econ. **76**(1), 39–51 (2002)
6. Hevner, A., March, S., Park, J., Ram, S.: Design science in information systems research. MIS Q. **28**(1), 75–105 (2004)
7. Horkoff, J., Barone, D., Jiang, L., Yu, E., Amyot, D., Borgida, A., Mylopoulos, J.: Strategic business modeling: representation and reasoning. Softw. Syst. Model. **13**(3), 1015–1041 (2014)
8. Kaplan, R., Norton, D.: The balanced scorecard - measures that drive performance. Harvard Bus. Rev., 71–79 (January–February 1992)
9. Kettinger, W., Teng, J., Guha, S.: Business process change: a study of methodologies, techniques, and tools. MIS Q. **21**(1), 55–80 (1997)
10. Lankhorst, M.: Enterprise Architecture at Work: Modelling, Communication and Analysis. Springer, New York (2013). doi:10.1007/978-3-642-29651-2
11. Laurier, W., Poels, G.: Invariant conditions in value system simulation models. Decis. Support Syst. **56**, 275–287 (2013)
12. Maes, R.: An integrative perspective on information management. In: Huizing, A., De Vries, E. (eds.) Information Management: Setting the Scene, pp. 11–28. Elsevier Science, Oxford (2007)
13. McCarthy, W.: The REA accounting model: a generalized framework for accounting systems in a shared data environment. Account. Rev. **57**, 554–578 (1982)
14. Neely, A., Adams, C., Kennerley, M.: The Performance Prism: The Scorecard for Measuring and Managing Business Success. FT Prentice-Hall, London (2002)
15. OMG: Business Architecture Body of Knowledge Handbook v.2.0 (2012)
16. Peffers, K., Tuunanen, T., Rothenberger, M., Chatterjee, S.: A design science research methodology for information systems research. J. Manag. Inf. Syst. **24**(3), 45–77 (2007)
17. Roelens, B., Poels, G.: Towards an integrative component framework for business models: identifying the common elements between the current business model views. In: Deneckère, R., Proper, H. (eds.) CAiSE 2013 Forum, pp. 114–121, Valencia (2013)

18. Roelens, B., Poels, G.: The creation of business architecture heat maps to support strategy-aligned organizational decisions. In: Devos, J., De Haes, S. (eds.) ECIME 2014, pp. 388–392, Academy Conferences Ltd. (2014)
19. Roelens, B., Steenacker, W., Poels, G.: Realizing strategic fit within the business architecture: the design of a process-goal alignment modeling and analysis technique. Softw. Syst. Model. (2017, in press)
20. Saaty, T.: How to make a decision: the analytic hierarchy process. Eur. J. Oper. Res. **48**(1), 9–26 (1990)
21. Sein, M., Henfridsson, O., Purao, S., Rossi, M., Lindgren, R.: Action design research. MIS Q. **35**(1), 37–56 (2011)
22. The Open Group: TOGAF v.9.1 (2011)
23. Tumay, K.: Business process simulation. In: Alexopoulos, A., et al. (eds.) WSC 1995, pp. 55–60. IEEE Computer Society, Washington (1995)
24. van der Aalst, W., Nakatumba, J., Rozinat, A., Russell, N.: Business process simulation: how to get it right? In: Computer science reports, vol. 0821. Technische Universiteit Eindhoven, Eindhoven (2008)
25. Wieringa, R.: Design Science Methodology for Information Systems and Software Engineering. Springer, Heidelberg (2014). doi:10.1007/978-3-662-43839-8

Supporting Multi-layer Modeling
in BPMN Collaborations

Flavio Corradini, Andrea Polini, Barbara Re, Lorenzo Rossi[✉],
and Francesco Tiezzi

School of Science and Technology, University of Camerino, Camerino, Italy
{flavio.corradini,andrea.polini,barbara.re,
lorenzo.rossi,francesco.tiezzi}@unicam.it

Abstract. In recent years, BPMN has acquired a clear predominance among the notations for modeling business processes. This is mainly due to its capability to close the communication gap between business and IT people. As a consequence, the quality of produced models is more and more important and, among the others, understandability plays a relevant role to permit to properly convey information in such a heterogeneous context. To improve understandability, it is generally recommended to not overwhelm models with to many details, and to use instead sub-process modeling elements to split collaborations into layers. However, the BPMN standard does not provide precise specifications on how the details, hidden at the given layer, should be included in the model, in particular considering message exchange. In particular, the consistency checking between collapsed sub-processes and their detailed representation is left to the modeler, and there is not much support to help him/her in this activity. In this paper, we analyze BPMN modeling tools with respect to their actual capabilities to support multi-layer collaborations. From the analysis we observed a general lack of support in the modeling environment. Then we propose a design methodology providing a set of guidelines to ensure consistency in multi-layer collaborations. These guidelines have been implemented in a stand alone tool, which enables their automated checking in any BPMN modeling tool.

Keywords: BPMN · Modeling guidelines · Messages exchange · Subprocesses

1 Introduction

Business process modeling is an important activity in order to understand and reason on how the work is performed within an organization. In order to support process modeling, several notations have been proposed and are currently available. This paper focus on Business Process Modeling Notation (BPMN) [1], an OMG standard that nowadays is one of the most used notations both in academic and in industrial contexts. This success is mainly due to its capability to close the communication gap between business and IT people. Its wide usage

© Springer International Publishing AG 2017
R. Pergl et al. (Eds.): EOMAS 2017, LNBIP 298, pp. 53–67, 2017.
DOI: 10.1007/978-3-319-68185-6_4

is also testified by the availability of more than 50 tools (for further details see www.bpmn.org) supporting the editing, and often other business process lifecycle phases (e.g., enactment and maintenance).

A largely used diagram of the notation is the *Collaboration* that, among the other aspects, permits to represent the message exchange between different participants collectively cooperating to reach specific goals. Involved participants in a collaboration diagram need to agree on the different aspects of the communication (message orders, message formats, etc.), so that they can effectively reach the objectives of the collaboration. In particular, the involved organizations will have to reconcile their internal processes to properly support the communication.

Collaboration diagrams can be fruitfully exploited for different purposes, that however can have contrasting needs. On the one hand, the diagram conveys relevant information for the involved stakeholders that need to understand and reasons on the impact of the collaboration on their organization. In general, this aspect, which relates to understandability of models, is favored when irrelevant details are hidden in the model and the dimension is kept to a manageable size. On the other hand, collaboration diagrams can be fruitfully exploited, given enough details, to set and deploy supporting software systems, applying for instance model-driven engineering techniques. The automatic derivation of software requires instead to include in the model a high degree of details.

Independently of the purpose of the models, their qualities must be ensured. In particular, to increase models understandability, modeling guidelines are proposed and used in practice. Among the others, it is recommended to split the collaboration into layers with a different focus on the process [2]. In order to do that, BPMN proposes sub-process elements to broke down a model from an abstract layer to a more detailed one (layer nesting is allowed). Indeed, in large and complex models sub-process elements are often used to abstract some part of the behaviour. In such a way it will be possible to achieve the desired trade off between the needs of understandability and precision. Nevertheless, modeling communications in collaboration diagrams could be tricky in multi-layer scenarios when sub-process elements are used.

The usage of multi-layer structures may lead to consistency issues concerning elements that do not represent the same concept in different layers. The OMG standard does not provide any detailed specification of what concerns this kind of situation, leading to modelling environments that behave differently. In particular, they do not support automatic consistency checking, leaving this cumbersome task to modelers. This is a major issue, considering that a manual check is obviously costly and error prone.

In this paper we want to give a solution to such an issue, supporting modelers to design consistent communications in multi-layer BPMN collaborations. More specifically, the contributions of the paper are:

- an analysis of the BPMN modeling tools regarding multi-layer consistency;
- a design methodology for ensuring multi-layer consistency;
- a stand alone tool for checking multi-layer consistency.

The rest of the paper is organized as follows. Section 2 discusses about multi-layer modeling approaches, and compares the most common BPMN modeling tools in terms of supporting mechanisms for multi-layer modeling and related consistency. Section 3 introduces the proposed methodology, providing the list of the defined guidelines. Moreover, it introduces the tool we developed. Section 4 presents most significant related works. Finally, Sect. 5 concludes by also touching upon directions for future work.

2   Multi-layer Modeling: Background Notions and State-of-the-Art

Modeling business processes is not a simple activity and several issues can arise. Business processes have to be considered in relation to size and complexity of the resulting models that in most of the cases need to be handled by introducing sub-process elements. In Sect. 2.1 we list the modeling approaches suitable for using sub-processes according to the OMG standard. Then, in Sect. 2.2, we show how modeling environments manage this kind of multi-layer modeling.

2.1   Multi-layer Modeling Approaches

According to the BPMN standard, expanded or collapsed sub-processes can be used [1]: (a) on the abstract layer (i.e., the main layer) when the sub-process is expanded, (b) on the abstract layer when the sub-process is collapsed using an independent model describing sub-process behaviour.

In practice, it is usually not recommended to use option (a) representing a sub-process in expanded form in the abstract layer, since collapsed sub-processes make the model more understandable. On one hand, the adoption of solution (a) presents issues related to consistency among layers, since all the elements are explicitly represented in the same diagram. Indeed, applying such an approach it is easy to see which task is sending or receiving the message and it is also possible to consider if each message is sent or received. On the other hand, keeping the sub-process expanded at a higher level makes the model and the working space more confusing.

Option (b), in which the sub-process is collapsed in the abstract layer and its specification is provided in an external model, can be a solution in term of modeling. Indeed, this approach solves the issues related to overcrowded models but it can pose issues in relation to the sub-process implementation and to the consistency of the message flows. For instance, inconsistency derive from a wrong naming or a missed specification of the same message in different layers.

The "correct" way of showing messages inside a sub-process is to include on the sub-process model the participants involved in the communication. Moreover, the messages exchange should be consistent among the different layers of the model. In this paper, we consider option (b) thanks to their ability to define multi-layer models giving the possibility to improve understandability.

We present now a multi-layer collaboration scenario, used as running example in the paper. We consider a BPMN collaboration combining the activities of three participants, *A*, *B* and *C*, organized into four layers (see Fig. 1). This example is intentionally kept simple, as it just aims at illustrating the main contributions of the paper. The abstract layer provides, in expanded way, each

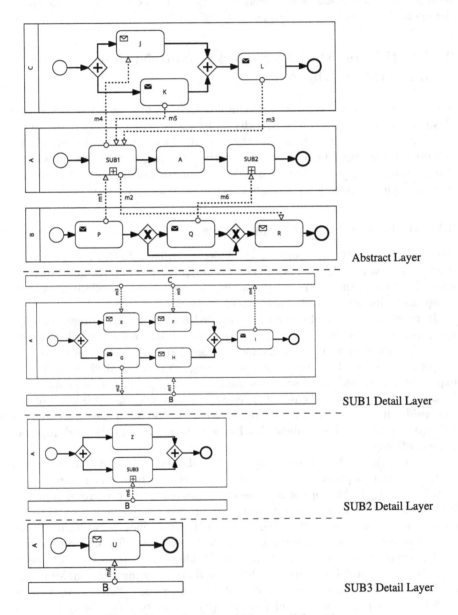

Abstract Layer

SUB1 Detail Layer

SUB2 Detail Layer

SUB3 Detail Layer

Fig. 1. Example of a multi-layer collaboration.

participant pool. This layer contains two sub-processes, *SUB1* and *SUB2*. Their specification processes are also provided, as well as the behavior of sub-process *SUB3* contained in *SUB2*.

2.2   Comparison of Modeling Environments

Considering multi-layer scenario, option (b), we made an assessment of 8 modeling environments widely used in order to check how they work in practice. In particular, the analysis of these tools relies on the features provided for modeling multi-layer collaborations. The analyzed tools are: ADOxx (www. adoxx.org), Aris Express (www.ariscommunity.com), Bizagi (www.bizagi. com), Camunda (www.camunda.com), Eclipse BPMN (www.eclipse.org/ bpmn2-modeler), Magic Draw (www.nomagic.com), Signavio (www.signavio. com) and Visual Paradigm (www.visual-paradigm.com).

Assessment results are provided in Table 1. The table shows, for the abstract layer, if a modeling tool introduces constraints on the number of message flows linkable to the sub-process. It results that AdoXX, Bizagi and Signavio limit the number of message flows that the designer can attach to the sub-process while the other tools do not set any limitation. Table 1 also shows the complexity of modeling tools of linking the abstract layer with the lower layers, hence their suitability to support a multi-layer approach. In this respect, Camunda is the only one that denies this possibility. For this reason, we do not consider it further in the detailed layer analysis. For those modeling environments having the possibility to consider the detailed layer, we compare the tools by analyzing the type of process that can be used in it. The process type can be private, without the possibility to include pools and communication, or public. All the modeling environments refer to public model including pools and messages, except Bizagi. Differently from the other environments, Visual Paradigm gives the possibility to add in the detailed layer pools, tasks and gateways modeled in the abstract

Table 1. Modeling environments comparison.

	Abstract Layer		Detailed Layer	
	Message flow constraints	Multi-layer support	Process type	Consistency check
ADOxx	Yes	Yes	Public	No
Aris Express	No	Yes	Public	No
Bizagi	Yes	Yes	Private	No
Camunda	No	No	-	-
Eclipse BPMN	No	Yes	Public	No
Magic Draw	No	Yes	Public	No
Signavio	Yes	Yes	Public	No
Visual Paradigm	No	Yes	Public	No

layer. Moreover, the tool maintains consistent names and types for the elements, even if, this feature does not consider messages. Thus, consistency is not guaranteed. Finally, Table 1 presents the capability to perform consistency checking focusing on multi-layer communications. We observe that none of the considered tools enables multi-layer consistency (e.g., see the case of Signavio in Fig. 2).

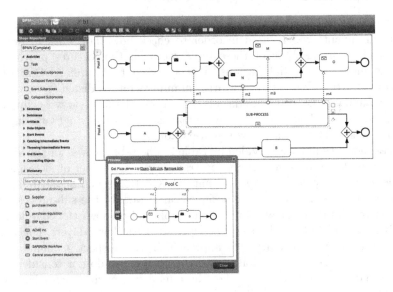

Fig. 2. Lack of consistency in signavio.

3   Methodology and Tool for Multi-layer Consistent Modeling

As we already said, the most effective modeling approach is the option (b), consisting of a collapsed sub-process in the abstract layer and its specification in the detailed one, to limit humans error in modeling. This allows to focus on details via external model view. We believe that in this approach, the designer should be assisted in modeling multi-layer collaboration, without the need to manually check consistency issues. Hence, what is expected from BPMN modeling environments is a reference practice in modeling multi-layer collaborations. Following, Sect. 3.1 discusses the proposed methodology and guidelines, and Sect. 3.2 introduces our consistency checking tool.

3.1   Design Methodology and Guidelines

We propose a top-down modeling approach in which the designer starts to model the abstract layer with collapsed sub-processes and then continue in the nested layers that will be linked to the abstract one. In terms of messages, the modeler should be allowed to attach more than one message flow to a sub-process element, in order to specify the number of communication tasks in the lower layers. Hence, going deeper in the detailed layers the modeler needs to be assisted by providing all the participant pools, and the related message flows, so that errors are limited. Finally, layer by layer, the designer fill the model by adding elements in the pool containing the sub-process and linking the provided messages.

Here are the proposed modeling steps that we propose to be supported by modeling environments in order to assist the model designer. The following four steps have to be applied in an iterative way for each sub-process and recursively for each layer.

S1: *In the abstract layer, the collaboration is provided including all the involved pools. If the process requires a sub-process specification, the designer has to use the collapsed sub-process element and each message exchanged by this element has to be specified in the message flow (Fig. 3).*

S2: *In the abstract layer, collapsed sub-processes have to be linked to their specification by using an external model.*

S3: *For each detailed layer, the modeling environment automatically includes pools and messages to be consistent with the abstract layer. By default, messages have to be attached to the relative pools (Fig. 4).*

S4: *For each detailed layer, the designer has to refine the model detailing the behavior of the sub-process and attaching the message flows to elements within the specified pool.*

Afterwards, a consistency check is expected. This relies on eight guidelines, detailed in the following, able to guarantee consistency at each level of abstraction. Each guideline is a necessary condition for consistency, but they do not represent a complete set of rules to fully ensure this property. It is worth noticing that the multi-layer consistency checking based on these guidelines is performed in the syntactic definition of the collaboration model, without resorting to any formal definition of its semantics. In fact our guidelines have been derived by referring to the semi-formal semantics of BPMN provided by the standard specification [1].

G1: **Message Propagation.** *Each incoming/outgoing message flow attached to a collapsed sub-process has to appear in the relative detailed layer with the same label.*

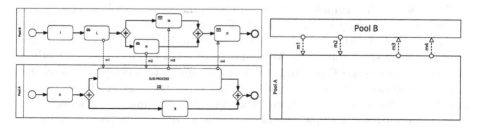

Fig. 3. Abstract Layer.   **Fig. 4.** SUB-PROCESS Detailed Layer - Step 3.

G2: Message Link. *Each incoming/outgoing message flow attached to a collapsed sub-process has to conclude its propagation in a message task or message event.*

G3: Message Number. *Further messages cannot be added to the ones in the abstract layer.*

G4: Message Direction. *Each message must keep the same sending and receiving participant in each layer.*

G5: Message Ordering. *For each couple of participants exchanging messages, if one of this performs a receive and after some steps a send, the other participant has to respect this order, by sending and than receiving the same messages independently from the layer in which are included (Fig. 5).*

G6: Optional Message. *For each couple of participants exchanging messages, each message sent by one of this participant in a non mandatory[1] branch has to be received by the other one in a non mandatory branch (Fig. 6).*

G7: Mandatory Message. *For each couple of participants exchanging messages, each message received by one of this participant in a mandatory branch has to be sent by the other one in a mandatory branch (Fig. 7).*

G8: Looping Message. *For each couple of participants exchanging messages, each message received by one of this participant in a loop branch has to be sent by the other one in a loop branch (Fig. 8).*

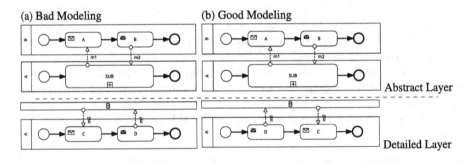

Fig. 5. Message Ordering example.

Considering the example we present in Sect. 2, here in the following we show the guidelines checking results. First of all we observe an issue referring to the message *m1* of the abstract layer that is linked in SUB1 to the border of the pool A. This is the result of the **Message Link - G2** check. We also underline the error of **Message Ordering - G5**. This regards to messages *m3* and *m4* following the order *m3 m4* in SUB1. Considering the abstract layer we can observe that the order is backward. Another problem impacts on message *m6*, in the abstract layer it is not mandatory, while we observe an issue referring to

---

[1] A non mandatory branch is a path of the process that starts from an exclusive, inclusive or event-based split gateway.

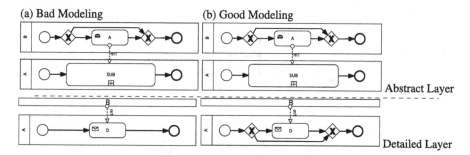

Fig. 6. Optional Message example.

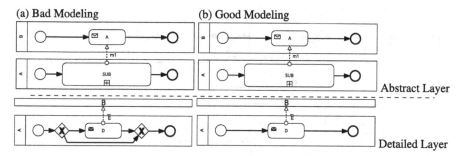

Fig. 7. Mandatory Message example.

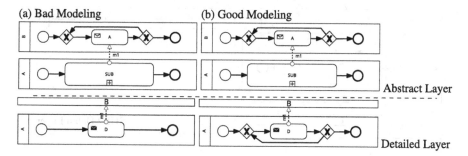

Fig. 8. Looping Message example.

the **Optional Message - G6** in SUB3 where the receiving task is mandatory. According to the suggested guidelines, in Fig. 9 we present the corrected multi-layer collaboration.

3.2 Consistency Checking Tool

In order to support the defined guidelines, we propose a *Java* based tool supporting designers in establishing whether their models are consistent. The tool is freely available[2]. It is independent from any modeling environment, hence can be used as an external service that can be integrated as a plug-in in other existing

---

[2] https://github.com/lorenzorossiunicam/ConsistencyChecking.

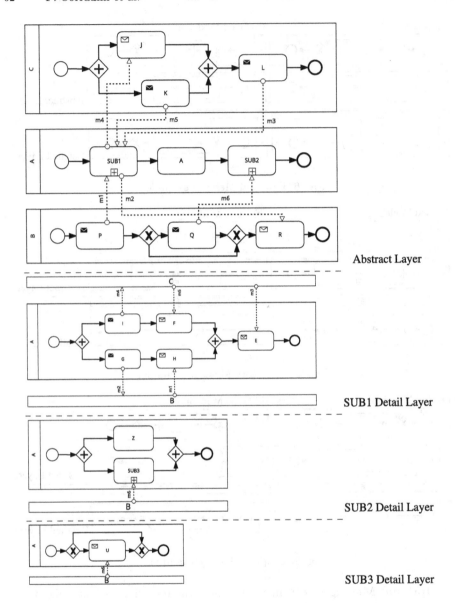

Fig. 9. Multi-layer collaboration (corrected version).

modeling tools, and eventually extended. The tool works with .bpmn files compliant with the OMG BPMN 2.0 standard. The input has to be provided as a set
of BPMN models organized with a tree structure, in which the root represents
the abstract layer and each leaf refers to a collapsed sub-process of the parent
model. Tree structure provides hence a link from each collapsed sub-process to
its process definition.

The consistency checking algorithm implemented in the tool, reported in Fig. 10, starts considering the abstract layer contained by the root of the dependency tree, then the other layers are analyzed using a depth first search navigation.

```
1  checkConsistency(Tree<Collaboration> tree){
2      Collaboration root = tree.getRoot();
3      for(Pool p : root.getPools())
4          for(Lane lane : p.getLanes())
5              lane.updateMessageSequence();
6      for(CollapsedSubProcess sub : root){
7          toCheck.addAll(sub.getMessages());
8          msgInRoot = toCheck;
9          goDeep(root.getChildrensOf(sub));
10     }
11     for (Message m : toCheck()){
12         //Guideline 1 and 2 Violation
13     }
14     checkMessageSequences();
15     //Guideline 5, 6, 7 and 8 violation
16 }
17
18 goDeep(Leaf l){
19     for(Pool p : l.getPools())
20         for(Lane lane : l.getLanes())
21             lane.updateMessageSequence();
22     for(Message m : l.getCollaboration().getMessages()){
23         if(!msgInRoot.contains(m))
24             //Guideline 3 Violation else
25         if(isWrongDirection(m))
26             //Guideline 4 Violation else
27         if(isSourceOrTarget(m))
28             toCheck.remove(m);
29     }
30     for(CollapsedSubProcess sub : l)
31         goDeep(l);
32 }
```

Fig. 10. Consistency checking algorithm

At each step of the navigation the messages attached to a collapsed sub-process element are added in a global set of messages considering its name, the communicating pools and if the source or the destination have to be checked. In addition, to this, for each participant guidelines G5, G6, G7 and G8 are checked. Then, the procedure removes elements in this set if the missing source/destination is found in the correct layer, the remaining messages suggest errors of missed source/destination. At the same time, messages that are further connected to a sub-process are kept into the set. Otherwise, if new message names are found, the tool notices the absence of their definition in the root model.

Consistency checking has to be done quickly in order to be used in real contexts. The computational complexity of this algorithm clearly depends on the number of layers and messages that have to be checked. Given a collaboration split into L layers, in which are exchanged M messages, the algorithm visits each layer with a computational complexity derived by the depth first search. This complexity is $O(V + E)$, where V is the number of nodes and E the number of edges. In our dependency tree the nodes number is equal to the number of layers while the number of edges is equal to the number of node minus one. Hence, the visit complexity is $O(V + E) = O(L + L - 1) = O(2L) = O(L)$. In addition to this, in each layer the algorithm controls each message. The number of messages in each layer is, in the worst case, equal to the number of messages in the abstract layer. Consequently, the overall computational complexity of the algorithm is $O(L \times M)$.

4   Related Works

Multi-layer consistency, which has been identified in the literature as a relevant issue [3], is still an open field of study. There is a lack of works both in methodological and in formal approaches. Here we first refer to modeling guidelines used into practice and then to those approaches discussing formal verification to support consistency.

Regarding modeling guidelines, valuable contributions can be found in the literature published before the release of BPMN 2.0 [2,4,5]. These works focus on other graphical languages for business process modeling, but many recommendations can also be applied to BPMN 2.0. Regarding BPMN 2.0, a relevant work that specifically focuses on guidelines is provided by Silingas and Mileviciene [6]; the authors analyzed six BPMN models, and identified the *bad smells* – i.e., modeling approaches negatively impacting on model quality – that they contained. On the application of guidelines, an interesting contribution is given by Leopold et al. [7]. The authors focus on quality issues of 585 BPMN 2.0 process models from industry, highlighting which guidelines (collected from specific works, [8–10]) are not followed. Another relevant work is provided by [9], who suggests the use of an approach called *method and style* to help the model designers. More generally on process model quality, the most complete overview is given by de Oca et al. [11]. The authors collected 72 papers addressing different aspects of modeling quality, e.g., understandability, readability, maintainability, correctness, modularity, perceived ambiguity, perceived usefulness, completeness, etc. Starting from this review, the authors provided a set of 27 problems and unified quality guidelines [12]. Summing up, these contributions have a larger scope than ours, since they consider multiple quality attributes. However, our work provides a deeper insight for what concerns the messages exchange in multi-layer scenario. Another difference with our work is that most of the authors do not always suggest a way to verify the application of those guidelines, that is needed to automatically check if the model fits with the guidelines or not.

Regarding the formalization and verification of BPMN model consistency, the notion of sub-process and multi-layer specification has not been extensively studied yet. Among the others, Christiansen et al. [13], Corradini et al. [14], Falcioni et al. [15] El-Saber and Boronat [16] and, Borger and Thalheim [17] provide a direct formalization for a minimal subset of BPMN elements. Others contributions provide a mapping toward well known formal specifications (e.g., process algebras and petri-nets). In particular, Van Gorp and Dijkman define a formalization using visual transformation rules [18]. Differently, Kossak et al. present a sub-process semantics. The paper skips the problem of messages flow saying that *"semantics, however, does not change with the graphical depiction, that is, a collapsed sub-process must have the same semantics as when it is expanded"* [19]. Dijkman et al. propose a mapping from BPMN to Petri nets. The paper introduces also sub-processes saying that *"the behavior of such a process is however not clear in the BPMN specification"* [20]. It has been used in practice in different application domains [21]. Relevant is the work of Conforti et al. [22]. It aims to present a technique for multi-layer discovery of BPMN models without considering issues derived by messages exchange. These papers do not take into account sub-processes in terms of multi-layer structures, hence it is clear that sub-process semantics are developed without taking into account consistency in message exchange.

Finally, consistency is not a specific matter of business process modeling. There exists several research largely focuses on checking consistency of individual model and of relationships between pairs of models [23].

5   Conclusions and Future Works

In this paper we provide the results of an analysis we conducted on eight BPMN modeling tools regarding their capabilities to support multi-layer collaborations. We observe that most of the tools support the multi-layer modeling, some of them do not implement any consistency check. To solve such an issue, we provide a design methodology based on a set of eight consistency guidelines for multi-layer collaborations. Moreover, we develop a stand alone Java tool for checking the proposed guidelines.

As a future work, we plan to investigate more in detail the notion of compliance in order to give a wider set of guidelines suitable to ensure process models correctness by design. We also plan to extend modeling tools to implement the methodology and to integrate the checking tool in the design process [24]. Moreover, we aim to address the problem in a more formal way, by using and, if necessary, extending formal semantics of BPMN collaborations.

Acknowledgments. The authors would like to thank Elisa Ballini for her support in the benchmarking of modelling environments.

References

1. OMG: Business Process Model and Notation (BPMN V 2.0) (2011)
2. Mendling, J., Reijers, H.A., van der Aalst, W.M.: Seven process modeling guidelines (7 pmg). Inf. Softw. Technol. **52**(2), 127–136 (2010)
3. Wong, P.Y.H., Gibbons, J.: A process semantics for BPMN. In: Liu, S., Maibaum, T., Araki, K. (eds.) ICFEM 2008. LNCS, vol. 5256, pp. 355–374. Springer, Heidelberg (2008). doi:10.1007/978-3-540-88194-0_22
4. Mendling, J., Reijers, H.A., Cardoso, J.: What makes process models understandable? In: Alonso, G., Dadam, P., Rosemann, M. (eds.) BPM 2007. LNCS, vol. 4714, pp. 48–63. Springer, Heidelberg (2007). doi:10.1007/978-3-540-75183-0_4
5. Mendling, J., Sanchez-Gonzalez, L., Garcia, F., La Rosa, M.: Thresholds for error probability measures of business process models. J. Syst. Softw. **85**(5), 1188–1197 (2012)
6. Silingas, D., Mileviciene, E.: Refactoring BPMN models: from 'Bad Smells' to best practices and patterns. In: BPMN 2.0 Handbook Second Edition: Methods, Concepts, Case Studies and Standards in Business Process Management Notation, p. 125 (2011)
7. Leopold, H., Mendling, J., Günther, O.: Learning from quality issues of BPMN models from industry. In: Proceedings of the 7th International Workshop on Enterprise Modeling and Information Systems Architectures, Vienna, Austria, 3–4 October 2016, pp. 36–39 (2016)
8. Allweyer, T.: BPMN 2.0 - Business Process Model and Notation: Einführung in den Standard für die Geschäftsprozessmodellierung. Books on Demand (2009)
9. Silver, B.: BPMN method and style: with BPMN implementer's guide, 2 edn. (2011)
10. White, S.A.: BPMN modeling and reference guide: understanding and using BPMN. Future Strategies Inc. (2008)
11. de Oca, I.M.M., Snoeck, M., Reijers, H.A., Rodríguez-Morffi, A.: A systematic literature review of studies on business process modeling quality. Inf. Softw. Technol. **58**, 187–205 (2015)
12. Moreno-Montes de Oca, I., Snoeck, M.: Pragmatic guidelines for business process modeling. Technical Report 2592983, KU Leuven, Faculty of Economics and Business, November 2014
13. Christiansen, D.R., Carbone, M., Hildebrandt, T.: Formal semantics and implementation of BPMN 2.0 inclusive gateways. In: Bravetti, M., Bultan, T. (eds.) WS-FM 2010. LNCS, vol. 6551, pp. 146–160. Springer, Heidelberg (2011). doi:10.1007/978-3-642-19589-1_10
14. Corradini, F., Polini, A., Re, B., Tiezzi, F.: An operational semantics of BPMN collaboration. In: Braga, C., Ölveczky, P.C. (eds.) FACS 2015. LNCS, vol. 9539, pp. 161–180. Springer, Cham (2016). doi:10.1007/978-3-319-28934-2_9
15. Falcioni, D., Polini, A., Polzonetti, A., Re, B.: Direct verification of BPMN processes through an optimized unfolding technique, pp. 179–188. IEEE, August 2012
16. El-Saber, N., Boronat, A.: BPMN formalization and verification using Maude. In: Proceedings of the 2014 Workshop on Behaviour Modelling-Foundations and Applications. BM-FA 2014, pp. 1:1–1:12. ACM, New York (2014)
17. Börger, E., Thalheim, B.: A method for verifiable and validatable business process modeling. In: Börger, E., Cisternino, A. (eds.) Advances in Software Engineering. LNCS, vol. 5316, pp. 59–115. Springer, Heidelberg (2008). doi:10.1007/978-3-540-89762-0_3

18. Van Gorp, P., Dijkman, R.: A visual token-based formalization of BPMN 2.0 based on in-place transformations. Inf. Softw. Technol. **55**(2), 365–394 (2013)

19. Kossak, F., et al.: A rigorous semantics for BPMN 2.0 process diagrams. A Rigorous Semantics for BPMN 2.0 Process Diagrams, pp. 29–154. Springer, Cham (2014). doi:10.1007/978-3-319-09931-6_4

20. Dijkman, R.M., Dumas, M., Ouyang, C.: Semantics and analysis of business process models in BPMN. Inf. Softw. Technol. **50**(12), 1281–1294 (2008)

21. Corradini, F., Polini, A., Re, B.: Inter-organizational business process verification in public administration. Bus. Process Manage. J. **21**(5), 1040–1065 (2015)

22. Conforti, R., Dumas, M., García-Bañuelos, L., La Rosa, M.: BPMN miner. Inform. Syst. **56**(C), 284–303 (2016)

23. Sabetzadeh, M., Nejati, S., Liaskos, S., Easterbrook, S., Chechik, M.: Consistency checking of conceptual models via model merging. In: 15th IEEE International Requirements Engineering Conference (RE 2007), pp. 221–230. IEEE (2007)

24. Flavio, C., Alberto, P., Barbara, R., Damiano, F.: An eclipse plug-in for formal verification of BPMN processes. In: 2010 Third International Conference on Communication Theory, Reliability, and Quality of Service, pp. 144–149, June 2010

Applying the Concept of Modularity to IT Outsourcing: A Financial Services Case

Shahzada Benazeer, Peter De Bruyn$^{(\boxtimes)}$, and Jan Verelst

Department of Management Information Systems,
University of Antwerp, Antwerp, Belgium
{shazdada.benazeer,peter.debruyn,jan.verelst}@uantwerp.be

Abstract. Information systems and information technology (IS/IT) services are often outsourced to external vendors for reasons of cost cutting or specialized expertise. Throughout the years, reports about high failure rates regarding IS/IT outsourcing initiatives have been repeatedly published. Therefore, the large variety of mitigating factors proposed in literature did not seem to be sufficient to significantly improve the success rate of these projects. This paper employs the concept of modularity to study the (un)successful execution of IT outsourcing projects. For this end, we present and analyze a single case study conducted at a financial institution in Belgium. It is shown how several modular structures can be identified and analyzed and might provide insight in the (un)successful outcome of IS/IT outsourcing initiatives.

Keywords: IS/IT outsourcing · Modularity · Case study research

1 Introduction

Due to globalization and advancements in information and communication technologies (ICT), information systems and/or information technology (IS/IT) outsourcing became a very common practice in developed and emerging economies. The global market of IS/IT outsourcing is predicted to be more than $260 billion in 2018 [7] and over 94% of the 'Fortune 500' companies are outsourcing at least one major business function [17]. Despite IS/IT outsourcing's importance and its worldwide acceptance, general performance reports on outsourcing initiatives indicate problematic situations. For instance, in some studies, failure rates as high as 50% and above (e.g., [10,20]) are reported. A large number of IS/IT outsourcing projects is being re-negotiated or prematurely terminated and many IS/IT outsourcing failures are even not publicly reported due to the fear of negative responses from the market and stakeholders [3]. Others suggest that in about 78% of IS/IT long-term outsourcing cases, the relationship between the customer and the vendor reaches the point of failure (e.g., [16]). Therefore, it is no surprise that some authors report satisfaction rates regarding IS/IT outsourcing projects of only 33% (e.g., [8]). Evolution over time tends to suggest some, but insufficient progress in this respect. For instance, one longitudinal

© Springer International Publishing AG 2017
R. Pergl et al. (Eds.): EOMAS 2017, LNBIP 298, pp. 68–82, 2017.
DOI: 10.1007/978-3-319-68185-6_5

study found that the percentage of failed IS/IT outsourcing projects (i.e., cancelled prior to completion or delivered and never used) had declined over time but still amounted to 44% in 2009 [13].

Many suggestions have been uttered by both scholars and practitioners on how these problems can be mitigated. Some suggest to streamline operations and 'fix the problem' before outsourcing IS/IT services (e.g., [18]). Other management-oriented suggestions include the 'Partnership Model [14]', the 'Seven steps to successful outsourcing' [9], knowledge sharing [15], 'knowledge transfer' [19], high quality 'service level agreements' (SLA) [11] or the reconfiguration of organizational resources (e.g., [26]). However, as the empirical research (as mentioned above) continues to report high failure rates of IS/IT outsourcing projects, it seems that these remedies turned out to be partially successful at best. The desire to be better equipped to understand potential IS/IT outsourcing issues has fueled the study presented in this paper. We present the use of a well-known and widely applied engineering concept (i.e., modularity) to study an enterprise challenge, i.e., the successful execution of IT outsourcing engagements. This perspective to analyze outsourcing initiatives is new as most existing approaches adopt a purely managerial focused perspective (e.g., focusing on issues such as trust or leadership). We illustrate our approach by presenting and analyzing a case study conducted at a Belgian financial institution. While in the past, we employed our perspective to analyze two theoretically based cases (i.e., based on case material available in literature), this paper presents the first case in which information was gathered via primary sources.

The remainder of this paper is structured as follows. Section 2 will describe the methodology adopted to analyze our case. Afterwards, the case is introduced (Sect. 3) and our analysis and findings are presented in Sect. 4. Our discussion and conclusions are offered in Sects. 5 and 6, respectively.

2 Methodology and Theoretical Background

We propose the lens of modularity to analyze outsourcing engagements. Modularity has been argued to reduce the complexity of systems [2] which makes it an interesting concept to apply to outsourcing engagements as these are typically considered to be highly complex as well. Baldwin and Clark [1, p. 86] state that a modular system is "composed of units (or modules) that are designed independently but still function as an integrated whole". The concept is recursive, in the sense that a module within a particular system can in itself be considered as a system as well, also being composed of a set of (sub) modules [21]. Good modular design should be characterized by high cohesion (modules consisting out of highly related parts) and low coupling (few dependencies between modules). The interaction between modules is captured by their interface, which should be exhaustive and invariant throughout time. In order to manage the modular architecture of a system, a set of design rules may be put forward, which formulate a set of boundary conditions to which all modules should adhere so they can communicate with one another [2]. While some authors have already suggested possible links between modularity and outsourcing (e.g., [6,23]), this connection has always been formulated in rather general or even vague terms. Little explicit knowledge is available regarding which specific aspects within outsourcing engagements can be studied by means of modularity and to which insights this might lead. Therefore, we formulate the following research question: "*How can the concept of modularity be applied to outsourcing engagements: which modularity specific aspects can be used and regarding which organizational issues can it provide additional insights?*"

Based on this research question and following the decision making structure of Wohlin [24], our research is to be seen as basic research (as we want to understand a phenomenon, here: IT outsourcing), inductive (aiming to infer general claims from observed data), having a descriptive goal (investigating the "how") and asks for a interpretivist approach. Therefore, a qualitative research process was deemed suitable as our goal is to gain an in-depth understanding of the manifestations of modularity within the context of IT outsourcing [25]. More specifically, a case study was chosen as the appropriate research method as this allowed us to investigate the relevance of the modularity concept within IT outsourcing initiatives in their natural setting [4,25]. Given the lack of preceding in-depth work on modularity in an outsourcing context, a more descriptive case study was considered appealing.

Our unit of analysis is a single company applying outsourcing in order to deal with its required IT functionalities. The selection of the case organization was performed purposefully based on a set of criteria. The case organization had to be engaged in IT outsourcing engagements of a certain amount of complexity. An organization was preferred which operated in a different industry than those in which our previous cases were performed (i.e., media broadcasting and higher eduction), and which was able to put an informant at our disposal who was willing to meet at least three times. The case organization as described in Sect. 3 was selected as it satisfied all criteria. It concerned a company within the finance industry which is particularly interesting as this industry is recently experiencing tendencies towards high digitization. Further, the company was involved in a multi-vendor package configuration, which also differed from our earlier cases in which one large outsourcing project was discussed.

Data gathering was mainly performed through interviews and analyzed by means of thematic analysis [24]. In a first stage, in-depth desk research about the Belgian banking sector and their IS/IT outsourcing strategies was performed. Next, publicly available documentation (including news papers and magazines) regarding the IS/IT outsourcing strategy adopted by the case organization was studied. In the second stage, a first exploratory meeting with the CIO of the company was performed. Here, the goal was to get a general overview of the organization. Therefore, the main questions were directed towards the current situation of the (IT) organization, their most important IT systems, the IT architecture and the different IT outsourcing initiatives undertaken in the past and present, etc. In order not to influence the answers provided by our informant, only the general goal of the research project was briefly discussed upfront (i.e., "we investigate the role between modularity and outsourcing") without mentioning specific concepts to be used during the analysis. In the third stage, a preliminary analysis of the first interview was jointly performed by the authors. The main goal of this initial analysis was to scope a set of potentially relevant issues (i.e., related to modularity) to be further investigated in the later stages. These issues were then systematically discussed and further elaborated during the second interview. In this interview, the basic ideas regarding modularity (decomposition, interfaces, coupling, etc.) were summarized for the informant. In the fourth and final stage, a more thorough analysis was performed by all authors. Also, a third interview was held in which the findings were presented and validated for factual correctness and appropriate interpretation. Any remaining questions of the informant were addressed during this interview, as well as a more in-depth discussion of the current state and findings of the research project in which the case is embedded. All interviews were conducted at the Belgian headquarter of the organization by the three authors, lasted each for about two hours, and were completed within a total time frame of about 2 months. The conversations were recorded digitally for future reference.

We acknowledge that the single-case approach presented in this paper limits the generalizability of our findings. It is however important to note that this case is embedded within a broader research project, in which several case studies (both theoretical and real-life) are performed. This should allow us to apply our perspective to various situations within different contexts, and to reflect on the generalizability of our findings in a more informed way.

3   Case Introduction

Our case organization concerns a Belgian banking organization (further referred to as "AB bank", a fictitious name in order to guarantee anonymity and confidentiality). AB bank focuses on private banking activities, implying that — compared to traditional retail bankers— their customer base is smaller but wealthier. Further, the bank's activities include asset management and merchant banking services. Within the Belgian financial services industry, the organization can be considered as medium sized in terms of its number of employees, number of clients, turnover, etc. While being a private bank in its core, the bank also welcomes investment clients with smaller budgets which can be served via an online investment portal. The portfolio management activities for bigger clients are offered through personal advice.

Due to its relatively limited size (about 10 employees), the IT department of AB bank is rather small as well. The bank considers its IT activities as operational and necessary but not as a strategic issue to obtain a competitive advantage. In that context, the bank has chosen over the years for a multi-vendor IT outsourcing strategy. This means that multiple and different external suppliers are used to provide different types of services. First, most of the development and maintenance work of the IT infrastructure is outsourced to external parties. Additionally, the IT department is dealing with many applications from different vendors. Given its relatively small internal team and the focus on outsourcing, AB bank has only developed three core applications internally: CRM, client on boarding (registering information of newly acquired customers), and an order management system. This aligns with the ambition of AB bank to limit the amount of customized products, while giving preference to the usage of package solutions. Therefore, the main activity of the in-house IT team of AB bank is concerned with the integration of all outsourced activities as well as its general management (package selection, vendor negotiations, etc.). Our informant was the head of the IT department (CIO). While sketching the current situation of his department as well as the outlook for the future, the integration of the different (often externally acquired) applications was already indicated as a major concern. As the previous two cases conducted in this research project [12] did not include multi-vendor configurations and were not situated within the financial services industry, this case allowed for a further exploration of our approach in a different setting. Moreover, the interviews with our informant allowed for a more interactive, iterative and in-depth way of information gathering.

4   Findings

We highlighted in Sect. 2 that modularity is inherently a recursive concept that can be applied at different levels. Our analysis revealed two major levels at which modularity could be clearly applied to the case at hand. Therefore, we subsequently discuss issues at an inter-organizational level (in which we consider the relationship of AB bank and its IT service providers) and at an intra-organizational level (in which we consider the internal organization of AB bank, such as the architecture of its different IT applications and their integration). This is visually illustrated by Fig. 1. On the one hand, the figure depicts a general overview of the IT system modules present within the case organization (the grey ovals indicate the internally developed and maintained applications). One can easily observe that a large majority of the IT applications (i.e., the white ovals) are outsourced to an external party. On the other hand, the figure shows that for these outsourced applications, a set of SLAs was agreed upon with a set of external IS service providers.

We adopt the same way of reporting for each of the identified modularity manifestations. First, we provide some relevant context related to the manifestation and identify the modular structure which is considered. Second, we ponder on which design prescriptions can be derived from the existing knowledge base regarding modularity for this situation. We refer to these prescriptions as modularity requirements. Third, we verify whether these requirements were actually adhered to in the specific situation at hand in the considered case. Based on such reasoning we can explore (1) which modularity aspects are relevant in an IT outsourcing context (2) to which organizational artifacts and modular structures can they be applied, and (3) to which extent this could clarify potential issues in the outsourcing engagement.

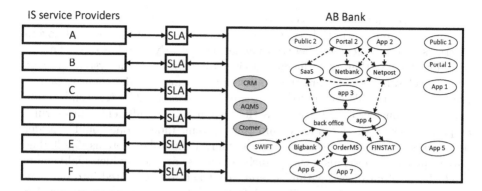

Fig. 1. Modular structures identified in the AB Bank case

4.1 Modularity Manifestations at the Inter-organizational Level

At the most general level, an outsourcing deal concerns an agreement or contract between (mostly two) parties in which one party (the vendor) agrees to deliver certain (in this case IT related) services to another party (the client). As these deals are often highly complex and of crucial importance for both parties, they need to be managed by good arrangements stipulating the roles and responsibilities of each of the involved actors. In the outsourcing industry, such contract is typically labeled as a *Service-Level Agreement (SLA)*. First, it is clear that such SLA is crucial from a legal point of view. Recall from Sect. 1 that many IT outsourcing projects fail and may result in non-satisfactory relationships between the vendor and the client which may sometimes even end up in a legal dispute. In such cases, obviously, the SLA serves as the starting point to analyze who has (not) fulfilled his or her responsibilities. In more general terms, the SLA can be regarded as the set of rules between the vendor and the client that govern the outsourcing relationship, which makes the SLA a crucial component of each and every outsourcing engagement. Given the importance of an SLA in an outsourcing context, we interviewed our informant in-depth about the SLAs adopted by the case organization during its outsourcing engagements. More specifically, we asked about how these SLAs were established during the initiation of an outsourcing deal. Furthermore, we obtained information regarding the extent to which the respondent believed that these SLAs were effective in providing a sufficient amount of guidance and coordination between the parties involved during the execution of the project. We also asked about the evolution of such SLA in case of long-term engagements: what if one of the parties wants to adapt certain conditions in the contract? (How) can this be done?

Identifying the Modular Structure and Requirements. At least two types of modular structures can be discerned when focusing on the role of an SLA within an outsourcing project. First, an SLA could be considered as the interface between the two organizations involved. Recall from Sect. 2 that an interface is the common boundary between modules, and manages the communication and interaction (input/output) between those modules. As the SLA should govern the rules and arrangements between parties, this clearly matches the definition of an interface. In that case, the outsourcing collaboration is the system in scope and the relevant modules are the vendor organization and the client organization. We refer to this configuration as *modular structure 1.1.* A second option could be to consider the SLA itself as the system and the different clauses, rules or paragraphs as the modules within that system. Indeed, one could consider documents, and legal documents in particular, as modular systems [5,22]. The paragraphs, items or clauses within such documents are clearly identifiable units —which are often reused within different contracts— aggregated into one specific contract acting as the specific SLA for a specific outsourcing agreement. We refer to this configuration as *modular structure 1.2.*

Regarding modular structure 1.1., and based on Sect. 2, we know that a good interface between modules should be exhaustive and complete. Applied to the SLA interpreted as the interface between the vendor and the client, this implies that all services required by AB bank from the vendor should be listed in the SLA (and other services than those embedded in the interface should not occur). We refer to this statement as *modularity requirement 1.1.*

Section 2 further mentioned that an interface should be kept constant throughout time (as otherwise changes in one module would cause unnecessary ripple effects within other modules). However, given the long-term duration of many outsourcing contracts, it is conceivable that mutually agreed upon changes in the SLA do need to happen or additional behavior of the involved parties is required (e.g., improved services from the vendor to the client). As this change of interface happens purposefully in order to change the behavior of one or both parties, this does not need to be problematic. However, in order to enable agility and flexibility regarding the SLA contract, it is required that the SLA itself consists out of subparts or modules itself (cf. modular structure 1.2). Each of these individual contract modules can then be updated or removed from the contract, or additional ones can be added. We refer to the existence of a fine-grained SLA contract which can be adapted at the level of individual clauses as *modularity requirement 1.2.*

Assessing the Modularity Requirements. It was remarkable to note that the SLA was mainly considered by the case organization as a "necessary obligation" attached to the beginning of each outsourcing initiative. The formulation of an outsourcing contract was primarily regarded as a legal issue to be dealt with by the legal department and not to be consulted except in cases where judicial actions were required:

> "For me a contract is something you make, you sign, and put it in a closet.
> (...) The moment you need that is because you have a problem."

Instead, our informant explained that AB bank was counting —to a large extent— on the professional behavior of the outsourcing partner and expected them to be reasonable. Stated otherwise, the "legal" SLA was indeed realized via a formal contract whereas the actual or "operational" SLA was mainly based on confidence and mutual trust: While in several situations such collaboration succeeded (due to personal contact between people at the vendor and the client side), the respondent acknowledged that this way of working had also clearly failed in numerous occasions:

> "(For instance,) when we see a problem (...) and ask to 'S' (pseudonym of a vendor): "why is this problem not noticed by you?" they answer that they were not monitoring that process. We tell the 'S' people that being a professional you should have monitored that problem. The 'S' people will reply that they have not been asked (by AB bank's SLA) to monitor that problem. (...) Both parties have done what is stated in the contract. Yes, but was that enough? No, probably not. It is not stated in the contract that we should make the design how the architecture (of the application) should look like and define it. But we expect them to operate the platform that runs the application."

From the above, it becomes clear that the description embedded within the SLA was by no means exhaustive. Ambiguous formulations were (often consciously) allowed within the contract as trust was considered to be the main driving force behind the collaboration. As a consequence, we conclude that modularity requirement 1.1 was not met.

While we do not underestimate or want to ignore the importance of human aspects (such as trust) in organizational collaborations, we find it interesting to note that this identified violation of requirement 1.1 (i.e., an insufficient specification of the way of interaction between the parties) was precisely considered by our informant as one of the most important reasons why outsourcing contracts were not always executed as expected. Discussions arose with vendors on who should do which tasks and it was highlighted that AB bank was unable to insist on getting the expected services performed properly due to their limited leverage over the respective vendors.

When asked for the possibility to adapt the SLAs with its vendors during the execution of an agreement, our informant indicated that such things simply did not happen at AB bank. Also here, our informant indicated that this is mostly assumed to be covered by mutual trust: an outsourcing contract is often negotiated and drafted as a whole, and there is not really a procedure in order to accommodate changes. Contracts are typically signed for a fixed duration (e.g., five years) and should therefore be renegotiated within the borders of this cycle. The only type of change which was explicitly taken into account was the (premature) termination of the contract initiated by the client (i.e., AB bank). This was again mainly included based on financial and legal motivations, such as stipulations regarding the maximum amount of costs for AB bank in order to leave the deal and be able to switch to another vendor. From these findings, it is clear that the SLA itself was considered as one monolithic block which was to be dealt with (and negotiated) as one whole. Parts (or modules) could not be changed during the stipulated duration of the contract. Therefore, we conclude that modularity requirement 1.2 was not met.

4.2   Modularity Manifestations at the Intra-organizational Level

At a more fine-grained level, an IT outsourcing project concerns the transferal of certain responsibilities regarding a (set of) IT application(s) from the client to the vendor. Clearly, at the client organization, these externally developed IT applications should be integrated (both with internal systems and with systems from other vendors) so that they can collaborate with one another if required. As described in Sect. 3 and illustrated in Fig. 1, AB bank adopted a multi-vendor outsourcing strategy encompassing numerous medium sized applications and only a limited amount of applications developed and maintained by themselves. The arrows within the figure depict the most important interactions between the systems.

Given the importance for AB bank of managing this set of applications, we interviewed our informant in-depth about how the organization dealt with this particular configuration. More specifically, we asked about how the integration between these applications was established. Was this easy or problematic? Whose responsibility was this? And how was this taken into account during the different phases of the outsourcing project (e.g., initiation, startup, execution, etc.)?

Identifying the Modular Structure and Requirements. The modular structure to study the communication between and integration of AB's IT systems can be easily identified. That is, each individual IT application is a module on its own. Our informant discussed the elaborate IT application landscape within AB bank (e.g., the different applications for the back office, front office, customer on board, etc.), some of them being internally managed and some of them externally. As the organization did not distinguish subparts within each application, the application level is the lowest granularity level available when studying the integration issue in this case. Therefore, we consider AB bank's IT application portfolio as the system, with every individual application being a module. In case an internal system has to communicate with an external IT system, this latter system should also be considered as a module. We refer to this configuration as *modular structure 2.1*.

We mentioned in Sect. 2 that a well-designed modular system should have a clear and well-established modular architecture. This means that the set of modules (here: IT applications) in the system should be identified and the dependencies between the IT applications (i.e., the interfaces) should be exhaustively documented. A set of design rules should be created, formulating conditions to which the IT applications have to comply (i.e., required inputs and outputs). Within these limitations, each IT application can freely choose its specific implementation. We refer to the existence of exhaustively documented inter-application interfaces and the adherence to centrally defined design rules as *modularity requirement 2.1*. Further, Sect. 2 explained that a good modular structure should exhibit high cohesion, meaning that every individual module should have a clearly focused responsibility. Applied to modular structure 2.1, this means that every IT application should be concerned with a clearly delineated functionality and, for instance, no overlap in functionalities among multiple IT applications should exist. We refer to this latter statement as *modularity requirement 2.2*.

Assessing the Modularity Requirements. At the start of the discussion of the IT application integration during the interview, we expressed our feeling that the architecture looked rather complicated and that we were wondering if and how integration occured. It was immediately noted by the informant that integration was an important IT challenge within AB bank as it was straightforward for him to enumerate a set of pertinent issues in this area. For example, it was stated that if a new customer is coming to open an account, the administrative employee needs to enter data manually in 7 different systems and that in some cases this number of systems can go up to 15. Or, if a customer likes to order a particular equity, the portfolio manager first has to look up the equity offers within a system A and then needs to go to system B to execute the order as no direct links between these two systems is established. Similarly, if a customer calls to AB bank and asks to buy a certain amount of a particular stock, the portfolio manager will enter this request into system B. System B sends this request automatically to the broker's system (typically another Belgian bank). The request comes back to system B confirming that the operation is executed at a particular price per share. The additional charges for this operation (e.g., commission, taxes, etc.) do not get incorporated in the invoice at that moment as it is not included within the interface between system B and the external broker. In fact, the information about the additional charges is only known to AB bank (and therefore its client) one day later. Stated otherwise, not all systems which can or should automatically interact were properly connected in the case of AB bank. Furthermore, this even did not seem to be a real priority when asking about the process of vendor and application selection:

> "When we select an application, the 1st thing we look at are the functional requirements. Do they match with our business requirements? Then we look at the non-functional requirements. We look at (...) are we able to manage the operating systems, the database systems, things like that. But indeed we don't take, let's say, some requirements there in terms of what kind of interfaces do we want."

Finally, it was interesting to note that the integration problem was not only technical or on a syntactical level, but equally semantic: the respondent acknowledged that different systems often used different (but similar) concepts which further hampers the integration. From this exemplary evidence, it becomes clear that the interfaces between the different applications of AB's IT portfolio were often not exhaustive, if they existed at all. Therefore, we can conclude that modularity requirement 2.1 was not met.

In order to investigate the degree of cohesion in the IT applications of AB bank, we asked our informant about how vendor and package selection was performed when a certain (new) functionality was required to be fulfilled. It became clear that the case organization performed its search in a purely supply based fashion. Stated otherwise, no explicit upfront delineation of IT application modules and their required functionalities was performed by AB bank when initiating the search for an outsourcing partner and packages. One can expect that such approach results in IT applications with rather broad responsibilities, which are quite likely to be frequently partially overlapping. This was largely confirmed by our informant:

> "Of course, if you go back to the packages, they come out-of-the box with a number of functionalities that you possibly already have in other systems. (...) At the end (...) you will end up with some double functionality in modules that provide the same function."

Based on this evidence, we can conclude that also modularity requirement 2.2 was not met.

5   Discussion

Table 1 summarizes the findings presented in the previous section. It is interesting to see that our analysis pointed out that modularity aspects could be applied to a variety of situations such as the collaboration as a whole, its SLA, as well as aspects within the IT application portfolio. While the manifestations found in this case did cover both organizational and technical (IT) related matters, they were exclusively situated within the outsourcing configuration and not the process (steps) for executing a project. It is important to realize that the observation of all modularity requirements not being met in this case does not mean that the application of the modularity concept was unsuccessful or irrelevant. In contrast, one can note that each of the violated modularity requirements could be associated with suboptimal situations within the outsourcing engagement and provided additional insights in potentially underlying reasons of the related issues.

As discussed in Sect. 2, we validated our analysis in phase four of the case study with our respondent. Here, we also wanted to know from our informant whether our approach offered a useful way for him to look at some of the IT challenges within AB bank and if so, in what way. It was interesting to note that the informant explicitly acknowledged that he indeed found our perspective to be relevant and it was triggering him to think about certain things in a new and fresh way. In order to prevent possible bias and "researcher pleasing" behavior, we asked for a more specific argumentation. Then, the informant for instance mentioned that he was not aware that their integration was a problematic issue in such large extent and that he was thinking about how he could incorporate ideas regarding design rules (which were currently absent) into his organization.

Nevertheless, our informant also indicated several practical issues which might arise when trying to avoid the above mentioned violations of modularity requirements. Consider for instance the identified need for complete and

Table 1. Summary of findings

Modular structure	Modularity requirement	Conformance
Outsourcing collaboration	Fully specified SLA	not met
SLA	Fine-grained clauses	not met
IT application portfolio	Exhaustive interapplication interfaces	not met
IT application portfolio	Cohesion and lack of duplication	not met

exhaustive SLAs (i.e., inter-organizational interfaces). Our informant acknowledged that a necessary amount of trust combined with a more complete and operationally defined interface was likely to improve their outsourcing collaborations:

> "We didn't provide (this service) in the SLA and perhaps we should have thought about it in advance that the system should function as designed and that the response times are within appropriate limits. Perhaps we also put the SLA at a too high level. We should have gone more into some detail points. (...) It is indeed more on operational levels that we didn't describe what we expected them to do. (...) Ok, (now) I understand, if we would have this kind of description, we could easily take it and discuss it with the party to see where the differences are."

However, the actual realization of such contracts in practice did not seem straightforward in all cases. For example, listing all activities that should ever be done in an outsourcing collaboration seems rather difficult as it is challenging to look ahead in this way:

> "In an outsourcing contract it is difficult to foresee what I need in six months or in one year. It is difficult to make it specific, therefore it is also difficult to foresee it already in a contract."

In contrast, what might be realistic is to have an independent industry standard, in which the generally accepted best-practices for such outsourcing deals are listed. Contracts based on these standards could probably already partially mitigate this problem.

A similar remark was made with respect to the modularization of the SLA contracts themselves. While the informant indicated that modular contracts would be highly appealing from a client organization viewpoint, it was also uttered that the realization of modular SLA contracts is not trivial either. First, the different parts (clauses) in a contract are typically not fully independent: changes or stipulations in one clause can influence other ones, hampering simple aggregation in a plug-and-play fashion. Second, easily changeable contracts might reduce the negotiation power of vendor organizations and therefore be in contradiction with their implicit business model: in typical outsourcing contracts, deals are made for a period of 3 to 5 years guaranteeing the supplier a revenue for the upcoming years.

The informant also agreed with the observation that the modular architecture resulting from the supply-based selection of packages (causing duplicate functionalities to arise) could be improved. It was indicated that it was likely that a more fine-grained modular approach was required to do this:

"We start in fact from an application which is in itself perhaps designed quite modular but we don't use it (in that way) because we use it as a complete functional box and now we are trying to cut pieces out of this complete box."

Finally, our informant acknowledged that the modular integration of the different IT applications within AB bank was far from optimal. AB bank had the ambition to improve this situation in the future. However, also this was considered to be non-evident due to multiple reasons. For instance, being a small to medium sized financial institution with a limited amount of customers, integration projects such as those related to the new customer registration process are very unlikely to obtain a sufficiently high priority. The informant additionally indicated that they also had some fundamental questions on how a good modular structure, in order to allow such integration, should be developed in the first place. While some basic and intuitive knowledge regarding modularity was present in the company, our informant indicated that in such case it would be required for him and his organization to acquire more in-depth knowledge regarding modular systems and sound integration practices.

6   Conclusions

IS/IT outsourcing is an important business strategy for many organizations. Unfortunately, failure rates remain high. This paper presented a new perspective on IT outsourcing initiatives, based on the concept of modularity. 4 modularity manifestations were identified, after which a set of modularity requirements was derived and tested for its (non) adherence in the context of a single case within the financial services industry. The ability to identify modularity manifestations and testing modularity requirements in a case study fulfills the main goal of our paper, i.e., demonstrating the relevance of modularity for interpreting and understanding IT outsourcing issues, and exploring the set of issues for which the approach can offer additional insights. Nevertheless, the observation of all 4 modularity requirements not being met in this case clearly reveals the need for future research: the actual feasibility of more modular-compliant outsourcing engagements in practice should be investigated (i.e., to which extent can modularity requirements be met in a realistic environment?). This necessity is also supported by the fact that our respondent indicated some practical issues in this respect. Additionally, our findings were exclusively situated within the outsourcing configuration and not the process (steps) of executing such project, so the latter aspect should be subject to future research efforts as well.

We believe this paper has theoretical and practical contributions. Regarding the first, several authors have already suggested the potential importance of the concept of modularity in the context of IT outsourcing. However, how our understanding of IT outsourcing projects can precisely be improved by using the concept is hardly ever discussed. Our paper clarifies some aspects of the relationship between modularity and IT outsourcing by listing a specific set of relevant issues to which modularity could be applied. A structured way of analyzing these manifestations (modular structure–modularity requirement–conformance) was offered in the context of an actual case. Regarding the second, practitioners could benefit from the examples provided in the paper. They describe how a well-designed modular structure within IT outsourcing projects can lead to (partial) improvements of their real-life outsourcing challenges and vice versa.

A limitation of this paper is the fact that it concerns a single case study, limiting its generalizability. However, as this case is part of an overarching research project (investigating the relevance of the concept of modularity in the context of IT outsourcing), this will be mitigated by the future integration of this case within the overall research project. Such overview could reveal which aspects from the theoretical knowledge base on modularity are, in general, most relevant for studying IT outsourcing. It could also offer interesting insights by highlighting those outsourcing risk factors (mentioned in management literature) of which our understanding could, in general, be improved by using a modularity perspective. As another limitation, it is important to remark that this paper does not propose an encompassing formalized model of IT outsourcing initiatives in terms of modularity (rather, our focus was put on demonstrating the mere relevance of modularity in this respect). Again, such efforts could be initiated once all case material in the mentioned research project has been integrated.

References

1. Baldwin, C.Y., Clark, K.B.: Managing in an age of modularity. Harv. Bus. Rev. **75**(5), 84–93 (1997)
2. Baldwin, C.Y., Clark, K.B.: Design Rules: The Power of Modularity, vol. 1. The MIT Press, Cambridge (2000)
3. Barthélemy, J.: The seven deadly sins of outsourcing. Acad. Manage. Executive **17**(2), 87–98 (2003)
4. Benbasat, I., Goldstein, D.K., Mead, M.: The case research strategy in studies of information systems. MIS Q. **11**, 369–386 (1987)
5. Blair, M.M., Connor, E.H., Kirchhoefer, G.: Outsourcing, modularity, and the theory of the firm. BYU Law Rev. **2011**(2), 263–314 (2011)
6. Campagnolo, D., Camuffo, A.: The concept of modularity in management studies: a literature review. Int. J. Manage. Rev. **12**(3), 259–283 (2010)
7. Fisher, J., Hirschheim, R., Jacobs, R.: Understanding the outsourcing learning curve: a longitudinal analysis of a large Australian company. Inf. Syst. Front. **10**, 165–178 (2008)
8. Gorla, N., Lau, M.B.: Will negative experiences impact future it outsourcing? J. Comput. Inf. Syst. **50**(3), 91–101 (2010)
9. Greaver, M.F.: Strategic Outsourcing: A Structured Approach to Outsourcing Decisions and Initiatives. AMACOM, New York (1999)

10. Hall, J.A., Liedtka, S.L.: Financial performance, CEO compensation, and large-scale information technology outsourcing decisions. J. Manage. Inf. Syst. **22**(1), 193–221 (2005)
11. Harris, M.D.S., Herron, D., Iwanicki, S.: The Business Value of IT: Managing Risks, Optimizing Performance and Measuring Results. Auerbach Publications, Boston (2008)
12. Huysmans, P., De Bruyn, P., Benazeer, S., De Beuckelaer, A., De Haes, S., Verelst, J.: Understanding outsourcing risk factors based on modularity: the BSKYB case. Int. J. IT/Bus. Align. Gov. **5**(1), 55–67 (2014)
13. Ćirić, Z., Raković, L.: Change management in information system development and implementation projects. Manage. Inf. Syst. **5**(2), 23–28 (2010)
14. Lambert, D.M., Emmelhainze, M.A., Gardner, J.T.: Building successful logistics partnerships. J. Bus. Logist. **20**(1), 165–182 (1999)
15. Lee, J.N.: The impact of knowledge sharing, organizational capability and partnership quality on is outsourcing success. Inf. Manage. **38**(5), 323–335 (2001)
16. Mehta, N., Mehta, A.: It takes two to tango: how relational investments improve it outsourcing partnerships. Commun. ACM **53**(2), 160–164 (2010)
17. Modarress, B., Ansari, A., Thies, E.: The impact of technology transfer through foreign direct investment in developing nations: a case study in the United Arab Emirates. Int. J. Econ. Fin. **6**(7), 108–126 (2014)
18. Peterson, B.L., Carco, D.M.: The Smart Way to Buy Information Technology: How to Maximize Value and Avoid Costly Pitfalls. AMACOM, New York (1998)
19. Rottman, J.W.: Successful knowledge transfer within offshore supplier networks: a case study exploring social capital in strategic alliances. J. Inf. Technol. **23**(1), 31–43 (2008)
20. Schmidt, N., Zöller, B., Rosenkranz, C.: The clash of cultures in information technology outsourcing relationships: an institutional logics perspective. In: Kotlarsky, J., Oshri, I., Willcocks, L.P. (eds.) Global Sourcing 2016. LNBIP, vol. 266, pp. 97–117. Springer, Cham (2016). doi:10.1007/978-3-319-47009-2_6
21. Simon, H.: The Sciences of the Artificial. MIT Press, Cambridge (1996)
22. Smith, H.: Modularity in contracts: boilerplate and information flow. In: American Law & Economics Association Annual Meetings Paper, p. 46 (2006)
23. Tiwana, A.: Does interfirm modularity complement ignorance? A field study of software outsourcing alliances. Strateg. Manage. J. **29**(11), 1241–1252 (2008)
24. Wohlin, C., Aurum, A.: Towards a decision-making structure for selecting a research design in empirical software engineering. Empir. Softw. Eng. **20**(6), 1427–1455 (2015)
25. Yin, R.K.: Case Study Research: Design and Methods, 4th edn. Sage Publications Inc., Thousand Oaks (2009)
26. Zheng, Y., Abbott, P.: Moving up the value chain or reconfiguring the value network? An organizational learning perspective on born global outsourcing vendors. In: Proceedings of the 21st European Conference on Information Systems (ECIS) (2013)

Modeling Business Rules Compliance for Goal-Oriented Business Processes

Patrizia Ribino$^{(\boxtimes)}$, Carmelo Lodato, and Massimo Cossentino

Institute of High Performance and Networking (ICAR),
National Research Council (CNR), Palermo, Italy
{patrizia.ribino,carmelo.lodato,massimo.cossentino}@icar.cnr.it

Abstract. For keeping up with competitive markets, organizations have to ensure their processes are compliant with the normative environment in which they are operating. Moreover, they must be able to adapt their processes to different normative contexts dynamically. In this paper, we propose a conceptual framework for modeling norm compliance in the context of goal-oriented systems. In particular, we provide a set of formal definitions where norms are conceived for regulating a system at a higher level of abstraction (i.e., goal level) and the norm compliance is related to the satisfiability of business process goals.

Keywords: Norm compliance · Norms · Goal-oriented systems

1 Introduction

Nowadays, organizations operate in a more complex and dynamic business environment that is subjected to an increasing number of regulations, many of them imposed by various governmental authorities. Organizations need to design and accordingly adjust their business processes, ensuring that they are properly operating within the boundaries delineated by the regulations. Compliance to legal regulations, business rules or best practices is becoming an increasingly important aspect of business process management [19]. Norm compliance is commonly defined as *"the set of activities and policies in place in an enterprise to ensure the business activities required to achieve the business goals of the company comply with the relevant normative requirements"* [11]. A process is compliant with a set of norms (i.e., normative system) if it does not breach the normative system.

Moreover, due to the rapid development of new technologies existing regulations might be changed and new rules might be imposed. Thus, to keep up with competitive markets organizations must be able to dynamically adapt to run-time their processes to different and changeable normative contexts.

Many efforts have been taken in the research of business process norm compliance [8]. The most compliance checking techniques are based on design-time approaches, which ensure that process instances will be norm compliant. On the contrary, a few run-time approaches target the verification of rules during execution time, thus preventing the actual execution of non-compliant tasks.

© Springer International Publishing AG 2017
R. Pergl et al. (Eds.): EOMAS 2017, LNBIP 298, pp. 83–99, 2017.
DOI: 10.1007/978-3-319-68185-6_6

In this paper, we propose a work arisen in the context of Self-Adaptive and Self-Organized systems (SASO), which are systems able to change their behavior for achieving the desired result. In particular, to pursue run-time norm compliance in dynamic business processes, we propose a conceptual normative framework for goal-oriented systems, where business rules are conceived for regulating a system at a higher level of abstraction (i.e., goal level) rather than task level. In the business process modeling community, attention is paid to the value of making goals explicit and incorporating the notion of goal into process modeling methods [3]. Goals express the desired state of the world the system wants to achieve [21,31]. In our model, business rules (i.e., norms) regulate the desired state of the world according to the normative context in which the system works. Thus, norm compliance is guaranteed at a higher level of abstraction respect to the system behavior.

The rest of the paper is organized as follows. Section 2 shows an overview of the literature. Section 3 introduces the theoretical background. Sections 4, 5 and 6 present the proposed approach. Finally, in Sect. 7 discussions and conclusions are drawn.

2   Related Works

Compliance to organizational rules poses new requirements for business process management. Organizations are therefore required to take measures for ensuring regulatory compliance [8]. Many efforts have been taken in the research of business process norm compliance. In particular, some approaches aim at ensuring that process instances will be norm compliant. In some cases, compliance rules may guide the design of a business process so that compliance is provided by design since compliance violations are identified in the course of process model creation. Other approaches use techniques like model checking for verifying some properties in already designed models but not yet deployed.

In [19] is presented an approach to automatically construct business process models that are compliant by design based on an existing artifact-centric framework. *Ghose et al.* [10] propose an approach based on predefined business process models for which compliance to regulations has been verified (compliance patterns). Such method relies mainly on the computation of the deviation of a given BP model to a particular compliance pattern. *Awad et al.* [2] introduced an approach to synthesizing business process templates out of a set of compliance rules expressed in linear temporal logic. In [17] a normative structure NNs to capture interrelations between regulations is proposed. NNs provide an expressive and flexible way of structuring rules, which is based on the formal theories of normative systems. In [7], authors address the problem of verifying business process compliance with norms by employing reasoning about actions in a temporal action theory. They proposed to specify business processes as action domains and norms with the notion of commitments and verify compliance of a business process with some regulations based on temporal answer sets.

Conversely, run-time approaches refer to executable business process models and, consequently, depend on the business process execution engine. Such kind of techniques commonly works by annotating business process models with assertions that are destined to be either used by compliance checking engines for verification or at later stages during execution. In this sense, regulations can either be defined in BP models, or they can require run-time information. The approach proposed by *M. Pesic et al.* in [23] introduces a framework in which process models are defined in a declarative way. The authors argue that constraint-based workflow models, avoiding over-specification, are more expressive and more flexible than procedural ones. *Birukou et al.* [4] presented a solution for run-time compliance governance in service-oriented architectures, supporting the whole cycle of compliance management from selecting compliance sources to run-time monitoring and reporting on violations. Several proposals also came from the domain of normative multi-agent systems where norm compliance checking is increasingly investigated. *Governatori and Rotolo* in [12] proposed a process compliance language (PCL) for the expression of violation conditions and reparation obligations intended to help agents reason about norm compliance. In [18] *Kazmierczak et al.* presented NORMC a model checker for reasoning about compliance in normative systems, which is implemented in the Haskell programming language. *Herzig et al.* [16] proposed a dynamic logic to reason about abilities and permissions of agents. Similar to these techniques our approach works at run-time with executable business process models. Differently, from our approach, they work at the task level. Ensuring norm compliance at goal level provides some advantages, respect to conventional methods, we find in working with open systems that evolve at run-time. Indeed, in such kind of system new services could be made available for satisfying process activities. By adopting the proposed approach, we do not need to modify anything to adapt the behavior of the system to manage new situations because the norm at the goal level spreads to the service level. Thus, the approach we propose allows maintaining the norm compliance although the service level is changed. Moreover, our approach avoids regulating all the possible ways the system can follow for reaching that goal. To the best of our knowledge, there are no existing works that consider run-time norm compliance for goal-oriented processes. In the field of software engineering, we found a work named Nomos [29]. Nomos is a goal-oriented approach to capturing high-level principles regarding goal realization for requirements guided by satisfiability of normative propositions obtained from rules embedded in law. This method deals with considering regulations during requirement analysis to build norm compliance systems by design. Thus, it could belong to the first category of design-time approaches.

3   Theoretical Background

The aim of this section is to provide the theoretical background the research presented in this paper is based on.

Organizational Rules - A common sense meaning about rule states: *"One of a set of explicit or understood regulations or principles governing conduct or procedure within a particular area of activity. . . a law or principle that operates* *within a particular sphere of knowledge describing, or prescribing what is possible or allowable"* [1]. Thus, organizational rules include laws, regulations, industry codes, business rules, standards, internal policies that can impose different limitations. A given *business rule* may permit that activity has to occur only if some preconditions are true. *Legislation* is the system of rules which a particular country or community recognizes as regulating the actions of its members and which it may enforce by the imposition of penalties. *Laws of Physics* ensure that data do not describe impossible physical world situation and they take into account interdependent proprieties of the physical world. *Standards* are set of imposed requirements to obtain a particular level of quality.

Despite their differences, organizational rules share a common aspect: they describe the obligations, prohibitions, and permissions an organization is subject during their business activities. *Obligations* define situations or actions that if they are not achieved or performed, the result is a violation of normative system. Conversely, a *Prohibition* indicates a situation or an action that must be avoided, and if it is achieved or performed, the results is a violation of normative system. Obligations and Prohibitions are constraints that define the boundaries of the processes. Finally, *Permissions* refer to something that is allowable if there are no obligations or prohibitions. Permissions cannot be violated, and they do not play a direct role in norm compliance.

In this paper, we adopt the definition given in *Governatori et al.* [11] where Business Process Compliance is defined as *"a relationship between the formal specifications of a process and the formal representation of the regulatory frameworks relevant of the process."*

BPMN and SBVR - A business process is commonly defined as a set of related activities (or tasks) that must be performed together to produce a defined set of results (products or services). The Business Process Modelling Notation (BPMN)[30] is widely recognized, and the well know standard that allows modeling a business process. BPMN is a graph-oriented notation developed by Object Management Group (OMG) that was conceived as being highly understandable by all business people interested into business processes. Practically, a BPMN model consists of nodes that can be connected through control flow arcs in arbitrary ways [22]. While BPMN models the dynamics of business processes, SBVR [13] allows modeling other complementary aspects of a business process such as business rules. Thus, SBVR allows modeling business vocabularies construction and business rules definitions (elements of guidance that govern actions). Nonetheless, SBVR does not standardize any particular language for representing vocabularies and rules. Instead, SBVR uses semantic formulation, which is a way of specifying the semantic structure of statements and definitions. This approach of defining structures of meaning, with its sound theoretical foundation of formal logic, gives a formal, language-independent means for capturing the semantics of a community's body of shared meanings.

4   Knowledge Modeling

The definition of organizational rules implicitly implies a formalization of a *"sphere of knowledge"* within a regulation operates. Moreover, to establish *"a relationship between the formal specifications of a process and the formal representation of the regulatory frameworks relevant of the process"* [11] thus realizing norm compliance, it is necessary to refer to the same semantic layer. These two requirements are satisfied by adopting a knowledge formalization we found in a proper ontology domain.

Domain Ontology - An ontology is a specification of a conceptualization made for the purpose of enabling knowledge sharing and reuse [14]. An ontological commitment is an agreement to use a thesaurus of words in a way that is consistent (even if not complete) respect to the theory specified by an ontology [15].

A Problem Ontology (PO) [26] is a conceptual model used to create an ontological commitment for developing complex systems. It describes what the elements of interest in a domain with their properties and how they act in the domain (see Fig. 1). In particular:

- A *Concept* is a general term usually used in a broad sense that has a unique meaning in a subject domain. In our approach we use the term Concept just for representing classes of domain entities;
- A *Predicate* is the expression of property, quality or a state of one (or more) concept(s). It could define a formal structure for statements and rules that relate instances of those concepts;

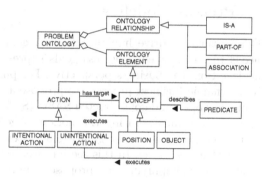

Fig. 1. Problem ontology metamodel

- an *Action* is defined as *"the cause of an event by an acting concept"* (adapted from [20]). Actions are classified as intentional and unintentional [9] where intentionality implies a kind of consciousness to act, whereas Unintentional Action is an automatic response governed by fixed rules or laws;
- a *Position* is a specialization of concept performing Actions (both Intentional and Unintentional).
- an *Object* represents all the concepts that can perform only unintentional actions.
- *is-a* (or is-a-subtype-of) that is the relationship that defines which objects are classified by which class, thus creating taxonomies;
- *part-of* relationship (or the counterpart has-part), in which ontological elements representing the components of something are associated with the ontological element representing the entire assembly;

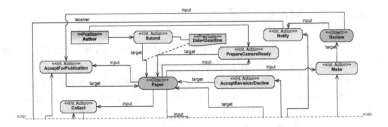

Fig. 2. A portion of PO taken from [26].

- *association* that is a general purpose relationship for establishing propositions that link two ontological elements. They are particularly useful for defining a formal structure for instances of related concepts.

In this work we use the PO for encoding a specific domain of interest as the baseline for realizing norm compliance. Figure 2 shows an excerpt of PO for a classical Conference Management System [26].

5 Process Modeling

Goals primarily drive human action. A goal is a desired state of affairs that needs to be attained. Business goals express what the organization wants to achieve from the business perspective. For pursuing run-time norm compliance in a dynamic business process, we propose a process specification model in the context of open and goal-directed SASO (Self-Adaptive and Self-Organized) systems. Hence, incorporating the notion of goal into process modeling, we can define business rules for regulating a system at a higher level of abstraction rather than task level. In this section, we provide a formal account of our approach. For exemplifying the proposed approach, we refer to a trivial BPMN business process (see Fig. 3) that models a workflow for submitting a paper. Such process consists of six activities performed by an author and two business rules that constrain the process. The domain ontology showed in Fig. 2 grounds such process.

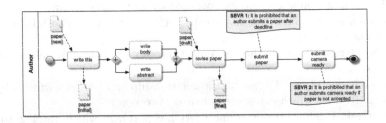

Fig. 3. A BMPN/SBVR model of a workflow for submitting a paper.

5.1 Process Specification

A Process Specification PS is defined by the elements of the following triple:

$$PS = \langle \mathcal{G}, \mathcal{R}, \mathcal{N} \rangle$$

where: $\mathcal{G}$ is a set of *Goals* the process has to reach; $\mathcal{R}$ is the set of *Roles* delegated for achieving goals; $\mathcal{N}$ is the set of norms that constrain the state of the world the process results in. Such definition grounds on three concepts that will be formally introduced in the following definitions.

Definition 1 (State of the world). *Let $\mathcal{D}$ be the set of concepts defining a business domain. Let $\mathcal{L}$ be a first-order logic defined on $\mathcal{D}$ with $\top$ a tautology and $\bot$ a logical contradiction, where an atomic formula $p(t_1, t_2..., t_n) \in \mathcal{L}$ is represented by a predicate applied to a tuple of terms $(t_1, t_2..., t_n) \in \mathcal{D}$ and the predicate is a property of or relation between such terms that can be true or false.*

A state of the world in a given time t ($\mathcal{W}^t$) is a subset of atomic formulae whose values are true at the time t:

$$\mathcal{W}^t = [p_1(t_1, t_2, ..., t_h), ..., p_n(t_1, t_2, ..., t_m)]$$

The state of the world represents a set of declarative information concerning events and relations among events at a given moment. It also describes conditions or set of circumstances in which the system operates at a specific time. Definition 1 is based on close world hypothesis [24] that considers all facts that are not in the state of the world are considered false.

An extract of the set of concepts defining the business domain for the business process shown in Fig. 3 are:

$$\mathcal{D} = \{paper, author, deadline, title, abstract, write, submit, ...\}$$

A state of the world at time t for the submitting paper process could be $\mathcal{W}^t = [before(deadline), done(submit(paper))]$. It means that at time t to which the state of the world refers, the time for submission is not expired yet and the author has submitted the paper.

Definition 2 (Goal). *Let $\mathcal{D}$, $\mathcal{L}$ and $p(t_1, t_2..., t_n) \in \mathcal{L}$ be as previously introduced in Definition 1. Let $t_c \in \mathcal{L}$ and $f_s \in \mathcal{L}$ be formulae that may be composed of atomic formulae by means of logic connectives AND($\wedge$), OR ($\vee$) and NOT ($\neg$).*

A Goal is a pair $\langle t_c, f_s \rangle$ where t_c (trigger condition) is a condition to evaluate over a state of the world $\mathcal{W}^t$ when the goal may be actively pursued and f_s (final state) is a condition to evaluate over a state of the world $W^{t+\Delta t}$ when it is eventually addressed:

$$a \ goal \ is \ active \ if \ t_c(\mathcal{W}^t) \wedge \neg f_s(\mathcal{W}^t) = true$$
$$a \ goal \ is \ addressed \ if \ f_s(\mathcal{W}^{t+\Delta t}) = true$$

As we said, the concept of goal is widely employed for describing a desired state of affairs that needs to be attained. In Definition 2, the desired state of affairs is represented by the final state. Moreover, goals are activated when some conditions occur.

About the previous example, a possible goal could be $g = \langle done(revise(pa-per) \wedge final(paper)), done(submitt(paper)) \rangle$. It means an author can achieve the desired state of affairs, namely the submission of his manuscript, only when the paper has finalized. Practically, only when the state of the world at a given time t is $\mathcal{W}^t = [\ldots, done(revise(paper)), final(paper) \ldots]$. Conversely, the author achieved the desired state of affairs only when exists a state of the world at a given time $t + \Delta t$ in which $done(submit(paper))$ is true, for example $\mathcal{W}^{t+\Delta t} = [done(revise(paper)), before(dead-line), done(submit(paper)), submitted(paper)]$.

Definition 3 (Norm). *Let $\mathcal{D}$, $\mathcal{L}$ and $p(t_1, t_2 \ldots, t_n) \in \mathcal{L}$ be as previously introduced in Definition 1. Let $\phi \in \mathcal{L}$ and $\rho \in \mathcal{L}$ formulae composed of atomic formula by means of logic connectives AND($\wedge$), OR ($\vee$) and NOT ($\neg$). Moreover, let $D_{op} = \{permission, obligati-on, prohibition\}$ be the set of deontic operators.*

A Norm is defined by the elements of the following tuple:

$$n = \langle r, g, \rho, \phi, d \rangle_{[scope]}$$

where

- *scope identifies the particular field of reference of the norm.*
- *$r \in \mathcal{R}$ is the Role the norm refers to. The special character "_" means any role.*
- *$g \in \mathcal{G}$ is the Goal the norm refers to. The special character "_" means any goal.*
- *$\rho \in \mathcal{L}$ is a formula expressing the set of actions or the state of affairs that the norm disciplines.*
- *$\phi \in \mathcal{L}$ is a logic condition (to evaluate over a state of the world $\mathcal{W}^t$) under which the norm is applicable;*
- *$d \in D_{op}$ is the deontic operator applied to ρ that the norm prescribes to the couple $(r, g) \in \mathcal{R} \times \mathcal{G}$:*

$$d(\rho) = \begin{cases} \rho & \text{if } d = \text{ obligation} \\ \neg\rho, & \text{if } d = \text{ prohibition} \\ \rho \vee \neg\rho & \text{if } d = \text{ permission} \end{cases}$$

In other words, given a state of the world $\mathcal{W}^t$ a norm prescribes to a couple (r, g) the deontic operator d applied to ρ if ϕ is true in $\mathcal{W}^t$. In particular, an *obligation* forces the system to obtain ρ. Conversely, a *prohibition* defines ρ as a non-admissible state. *Permission* do not have a restrictive role. Moreover, a norm could be defined for a specific field of reference (e.g.: security, data protection etc. . .).

It is worth noting that because ρ may also refer to a state of the affair could happen that it coincides with the desired state of the world (i.e.: $\rho = f_s$).

Concerning the previous goal, a norm could be $n = \langle \_, g, done$ $(submit(paper)), after(deadline), prohibition\rangle$ which prescribes to anyone that wants to achieve the goal g the prohibition to submit a paper after the deadline. In such case $\rho = done(submit(paper))$ is a non-admissible state under certain conditions.

According to the proposed specification, the process depicted in Fig. 3 could be modeled by the following triple:

$$
\mathcal{G} = \left\{
\begin{array}{l}
g_0 = \langle new(paper), [accepted(paper) \wedge done(submit(CR))]\rangle \\
g_1 = \langle new(paper), [initial(paper) \wedge done(write(title))]\rangle \\
g_2 = \langle [initial(paper) \wedge done(write(title))], done(write(body))\rangle \\
g_3 = \langle [initial(paper) \wedge done(write(title))], done(write(abstract))\rangle \\
g_4 = \langle [draft(paper) \wedge done(write(title)) \wedge done(write(abstract))], \\
\quad\quad [final(paper) \wedge done(revise(paper))]\rangle \\
g_5 = \langle [final(paper) \wedge done(revise(paper))], done(submit(paper))\rangle \\
g_6 = \langle done(submit(paper)), done(submit(CR))\rangle
\end{array}
\right\}
$$

$$
\mathcal{R} = \{author\}
$$

$$
\mathcal{N} = \left\{
\begin{array}{l}
n_1 = \langle author, g_5, done(submit(paper)), after(deadline), prohibition\rangle \\
n_2 = \langle author, g_6, done(submit(CR)), \neg accepted(paper), prohibition\rangle
\end{array}
\right\}
$$

6   Norm Compliance

In the previous section, we have introduced the formalism we used for specifying a business process with Goals, Roles, and Norms. Here, we focus on the mechanism for determining norm compliance.

Definition 4 (Inadmissible State of the World). *A state of the world at a given time t*

$$
\mathcal{W}^t = [p_1(t_1, t_2, ..., t_h), ..., p_n(t_1, t_2, ..., t_m)]
$$

is an Inadmissible State of the World iff $\exists \, n = \langle r, g, \rho, \phi, d\rangle \mid$

$$
\begin{cases}
\phi(\mathcal{W}^{t-\Delta t}) \wedge \neg\rho(\mathcal{W}^{t-\Delta t}) = true \\
p_1(t_1, t_2, ..., t_h) \wedge ... \wedge p_n(t_1, t_2, ..., t_m) \wedge d(\rho) = \bot
\end{cases}
$$

The first condition to be evaluated in Definition 4 allows ensuring the non-retroactive effect of a norm. It disciplines the case where the state of affair regulated by a norm has occurred before the norm is applicable. Therefore, if n is a prohibition and $\rho = true$ before the rule came into force, we do not consider the state as inadmissible. The same consideration is applicable if n is an obligation, even if in this case there is no conflict.

Resuming the previous example, let us consider the norm that prohibits the submission of paper after the deadline

$$n_1 = \langle \_, \_, done(submit(paper)), after(deadline), prohibition \rangle$$

Let assume that at time t the state of the world is

$$\mathcal{W}^t = [done(revise(paper)), final(paper), after(deadline)]$$

Then, let us suppose that in some way someone or something has changed the state of the world and at time $t + \Delta t$

$$\mathcal{W}^{t+\Delta t} = [after(deadline), done(submit(paper)), submitted(paper)]$$

According to the previous definition, $\mathcal{W}^{t+\Delta t}$ is an inadmissible state of the world because

$$\underbrace{after(deadline)}_{\phi(\mathcal{W}^t)} \wedge \underbrace{\neg done(submit(paper))}_{\neg \rho(\mathcal{W}^t)} = true$$

$$\underbrace{after(deadline) \wedge done(submit(paper)) \wedge submitted(paper)}_{\mathcal{W}^{t+\Delta t}} \wedge \underbrace{\neg done(submit(paper))}_{d(\rho)} = \bot$$

The second condition generates a logical contradiction.

Analogously, let us consider a norm that obligates the submission of camera ready before a deadline if the paper was accepted.

$$n = \langle \_, \_, \underbrace{done(submit(CR))}_{\rho}, \underbrace{accepted(paper) \wedge before(CR\_deadline)}_{\phi}, obligation \rangle$$

Let assume that at time t the state of the world is

$$\mathcal{W}^t = [accepted(paper), before(CR\_deadline)]$$

Then, let us suppose at time $t + \Delta t$ that nothing is changed in the state of the world except the time

$$\mathcal{W}^{t+\Delta t} = [accepted(paper), after(CR\_deadline)]$$

According to the previous definition, $\mathcal{W}^{t+\Delta t}$ is an inadmissible state of the world

$$\underbrace{accepted(paper) \wedge before(CR\_deadline)}_{\phi(\mathcal{W}^t)} \wedge \underbrace{\neg done(submit(CR))}_{\neg\rho(\mathcal{W}^t)} = true$$

$$\underbrace{accepted(paper), after(CR\_deadline)}_{\mathcal{W}^{t+\Delta t}} \wedge \underbrace{done(submit(CR))}_{d(\rho)} = \bot$$

In $\mathcal{W}^{t+\Delta t}$, $done(submit(CR))$ is false for the close world hypothesis. This situation is equivalent to explicit in $\mathcal{W}^{t+\Delta t}$ the following formula $\neg done(submit(CR))$. Moreover, in the case of obligation $d(\rho) = done(submit (CR))$ is true by default. As a consequence, in $\mathcal{W}^{t+\Delta t}$ a contradiction is generated.

Definition 5 (State of Norm). *Let a norm* $n = \langle r, g, \rho, \phi, d \rangle$ *where* $g = \langle t_c, f_s \rangle$ *and let a state of the world in a given time* t *(* $\mathcal{W}^t$ *). A norm can assume the following states:*

- n *is applicable at time* t *if* $\phi(\mathcal{W}^t) = true \vee \phi = \top$
- n *is active at time* t *if* n *is applicable and* $t_c(\mathcal{W}^t) = true$
- n *is logically contradictory if* ϕ *is* $\bot$
- n *is in opposition to goal if* $f_s \wedge d(\rho)$ *is* $\bot$

Moreover, let a state of the world in a given time t *(* W^t *) and let two norms* $n_1 = \langle r_1, g_1, \rho_1, \phi_1, d_1 \rangle$ *and* $n_2 = \langle r_2, g_2, \rho_2, \phi_2, d_2 \rangle$ *where* $r_1 = r_2$, $g_1 = g_2$ $\rho_1 = \rho_2$

- n_1 *and* n_2 *are deontically contradictory iff* $\begin{cases} \phi_1(\mathcal{W}^t) \wedge \phi_2(\mathcal{W}^t) = true \\ d_1 \neq d_2 \end{cases}$

It is worth noting that we talk about *logically contradictory* when the contradiction concerns the logical conditions ($\phi \in \mathcal{L}$) under which the norm is applicable. Conversely, we talk about *deontically contradictory* when the contradiction concerns the semantic meaning of the deontic operator ($d \in D_{op}$) the norms apply.

Let us consider the norm $n_1 = \langle author, g_5, done(submit(paper)), after (deadline), prohibition \rangle$ and $n_2 = \langle author, g_6, done(submit(CR)), \neg accepted(paper), prohibition \rangle$ previously exemplified. Let us suppose that at a given time t

$$\mathcal{W}^t = \{done(revise(paper))\}$$

The norm n_1 is not applicable because $\phi_{n_1} = after(deadline)$ is false in $\mathcal{W}^t$ while the norm n_2 is applicable because $\phi_{n_2} = \neg accepted(paper)$ is true in $\mathcal{W}^{t1}$.

Let us suppose that at a given time $t + \Delta t$ the state of the world is the following:

$$\mathcal{W}^{t+\Delta t} = \{after(deadline), accepted(paper)\}$$

In this case, the norm n_1 is applicable because $\phi_{n_1} = after(deadline)$ is true in $\mathcal{W}^{t+\Delta t}$ while the norm n_2 is not applicable because $\phi_{n_2} = \neg accepted(paper)$ is false in $\mathcal{W}^{t+\Delta t}$. For space constraints, we do not provide examples for each state of a norm.

---

[1] All facts that are not in the state of the world are considered false.

Definition 6 (Norm Compliance). *Let us consider a norm $n = \langle r, g, \rho, \phi, d \rangle$ and a goal $g = \langle t_c, f_s \rangle$. Let us consider a state of the world $\mathcal{W}^t$ in a given time t in which n is active and let $\mathcal{W}^{t+\Delta t}$ be the state of the world in which f_s is true. Pursuing the goal g is compliant with the norm n if $\mathcal{W}$ is an admissible state of the world where:*

$$\mathcal{W} = \begin{cases} \mathcal{W}^{t+\Delta t} & f_s = \rho \\ \bigcup_{k=t}^{t+\Delta t} \mathcal{W}^k & f_s \neq \rho \end{cases}$$

In the following, we show two examples for $f_s = \rho$ and $f_s \neq \rho$.

Let us consider the goal g_6 previously introduced and a norm that obligates the submission of camera ready if the paper was accepted.

$$n = \langle \_, g_6, \underbrace{done(submit(CR))}_{\rho}, \underbrace{accepted(paper) \wedge before(CR\_deadline)}_{\phi}, obligation \rangle$$

Let assume that at time t the state of the world is

$$\mathcal{W}^t = [accepted(paper), before(camera\_ready\_deadline)]$$

In $\mathcal{W}^t$ n is active (see Definition 5). Pursuing g_6 leads the system to a new state of the world

$$\mathcal{W}^{t+\Delta t} = [accepted(paper), done(submit(camera\_ready))]$$

In this case $f_s = \rho$, then according to the previous definition, $\mathcal{W} = \mathcal{W}^{t+\Delta t}$ is an admissible state of the world

$$\underbrace{accepted(paper) \wedge before(CR\_deadline)}_{\phi(\mathcal{W}^t)} \wedge \underbrace{\neg done(submit(CR))}_{\neg\rho(\mathcal{W}^t)} = true$$

$$\underbrace{accepted(paper), done(submit(CR))}_{\mathcal{W}^{t+\Delta t}} \wedge \underbrace{done(submit(CR))}_{d(\rho)} \neq \perp$$

In $\mathcal{W}^{t+\Delta t}$, $done(submit(CR))$ is true as well as the obligation prescribes.

Similarly, let us consider a norm that obligates to sign a paper for submitting it.

$$n = \langle \_, g_5, \underbrace{signed(paper)}_{\rho}, \underbrace{true}_{\phi}, obligation \rangle$$

Let assume a state of the world $\mathcal{W}^t$ in which n is active.

$$\mathcal{W}^t = \{done(revise(paper)), before(deadline), final(paper)\}$$

Let us suppose that g_5 could be satisfied by following a path, which at times $t+1, t+2, ...,$ and $t+\Delta t$ leads the system to evolve toward the following states of the worlds:

$$\mathcal{W}^{t+1} = \{logged(author, system), done(revise(paper)), before(deadline), final(paper)\}$$
$$\mathcal{W}^{t+2} = \{logged(author, system), done(revise(paper)), before(deadline), signed(paper)\}$$
$$\mathcal{W}^{t+\Delta t} = \{done(submit(paper)), submitted(paper)\}$$

In this case $f_s = \rho$, thus pursuing g_5 is compliant with n because

$$\mathcal{W} = \bigcup_{k=t}^{t+\Delta t} \mathcal{W}^k$$

$$= \{logged(author, system), done(revise(paper)), before(deadline),$$
$$final(paper), signed(paper), done(submit(paper)), submitted(paper)\}$$

is an admissible state of the world according to Definition 4.

The interpretation of norm compliance according to Definition 6 influences a fundamental process of goal-oriented systems, the Practical Reasoning. *Practical Reasoning* is reasoning directed towards actions; it is the process of figuring out what to do [5]. It consists of two activities: *deliberation* - deciding what goals to achieve and *means-ends reasoning* - determining how to meet these goals.

The central aspect of goal deliberation is *"How can the system deliberate on its goals to decide which ones shall be pursued?"* [6]. A goal-oriented system sees some of its goals merely as possible options. Goal deliberation has the task to decide which goals a system actively pursues, which ones it delays and which ones it abandons. Conversely, means-ends reasoning aims at providing operalization of goals. It is the process of deciding how to achieve a goal using the available means (e.g., actions, services, etc.). The definition we introduce about norm compliance directly influences the process of goal deliberation. The first condition of Definition 6 has a direct impact on the choice of goals that can be pursued. A system can deliberate to pursue a goal based on run-time conditions by envisaging normative effects of the goal. Conversely, means-ends reasoning is a process that allows choosing the appropriate ways to fulfill a deliberated goal. The second condition of norm compliance is implicitly related to this process. A system can determine the way to reach a goal by envisaging the normative effects of available means that it can choose.

We have concretely applied the theory we have presented in this paper in different contexts and for different purposes. We discuss them in the next section.

7   Discussions and Conclusions

The increasing employment of self-adaptive and self-organized systems (SASO) in the field of business process management poses new challenges also in norm compliance checking. SASO systems can effectively adapt their behavior to changes in the environment and self-organize their internal structure for finding composed solutions to achieve collaborative goals. In particular, they are commonly goal-directed systems. Goals are motivators for these systems providing them the reason for doing something. Goals express user requirements to be satisfied. Moreover, they are open systems that evolve at run-time because: (i) new services could be made available for satisfying user requirements; (ii) the satisfaction of new user requirements may be demanded to the system. In this context, we presented a normative framework for ensuring business rules compliance for goal-oriented business processes. As far as we know, there are no run-time norm compliance approaches that work at the goal level. The normative framework we propose, allowing to reason about norm compliance in a more high-level of abstraction than the task level, is coupled with the goal-driven nature of currently software systems. Thus providing several advantages related to a key feature of the goal-oriented paradigm that is the possibility to reason about alternative paths against possible situations of benefit, drawback or, in our case, norm compliance. Moreover, for allowing business analysts to take advantage of our normative framework, we are completing a suite of tools for supporting the conversion of our business process specification in a standard BPMN/SBVR and vice-versa. To evaluate our approach, we concretely adopt it in several application scenarios described in the following.

Business Process Merging - Business Process merging or workflow merging is the problem to create a process model by unifying several process models that share process fragments. Processes are commonly defined both by specifying the flow of the activities they are composed of but also rules that constraints the activities. In [25] we present a merging approach that adopts the proposed normative framework to consider also normative specifications. The concept of norm with its formal specification allow us to reason also about constraints and rules (or commonly business rules) during the merging process thus unifying them in the merged process.

Merging Conflicts - We study the problem of norm conflict in the context of business process merging [25]. The presence of regulations in processes to be merged may generate conflicts defined for the same activity in the merging workflows. We adopt the normative framework for identifying two kinds of conflicts that can occur: (i) conflicts determined by merging two or more norms that generate a combined norm that is logically contradictory; (ii) conflicts between norm and goal when the fulfillment of goal always causes a norm violation.

Personalization of Smart Environments - In recent years, a growing trend is the development of smart systems to improve the well-being of individuals in their environment by making everyday activities more convenient and enjoyable. Smart systems aim at augmenting real environments to create smart spaces where users are provided with pervasive electronic devices. A smart system connects such electronic devices into a network and controls them by using advanced ICT technologies in such away the devices satisfy user requirements. The use of a smart environment is variable from a user to another. Designing ad-hoc systems for each is not realistic economically. As well as, it is not possible to hard-wire all possible user scenarios. In [27], we adopt the proposed normative framework for constraining user requirements using non-functional requirements (norms) expressed using permissions, obligations or prohibitions.

Run-time injection of norms - A great challenge in complex systems is to adequately deal with the unpredictability and the dynamics changing of the application context the systems are plugged in. Smart environments are complex systems that are affected by these issues. A way to provide system flexibility is given by implementing statically normative frameworks in which norms for regulating the behavior of the system are specified at design time. This kind of solution is not useful when we face with unexpected situations that have not been considered at design time. We defined appropriate algorithms [28] based on the proposed normative framework that allows to introduce and manage run-time norms. In such approach, we consider the goals as a particular kind of obligation that have to be satisfied under certain conditions. Besides, we see permission and prohibition norms as promoters or inhibitors of the system in pursuing its goals. By introducing norms to run-time, we also make the system more flexible to environment changes and able to self-adapt to new normative contexts.

Conflict Detection - Currently, we are working on detecting conflicts in normative systems. By adopting the proposed framework, we are developing appropriate algorithms for detecting the following anomalous situations: (i) Inconsistent norms. It means that a norm is self-contradictory because it contains a logical contradiction (i.e., the conjunction of a statement S and its denied, not S); (ii) Antinomy. An antinomy designates a conflict of two norms that are mutually exclusive or that oppose one another. (iii) Norms incompatible with system requirements. A norm is incompatible with a system requirement when it always makes that system requirement not satisfiable.

Cloud For Europe - In many application contexts, legal requirements constrain the usage of cloud computing. Each country may be subjected to different types of regulations. To work in the scope of European single digital market that provides cloud services, a great challenge to be addressed is to make Public Administrations processes able to move inside the boundary of the applicable legislation by introducing legislation awareness inside the system that manages such processes. Cloud For Europe[2] is tendering research to assist take-up of cloud computing in the public sector. A challenge of the project is to provide legislation execution. It aims at ensuring legal requirements constraints for cloud services. In this project, we are implementing the proposed normative framework in a web service component to be used by Public Administration for verifying the normative compliance of their run-time processes.

---

[2] Cloud For Europe is funded from the European Union's Seventh Framework Programme for research, technological development, and demonstration under grant agreement no 610650.

References

1. Abate, F., Jewell, E.J.: New Oxford American Dictionary (2001)
2. Awad, A., Goré, R., Hou, Z., Thomson, J., Weidlich, M.: An iterative approach to synthesize business process templates from compliance rules. Inform. Syst. **37**(8), 714–736 (2012)
3. Bider, I., Johannesson, P., Soffer, P., Wand, Y.: On the notion of soft-goals in business process modeling. Bus. Process Manage. J. **11**(6), 663–679 (2005)
4. Birukou, A., D'Andrea, V., Leymann, F., Serafinski, J., Silveira, P., Strauch, S., Tluczek, M.: An integrated solution for runtime compliance governance in SOA. In: Maglio, P.P., Weske, M., Yang, J., Fantinato, M. (eds.) ICSOC 2010. LNCS, vol. 6470, pp. 122–136. Springer, Heidelberg (2010). doi:10.1007/978-3-642-17358-5_9
5. Bratman, M.E., Israel, D.J., Pollack, M.E.: Plans and resource-bounded practical reasoning. Comput. Intell. **4**(3), 349–355 (1988)
6. Braubach, L., Pokahr, A., Moldt, D., Lamersdorf, W.: Goal representation for BDI agent systems. In: Bordini, R.H., Dastani, M., Dix, J., El Fallah Seghrouchni, A. (eds.) ProMAS 2004. LNCS, vol. 3346, pp. 44–65. Springer, Heidelberg (2005). doi:10.1007/978-3-540-32260-3_3
7. D'Aprile, D., Giordano, L., Gliozzi, V., Martelli, A., Pozzato, G.L., Theseider Dupré, D.: Verifying business process compliance by reasoning about actions. In: Dix, J., Leite, J., Governatori, G., Jamroga, W. (eds.) CLIMA 2010. LNCS, vol. 6245, pp. 99–116. Springer, Heidelberg (2010). doi:10.1007/978-3-642-14977-1_10
8. El Kharbili, M., de Medeiros, A.K.A., Stein, S., van der Aalst, W.M.P.: Business process compliance checking. MobIS **141**, 107–113 (2008)
9. Frankfurt, G.H.: The problem of action. Am. Philos. Q. **15**(2), 157–162 (1978)
10. Ghose, A., Koliadis, G.: Auditing business process compliance. In: Krämer, B.J., Lin, K.-J., Narasimhan, P. (eds.) ICSOC 2007. LNCS, vol. 4749, pp. 169–180. Springer, Heidelberg (2007). doi:10.1007/978-3-540-74974-5_14
11. Governatori, G.: Business process compliance: an abstract normative framework. it-Inform. Technol. it-Inform. Technol. **55**(6), 231–238 (2013)
12. Governatori, G., Rotolo, A.: How do agents comply with norms? In: International Joint Conference on Web Intelligence and Intelligent Agent Technology, vol. 03, pp. 488–491. IEEE Computer Society 2009
13. Object Management Group. Semantics of business vocabulary and business rules (SBVR). version 1.3, May 2015
14. Gruber, T.R., et al.: A translation approach to portable ontology specifications. Knowl. Acquisition **5**(2), 199–220 (1993)
15. Guarino, N., Carrara, M., Giaretta, P.: Formalizing ontological commitment. In: AAAI, vol. 94, pp. 560–567 (1994)
16. Herzig, A., Lorini, E., Moisan, F., Troquard, N.: A dynamic logic of normative systems. IJCAI **2011**, 228–233 (2011)
17. Jiang, J., Aldewereld, H., Dignum, V., Tan, Y.-H.: Compliance checking of organizational interactions. ACM Trans. Manage. Inform. Syst. (TMIS) **5**(4), 23 (2015)
18. Kazmierczak, P., Pedersen, T., Ågotnes, T.: Normc: a norm compliance temporal logic model checker. In: STAIRS, pp. 168–179 (2012)
19. Lohmann, N.: Compliance by design for artifact-centric business processes. Inform. Syst. **38**(4), 606–618 (2013)
20. Lowe, E.J.: A Survey of Metaphysics. Oxford University Press, Oxford (2002)
21. Markovic, I., Kowalkiewicz, M.: Linking business goals to process models in semantic business process modeling. In: 12th International IEEE Enterprise Distributed Object Computing Conference, EDOC 2008, pp. 332–338. IEEE (2008)

22. Ouyang, C., Dumas, M., Van Der Aalst, W.M., Ter Hofstede, A.H., Mendling, J.: From business process models to process-oriented software systems. ACM Trans. Softw. Eng. Methodol. (TOSEM) **19**(1), 2 (2009)

23. Pesic, M., Schonenberg, M.H., Sidorova, N., Van Der Aalst, W.M.P.: Constraint-based workflow models: change made easy. In: Meersman, R., Tari, Z. (eds.) OTM 2007. LNCS, vol. 4803, pp. 77–94. Springer, Heidelberg (2007). doi:10.1007/978-3-540-76848-7_7

24. Reiter, R.: On closed world data bases. In: Gallaire, H., Minker, J. (eds.) Logic and Data Bases, pp. 55–76. Springer, Boston (1978)

25. Ribino, P., Cossentino, M., Lodato, C.: A workflow merging approach for emergency procedures. In: ICAR Technical report N: RT-ICAR-PA-16-01, February 2016

26. Ribino, P., Cossentino, M., Lodato, C., Lopes, S., Sabatucci, L., Seidita, V.: Ontology and goal model in designing BDI multi-agent systems. WOA@ AI* IA **1099**, 66–72 (2013)

27. Ribino, P., Lodato, C., Cavaleri, A., Cossentino, M.: A norm-based approach for personalising smart environments. In: De Pietro, G., Gallo, L., Howlett, R.J., Jain, L.C. (eds.) Intelligent Interactive Multimedia Systems and Services 2016. SIST, vol. 55, pp. 659–670. Springer, Cham (2016). doi:10.1007/978-3-319-39345-2_59

28. Ribino, P., Lodato, C., Cavaleri, A., Cossentino, M.: Run-time injection of norms in simulated smart environments. In: Federated Conference on Computer Science and Information Systems (FedCSIS), pp. 1481–1490. IEEE (2016)

29. Villafiorita, A., Weldemariam, K., Susi, A., Siena, A.: Modeling and analysis of laws using BPR and goal-oriented framework. In: Fourth International Conference on Digital Society, ICDS 2010, pp. 353–358. IEEE (2010)

30. White, S.A.: Business process modeling notation, p. 21 (2004). BPMI.org

31. Eric, Y.: Modelling strategic relationships for process reengineering. Soc. Model. Requirements Eng. **11**, 2011 (2011)

Symmetries of Modelling Concepts and Relationships in UML - Advances and Opportunities

Vojtěch Merunka[1,2(✉)]

[1] Department of Information Engineering, Faculty of Economics and Management,
Czech University of Life Sciences Prague, Prague, Czech Republic
vmerunka@gmail.com
[2] Department of Software Engineering, Faculty of Nuclear Sciences and Physical Engineering,
Czech Technical University in Prague, Prague, Czech Republic

Abstract. The article deals with the problem of asymmetry and redundancy of UML concepts that lead to overly complex modelling process without the possibility of efficient generalisation and decomposition of the modelled system to keep UML documentation to a manageable size, to improve user understanding, and simplify documentation and maintenance. The article includes a description of the original way of solving this problem.

Keywords: UML concepts and relationships · Symmetries · Diagraming techniques in UML · Decomposition in UML

1 Introduction - What Is UML?

Software engineers and practitioners are confronted with the question of what is actually UML. Is it mainly a standard of 14 UML-style diagrams or it is mainly a standard for modelling concepts, their properties and their mutual links, where diagrams are secondary as the most commonly used combinations of those more or less diagram-independent elements and links?

Of course, from a practical perspective, the UML standard is a standard for diagrams. But the idea of UML is larger. UML has its metamodel, UML also has its declarative programming language OCL, etc. UML has extension mechanisms (such stereotypes). Theoretically, we can imagine that we can have more new diagrams that would also respect the principles of UML. Moreover, maybe UML will absorb technology BPMN and yet some another tool.

But UML suffers by growing serious problems which were pointed by Simons and Graham (1999) several years ago. Leaving aside criticism of UML semantics, such as the direction of arrows, ugly aesthetics of some shapes, and other possibly confusing features of UML, we still need to stress following serious problems:

1. UML has too many species of terms in a very long but weakly-ordered list. Among these species, there is almost missing any taxonomy and hierarchy. It is in great contrast with the older techniques such Yourdon's structured method that sufficed

© Springer International Publishing AG 2017
R. Pergl et al. (Eds.): EOMAS 2017, LNBIP 298, pp. 100–110, 2017.
DOI: 10.1007/978-3-319-68185-6_7

with easily logical and simple diagrams ERD and DFD having only a few of well-defined concepts. It is obvious that the UML is designed by engineers and practitioners, but not mathematicians. In short, the difference between UML diagrams and ERD & DFD is like the gap between the gigantic programming language C++ and smart programming language Scheme.

2. UML has almost no support for the composition and decomposition of the modelled system. This problem is often multiplied at the enterprise level, where UML diagrams typically consist of hundreds or even thousands of elements. The only diagram that allows this property is a diagram of states and transitions. Instead of it, UML defines too complicated and confusing expansion-like relationships between various elements in different diagrams, such as in Fig. 1.

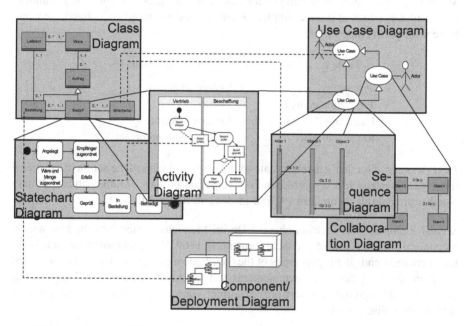

Fig. 1. Relations of UML diagrams and UML concept (Davis and Brabander 2007)

3. UML has strong opposition in the agile programming community. These people say that they prefer «working software over comprehensive documentation» (AP manifesto 2001). The above problems of UML led these people to the radical conclusion that better than a bad conceptual documentation is no conceptual documentation. They decided to spend the saved time to full use of object-oriented development environments (e.g. refactoring, testing, code sharing) of platforms such as .NET, XCode, Ja-vaBeans, VisualWorks…, which are not sufficiently reflected in UML.

We dare to say that the limited possibility of making system composition-decomposition and the absence of symmetries among concepts in the UML is the greatest weakness of UML. Therefore, we think that UML will continue to swell more and more new concepts and will be yet more complex than now. UML is not able to keep pace with new programming languages and new development environments in another way than by swallowing yet more new concepts, which degrade the original idea. UML is losing its potential power to motivate the evolution of development environments and languages in a similar way as UML predecessors Coad-Yourdon and Booch methods did.

2   The Motivation - Symmetries and Analogies in the Real World

In the physical world, the symmetry is an observable mathematical feature of a real system that remains unchanged under some transformation. The analogy is an effect of mapping some structure of one subsystem to another structure of another subsystem. Symmetries and analogies are maybe the essential principles how the God is building the world. Let's look at three examples of making systems more understandable using these principles (Table 1):

Table 1.   symmetries and conservation law examples

Symmetry	Conserved quantity
Translation in time	Energy
Linear translation in space	Linear momentum
Rotation in space	Angular momentum

First example; Noether's theorem states that every symmetry of the action in a physical time-space system has a corresponding conservation law. Mathematician Emmy Noether proved this theorem in 1915 (Banados and Reyes 2016).

Second example; The Russian chemist Dmitri Mendeleev published the first widely recognised periodic table of chemical elements in 1869. He developed his table to illustrate periodic trends in the properties of the then-known elements, and he also predicted some properties of then-unknown elements that would be expected to fill gaps in this table. Most of his predictions were proved correct when the new chemical elements were subsequently discovered.

Finally; The Occam's razor is a general principle from philosophy which says if there exist more different models explaining some occurrence, the simplest one is usually the best one.

3   Solution

Fortunately, we have the hoped solution at our fingertips. Let us look at the UML standard primarily as a standard for software elements and their relationships, where UML diagrams are secondary. From this perspective, the UML sequence diagram and UML interaction diagram can be interpreted as the 2D projections of the single hypothetical 3D diagram, that shows everything in one (see Fig. 2). This is well known in better CASE tools (e.g. Visual Paradigm, Rational Rose,…) that allow creating an interaction diagram automatically from the current sequence diagram and vice-versa.

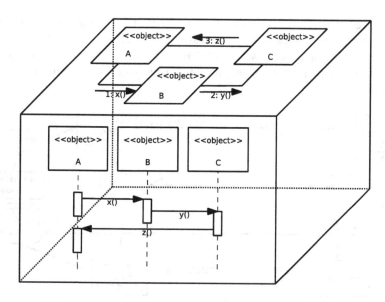

Fig. 2. 3D combination of a sequence and interaction diagram. [author]

If we generalise this effect to another UML concepts, we can combine also other UML diagrams in a similar way. In Fig. 3, there are two standard diagrams of states and transitions. The left diagram describes the behaviour of a borrower and right diagram describes the behaviour of a book in some library.

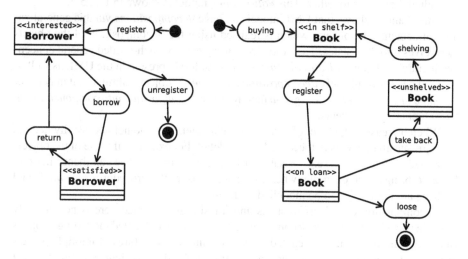

Fig. 3. State-transition diagrams of a borrower and a book in a library. [author]

If the object states will be considered as the greater detail of standard objects, then we can link them via associations, which we know from a standard UML class or instance diagrams. Likewise, based on the expected symmetry, we can also consider the transitions between states as the activities (or methods), then we can connect these transitions via messages. It is interesting that as associations can have expressed their quantity as *cardinalities* of *associations*, also behaviours (e.g. messages) can have a similar concept, which we propose to call *frequencies* of *communications*. The overall result is shown in Fig. 4.

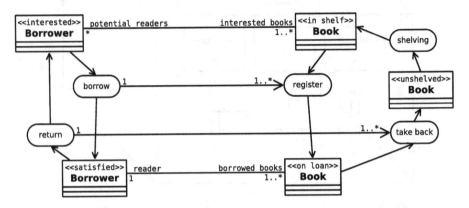

Fig. 4. Associations between states and communications between transitions. [author]

The composite model from Fig. 4 offers a very interesting option: Different states describe the behaviour of the same object during its whole existence, so we can create a simplified model that describes the same situation, but in the aggregate way of all individual time steps together. This «*all-in-one*» model is shown in Fig. 5.

This example shows that UML model can have *decompositions* via this generalization-refinement relationship, which is realised using the decomposition of the objects themselves into their states. Therefore, we can say that so much-needed general conceptual hierarchy of *generalization-refinement* is seamlessly present in the UML as well. It does not need to be the only *decomposition into states* of objects. Similarly, it may occur *decomposition into subtypes* (e.g. *is-a* hierarchy) or *decomposition into components* (e.g. *has-a* hierarchy) of objects.

When increasing the level of detail (e.g. refinement), we do not necessarily need to disaggregate all elements in the same level of detail. For example, if some of the objects are already implemented (e.g. reusable or legacy components), we can them filter out. Figure 6 brings such example, where, for some reason, the procedures *take back*, and *shelving* are not needed to be modelled in detail.

Decomposition of objects to states and transitions presented here is not the only possible way to introduce the decomposition into the object-oriented modelling. Objects can be decomposed (and aggregated back), also into the structures of multiple objects of more different classes, which are interconnected by the inheritance and whole-part relationships.

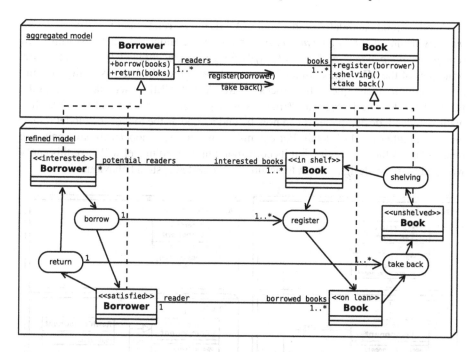

Fig. 5. Aggregation and refinement of the model. [author]

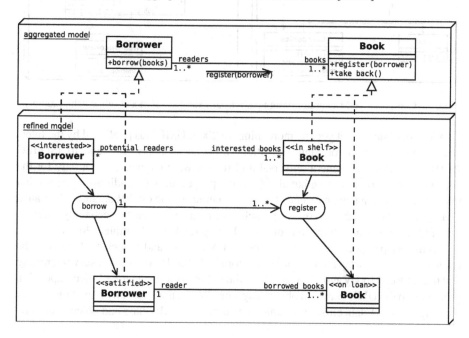

Fig. 6. Refined model with filtration of some unnecessary details. [author]

Another good candidate for this kind of UML model refinement is applying *design patterns* technique. *Design patterns* is already a technique which transforms CIM (*computer-independent model*) to PIM (*platform-independent model*) according to the principles of the MDA (*model-driven-architecture*) approach. The possibility of using *design patterns* technique in the process of MDA with UML is well described in the paper of Kardos and Drozdova (2010). Figure 7 presents an example of such transformation. Indeed, design patterns can now be understood as the tool of the model refinement to a higher level of detail. For example, a generalised model will have only one object class as the only entity, but its corresponding refined model will have this entity wrapped by some design pattern to ensure the requested system behaviour.

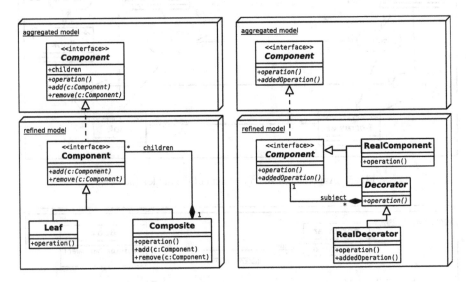

Fig. 7. Composite and Decorator design patterns as examples of model refinement. [author]

We should not forget yet one more thing. In 2005, UML was published by the International Organization for Standardization (ISO) as an approved standard ISO/IEC 19501:2005. It has become a universal tool for software engineering not only for the object-oriented programming but also for other programming paradigms. It means that UML also covers and even extends the full semantics of the old ER database diagrams. UML profiles for database modelling, including relational database technology, can be found for example in publications of Lo and Hung (2014) and Ambler (2003).

From this perspective, the semantics of UML class and object diagrams can be regarded as a superset (or evolution) of the former ERD. Therefore, it is very interesting that the authors Moody and Flitman (2000) did not try to apply their ERD decomposition principles to the UML class and object diagrams. We do not know any impediment, why their algorithm of data clustering cannot be applied to UML class and object diagram.

4   Discussion

Figure 8 gives a general overview of the proposed hierarchical approach to the UML modelling.

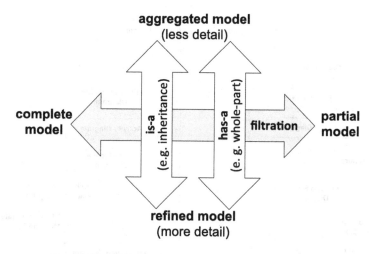

Fig. 8. Hierarchical approach to UML modeling. [author]

We have tried to describe a new approach in the form of a 2D table (see Table 2). This table has two major and mutually symmetrical rows, which correspond to the basic classification of UML 2.5 diagrams from Fig. 9. Four columns of this table show the scope from the highest level of abstraction (on the left) to the level of greatest detail (on the right). Of course, it would be possible to find yet more columns, but we think that

Table 2. Hierarchical approach to UML classification. [author]

Scope			System	Component	Object	Object interior
Structure	**Elements**		system and actors	component	object	state
	Relationships btw elements		actor - usecase link only	association	association	association with cardinalities
	Hierarchies	is-a	supertype-subtype of actors		inheritance of objects	
		has-a	actor or subsystem whole-part	package decomposition	whole-part links of objects	state diagram decomposition
Behaviour	**Elements**		use case	interface	method	transition
	Relationships btw elements		actor - usecase link only	connectors and ports	message	*communication with frequencies*
	Hierarchies	is-a	usecase link «extends»	interface inheritance	inheritance of methods	
		has-a	usecase link «includes»		method code decomposition	state diagram decomposition

our four columns (*system - component - object - object interior*) will be entirely sufficient to illustrate our approach.

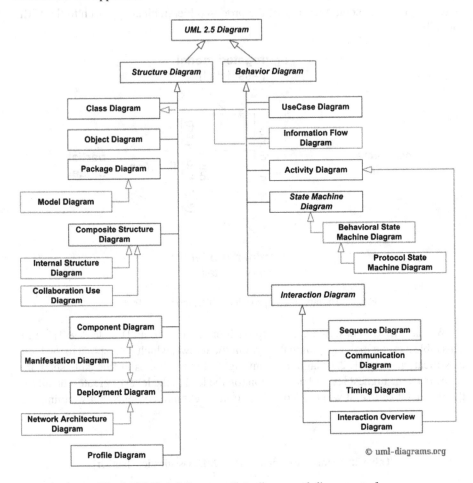

Fig. 9. UML 2.5 diagrams. [http://www.uml-diagrams.org]

4.1 New Concept of Communication with Frequencies

The newly designed concept of *communication* with *frequencies* between transitions (implemented by object methods) is in the symmetrical position with the concept of *association* with *cardinalities*. It should be noted that similar frequency (or cardinality) can be found in the links between actors and usecases in the detailed use-case diagrams. For us, it is not surprising, because the actor - use-case links are regarded as the highest-level generalisation of the communications with frequencies. Even, frequencies can also be added to messages and links between connectors and ports, where should also make sense. Analogously, we can anticipate the inclusion of other new concepts. The empty cells in Table 2 are candidates for these new concepts.

4.2 Solution of the Problem with Association and Whole-Part Relationship

In UML, the concept of a *whole-part* relationship seems to be a special kind of *an association*. Novices in the UML modelling have problems because they do not know which link you choose in a particular case. Similarly, this mistake often happens to professionals having years of experience in programming; database programmers tend to prefer *associations* everywhere, but object-oriented programmers tend to prefer *whole-part object relationships*. The most used database technology is based on the concept of the relation between data, but the object-oriented programming directly supports only object whole-part relationships. Object-oriented programming technology and the most used database technology are real, everybody is very likely working with both, and they are here to stay and must be supported by the UML. Unfortunately, these two programming technologies have a difference which is called «the object-relational impedance mismatch» (Ambler 2013).

Our solution is following:

- Objects in the *whole-part* relationship are in a dependency relationship like the object *inheritance* relationship. Both *whole-part* and *inheritance* relationships (better naming would be *hierarchies*) are used to describe some higher or lower level of abstraction and are subject to aggregation/refinement procedures.
- *Associations* between objects are the relationship between the independent elements of the same level of abstraction. Associations are subject to aggregation/refinement procedures, only if their objects have own hierarchies.

5   Conclusion

This paper has presented an alternative approach to classification of UML concepts and their relationships. This approach enables a manual procedure for decomposing and composing UML models into hierarchies of manageable size, which allows a human to improve the quality of the result, reduce uncertainty and improve conceptual consistency among members of the development team.

The major theoretical contribution of this paper is an alternative perspective on the current UML standard, which provides a solid foundation for both future theoretical research and practical implementation of new CASE tools.

1. We confirmed the roles of the *inheritance* and the *whole-part* relationship as tools for *generalisation* and *refinement* of UML models.
2. We explained the conceptual difference between *association* (which is not directly included in object-oriented programming languages) and *whole-part* relationship (which is directly included in object-oriented programming languages).
3. Based on symmetry with *associations* and *cardinalities* which inform about the quantity of *association* relationship between object species, we recognised the existence of *communications* and *frequencies* which inform about the amount of *communications* between object behaviours.
4. We demonstrated that UML does not need to grow and mindlessly absorb new concepts at any cost but just refine what is already done.

Our future research will focus on the empirical justification of our statements and find new algorithms of model transformation that would automatically perform proposed model transformations.

Acknowledgments. This paper was elaborated under the support of the grant project SGS17/197/ OHK4/3T/14 of the CTU in Prague.

References

Agile programming manifesto (2001). http://agilemanifesto.org/

Ambler, S.W.: Agile Database Techniques: Effective Strategies for the Agile Software Developer. Wiley Publishing Inc., New York (2003). ISBN 978-0-471-20283-7

Ambler, S.W.: The Object-Relational Impedance Mismatch, in Agile Essays by AmbySoft Inc. (2013). http://www.agiledata.org/essays/impedanceMismatch.html

Banados, M., Reyes, I.: A short review on Noether's theorems, gauge symmetries and boundary terms. Universidad Catolica de Chile (2016)

Davis, R., Brabander, E.: Aris Design Platform, Chapter 2 - UML Designer (2007). ISBN 978-1-84628-612-4

Kardoš, M., Drozdová, M.: Analytical method of CIM to PIM transformation in Model Driven Architecture (MDA). J. Inf. Organ. Sci. **34**(1), 89–99 (2010)

Lo, C.-M., Hung, H.-Y.: Towards a UML profile to relational database modelling. Appl. Math. Inf. Sci. **8**(2), 733–743 (2014). http://dx.doi.org/10.12785/amis/080233

Moody, D.L., Flitman, A.R.: A decomposition method for entity relationship models: a systems theoretic approach. In: Proceedings of the First International Conference on Systems Thinking in Management, Geelong, Australia (2000)

Simons, A.J.H., Graham, I.: 30 Things that Go wrong in object modelling with UML 1.3. In: Kilov, H., Rumpe, B., Simmonds, I. (eds.) Behavioral Specifications of Businesses and Systems. The Springer International Series in Engineering and Computer Science, vol. 523, pp. 237–257. Springer, Boston (1999). doi:10.1007/978-1-4615-5229-1

A Rules Based Decision Making Model for Business Impact Analysis: The Business Function Criticality Classifier

Athanasios Podaras[(✉)]

Department of Informatics, Faculty of Economics,
Technical University of Liberec,
Voroněžská 13, 460 01 Liberec 1, Czech Republic
athanasios.podaras@tul.cz

Abstract. The present article aims to present a rules based decision making model for a crucial business impact analysis task, namely the non-arbitrary criticality ranking of an individual business function. The model aims to serve as a classifier for the specific task. The components of the developed classifier are the inducted decision trees based on a data set and their supporting business rules. Moreover a business process representation with the Business Object Relation Modeling approach is included. The data set for creating the classifier has been based on computations of specific recovery complexity parameters. The parameters are included in the proposed by the author business continuity points method for estimating the recovery complexity of a business function, which, in its turn, stems from the use case points approach for software complexity estimation. The current work includes primary results of computations based on the default recovery case.

Keywords: Business continuity · Business impact analysis · Business function · Business rules · Business function criticality ranking · Recovery complexity · Decision trees · BORM

1 Introduction

The complexity of modern industrial and organizational information systems and business processes hardens the formulation of a recovery strategy against their unexpected interruptions. Business Continuity Management deals with the above stated demanding issue. The industry experts nowadays have increased their interest in exploring, recognizing and, in multiple cases, incorporating the solutions provided by the academic researchers with respect to the specific domain. Multiple researchers have presented results of high value regarding business continuity management software tools [4], decision making models [5] as well as process modeling tools [2] which are aimed to the amelioration of the currently provided business continuity management standards [11]. The question rising from the thorough study of all the above mentioned material is "how can an organization deal with the major issue of predicting the recovery time of an interrupted business function (BF) in this complex environment?" The author dealt with this issue by introducing the business continuity points method

© Springer International Publishing AG 2017
R. Pergl et al. (Eds.): EOMAS 2017, LNBIP 298, pp. 111–124, 2017.
DOI: 10.1007/978-3-319-68185-6_8

[20] for measuring the recovery complexity of a business function. The approach is based on the Karner's use case points [12] method for software complexity estimation.

The goal of the current paper is to enhance the method's value by creating a model (classifier) [14] for supporting the binary classification of the business function as critical/non-critical, via the induction of analytical decision trees. The paper illustrates the initially inferred results of the research which focuses on the induction of decision trees for the so called *default classification path*. The results are based on an initial learning dataset which is validated with the help of the confusion matrix technique. Moreover, the initial dataset is split into a training and a testing subset for further validation. The generated business rules [1] enhance the classifier's performance as well as the transparency and the accuracy in implementing recovery scenarios. Additionally, a business process model of the general recovery complexity estimation procedure for a given function is also represented with the Object Relation Diagram (ORD) [22].

1.1 Motivation

The main fact which triggered the necessity to model the recovery complexity based decision making procedure regarding the criticality ranking of a single business function, is the fact that the modern business and industrial environment require plain, comprehensible and scientific description of any method or model proposed by the scientific community. Currently, the overall Business Impact Analysis process, part of which is the criticality ranking of individual business functions, is arbitrarily determined [7]. A BIA predicts the effects of a disruption for critical business functions and processes, gathering information required to develop the best recovery strategy [2].

Neither academics nor the practitioners have so far proposed a mathematical and non-arbitrary method for the criticality classification of an individual business function. The business continuity points [19, 20] contribution deals with this issue. The author proposed a method for classifying business functions in 2 ways. At first, an early and speedy classification is determined with the computation of the Unadjusted Business Function Recovery Points (UBFRP) value. A second and more analytical way is to calculate the precise Recovery Time Effort (RTE) after considering the Adjusted Business Function Recovery Points (ABFRP). The RTE permits to classify a given function as critical/non-critical (see Table 1). For further interpretation the study of the two previous papers is necessary. However, the model's further scientific justification for its acceptance from both the academic as well as the industrial sphere has been proved a necessity since the model is based on mathematical computations.

In this paper a standard decision making model (classifier) with specific business rules is proposed. Moreover, a business process aspect of the classifier is provided with the broadly accepted BORM approach for modeling business processes. Business process models show and animate (when they are simulated) the collaboration of more participants within the solved system [10].

2 Methods and Tools

2.1 The Business Continuity Points Method – Preparation of the Dataset

The method has been introduced by the author as a theoretical approach for estimating the recovery complexity of a business function. Analysis of the method is provided by the specific contributions. For the needs of the current paper a learning dataset has been prepared based on the calculations of the parameters which are demanded by the proposed model and stem from the use case points method. The dataset has been organized in Microsoft Excel worksheet, and includes empirical calculations of both the Unadjusted and the Adjusted recovery complexity parameters as well as the esti- mation of the recovery time regarding 47 business functions. The elements of every business function (i.e. number of actors, number of technical, environmental and unexpected factors) are selected as data for testing purposes based on similar values considered for the use case points. The equations which provide the recovery com- plexity parameters of a business function have been analyzed in previous publications of the author [19, 20].

The calculated parameters are:

- The **Unadjusted Business Function Recovery Points** (hereinafter *UBFRP* Value).
- The Estimation of the **Technical, Environmental and Unexpected Recovery Factor** (hereinafter *TRF, ERF, URF* values).
- The **Adjusted Business Function Recovery Points** (hereinafter *ABFRP* value).
- The estimation of the **Recovery Time Effort** (hereinafter *RTE* value), calculated in hours[1].

The equations which provide the ABFRP and RTE values (Recovery Time) are:

$$ABFRP = TRF * ERF * URF * UBFRP \tag{1}$$

$$RTE = (5000/ABFRP^\wedge 2) - 3 \tag{2}$$

The aforementioned parameters (variables) behave as predictors in the proposed classification model. The predicted variable is the impact value level (hereinafter, IVL). The specific levels are based on Gibson's criticality ranking which is depicted in the following Table (Table 1).

According to Gibson, who is an expert in Business Continuity Management, the above estimated values are internal, which means that recovery objectives used by one organization can be completely different from those used by another organization [8]. Nevertheless, though flexible due to the presence of recovery time intervals, the pro- posed values are considered as reliable, due to the fact that both direct and indirect costs have been considered for their calculation. Direct costs include, i.e. loss of immediate sales and cash flow or equipment/building replacement costs, while indirect costs include i.e. lost opportunities during recovery.

---

[1] Based on the Use Case Points no units are used for the UBFRP, TRF, URF, ERF and ABFRP.

Table 1. Criticality ranking of business functions [8]

Impact Value Level	Criticality of a BF	RTO[a]	MAO[b]
IVL = 4	BF maybe interrupted for extended period	<168 h	= 168 h
IVL = 3	BF maybe interrupted for 1 or more days	<72 h	= 72 h
IVL = 2	BF maybe interrupted for a short period	<24 h	= 24 h
IVL = 1	BF should be running without interruption	<2 h	= 2 h

[a] RTO = Recovery Time Objective [11].
[b] MAO = Maximum Accepted Outage [11].

2.2 Decision Tree and Business Rules Induction in R Software

The R software is an open source statistical software with many advantages [6]. The R-Studio software tool [24] has been selected by the author for decision tree induction, due to the fact that it supports tree induction with various algorithms, i.e. ID3, C4.5 and CART. Classification and Regression Trees (CART) [3, 9] has been found ideal for the current model due to the fact that it supports classifications for both binary and continuous variables. For the implementation of the CART algorithm the package in R-Studio which had to be utilized is the (rpart) package. The decision tree was formulated after importing the dataset with all the UBFRP values in Ms Excel, from a corresponding.txt file.

The derivation of business rules requires in R-Studio requires importing of the data set, creation of a corresponding testing data set and installation of the appropriate packages and libraries for decision tree induction and business rules generation. The demanded code for implementing the aforementioned tasks is the following:

```
> install.packages("rattle")    #package for business
rules
> install.packages("rpart")     #package for decision
trees using CART
> install.packages("rpart.plot")  #package for better
visualization of the DT
> library(rpart)
> library (rpart.plot)
> library(rattle)
> require(rattle)
> datafile <- read.csv("C:/Users/.../datafile.csv",
sep=";")
>   View(datafile)
> fit<- rpart(PredictedValue~Predictor1+Predictor2,
data=datafile)
> asRules(fit) #command for creating business rules
```

Aditionally, the constructed data set had been splitted into a into a subset training (70% of the records) and a testing dataset (30% of the records) for its further validation. The code in R-Studio for splitting a dataset into a training and a testing dataset is the following:

```
>install.packages("caTools")
>library(caTools)
>require(caTools)
>dataset <- read_delim("C:/…../Case1.csv",
+       ";", escape_double = FALSE, trim_ws = TRUE)
View(dataset)
sample = sample.split(dataset, SplitRatio = .7)
train = subset(Case, sample == TRUE)
test = subset(Case1, sample == FALSE)
```

2.3 Business Process Representation with BORM

The BORM (Business Object Relationship Modelling) approach is considered ideal for representing the process workflow. The method has been in development since 1993 and has been a considerably effective and popular tool for both users and analysts. BORM [13, 15, 16] was intended to provide seamless support for the building of object oriented software systems based on pure object-oriented languages, databases and distributed environments [10]. Moreover, BORM has been applied to various projects and case studies [17, 18]. This makes it easy to understand even for the first-time users with almost no knowledge of business analysis [19]. The BORM method uses for visual presentation of the information a simple BORM diagram (Fig. 2) that contains the following concepts [22]:

- **Participant:** an object representing the stakeholder involved in one of the modelled processes, which is recognized during the analysis.
- **State:** sequential changes of the participants in time are described by these states.
- Association: data-orientated relation between the participants.
- **Activity:** represents an atomic step of the behaviour of the object recognized during the analysis.
- **Communication:** represents the data flow and dependencies the activities. Data may flow bidirectionally during the communication.

3 Results

3.1 Decision Tree for a Rules Based Default Recovery Case (Default Classification Path) – Prediction of the IVL of a BF

According to the business continuity points method a default recovery case includes the following categories and Recovery Scenarios (RS) [20, 21]:

- Simple Case: UBFRP = 9, RS: Simple, Classification: IVL = Level 4 (Non-Critical Business Function)

- Average Case: UBFRP = 15, RS: Average, Classification: IVL = Level 3 (Non-Critical) or IVL = Level 2 (Critical).
- Complex Case: UBFRP = 21. Classification: IVL = Level 1 (Critical).

Moreover, the same recovery case, assumes the following values for three different categories of recovery scenarios:

- Simple RS: TRF, URF, ERF = 0.85, ABFRP = 5,5 and RTE = 160 h
- Average RS: TRF, URF, ERF = 1, ABFRP = 9 and RTE = 20 h
- Complex RS: TRF, URF, ERF = 1.15 ABFRP = 31,5 and RTE = 1,9 h.

The above mentioned scenario is the most representative recovery case for the business continuity points. However, when calculating the recovery time effort for BFs with 9 < UBFRPB < 15, their criticality ranking is not exactly as the one described by the representative RS. Thus, the training data set which had been imported to R-Studio enabled us derive the below depicted decision tree (see Fig. 1). It can be observed that the criticality levels are L4 (Non-Critical BF) when UBFRP <= 13.29. The category L3 (Non-Critical) does not emerge in this the specific DT because of the small number of the observed values. However, this classification exists for the interval 13.29 < UBFRP < 14.40.

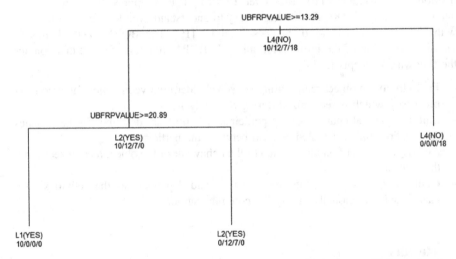

Fig. 1. The decision tree default recovery case for an unexpectedly interrupted business function

The creation of a classifier, such as a decision tree, promotes the rapid estimation of an impact value level as well as the approximate (not precise) value of the RTE. For the specific classifier predictor is the UBFRP Value and predicted variable is the IVL of a BF. The above depicted decision tree can serve as a helpful tool towards the criticality ranking of a BF as critical/non-critical (binary classification) by considering only the

UBFRP Value (Unadjusted Points). The computation of the adjusted points in this case is not required which is a time saving achievement especially for business managers. Finally, the following business rules have been derived with respect to the default recovery case:

```
Rule number: 3 [IVL_RTE=L4(NO) cover=18 (38%) prob=18.00]
    UBFRPVALUE< 13.29

Rule number: 5 [IVL_RTE=L2(YES) cover=19 (40%) prob=0.00]
    UBFRPVALUE>=13.29
    UBFRPVALUE< 20.89

Rule number: 4 [IVL_RTE=L1(YES) cover=10 (21%) prob=0.00]
    UBFRPVALUE>=13.29
    UBFRPVALUE>=20.89
```

In order to ensure the classifier's accuracy regarding the recovery complexity based criticality ranking of a BF, the confusion matrix technique has been applied for IVL prediction based on, firstly, the UBFRP and, secondly the RTE. The method has been implemented in R-Studio software. The performance of the classifier was more than satisfactory with almost 90% accuracy rate. The code for implementing the confusion matrix technique is the following:

```
Require (caret)
install.packages("e1071")
K<-confusionMatrix("CaseCM$IVL_RTE", "CaseCM$IVL_UBFRP")
#CaseCM is the dataset with only 2 columns
Print(K)

Confusion Matrix and Statistics

              Reference
Prediction L1(YES) L2(YES) L3(NO) L4(NO)
    L1(YES)      10       0      0      0
    L2(YES)       0      12      0      0
    L3(NO)        0       0      7      0
    L4(NO)        0       0      5     13

Overall Statistics

              Accuracy : 0.8936
                95% CI : (0.769, 0.9645)
    No Information Rate : 0.2766
    P-Value [Acc > NIR] : < 2.2e-16
```

However, in order for the dataset to be valid, when splitting into a subset training and a testing dataset the inferred results should be similar, if not precisely equal regarding the decision making rules for criticality ranking of a BF. In our case, the testing dataset included the 30% of the records. The inducted decision trees for firstly the training and secondly the testing dataset are also illustrated. Significant differences between the subset training (see Fig. 2) and the testing datasets (see Fig. 3) have not been observed. A slight difference in the predicted Impact Value level is observed for a BF with UBFRP > 12.65p. The difference is, yet, of minor importance since the BF is in both cases classified as critical (L1 (YES), L2 (YES)).

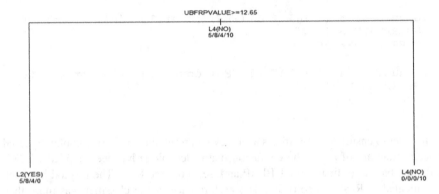

Fig. 2. The decision tree for default recovery case (subset training dataset, 70% of records)

Fig. 3. The decision tree for default recovery case (testing dataset, 30% of records)

3.2 Decision Tree for a Rules Based Default Recovery Case (RTE Estimation)

The constructed data set, additionally, permits the approximate estimation of the RTE Value. The predictors in that circumstance, are: the UBFRP value, and the Recovery Scenario. The classifier, in this case considers the Adjusted Points data, predicts the RTE value (see Fig. 4) and determines the specific IVL. In this way a BF is characterized as critical/non/critical.

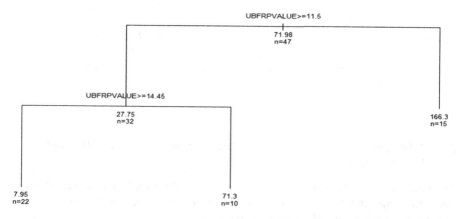

Fig. 4. The decision tree default recovery case for predicting the RTE value for a BF

The above mentioned default recovery case indicate that when business managers need to estimate the RTE value, they have to consider also the corresponding TRF, ERF and URF Values. The UBFRP value is not sufficient for predicting the criticality level of a business function since criticality ranking is strongly related to the RTE. As a consequence, the classification of a given business function without computing all these parameters is a hard task. Thus, the ranking which is based on RTE is highly recommended. However, it can be noticed from both diagrams, that when the UBFRP value has very high (UBFRP > 21) or very low (UBFRP < 9) values, a direct classification is also secure. The derived business rules for the criticality ranking based on the RTE estimation are the following:

```
Rule number: 4 [RTE=7.95 cover=22 (47%)]
    UBFRPVALUE>=11.5
    UBFRPVALUE>=14.45

Rule number: 3 [RTE=166.33 cover=15 (32%)]
    UBFRPVALUE< 11.5

Rule number: 5 [RTE=71.3 cover=10 (21%)]

    UBFRPVALUE>=11.5
    UBFRPVALUE< 14.45
```

The following code provides also information about the predictor (UBFRP) as well as the predicted value (RTE):

```
> fit1b<-rpart(RTE~UBFRPVALUE+SCENARIO, Case1)
> plot(fit1b, uniform=TRUE,margin=0.2)
> text(fit1b, use.n=TRUE, all=TRUE, cex=.8)
> asRules(fit1b)
```

3.3   A Business Process Model of the Business Continuity Points (Default Recovery Case)

The final output of the current paper is the Object Relation Diagram (ORD) which stems from the BORM approach to business process modeling and simulation. The specific diagram includes the following elements:

Participant A: Business Manager. A business manager may be any user who participates in daily operations involved in the business function, a business continuity consultant or any stakeholder who has an active role in the recovery process of any unexpectedly interrupted business function.

Participant B: The BIA-Data warehouse. For efficient business continuity management decisions business intelligence tools are ideal According to business continuity experts the resilient organization, through an enhanced sensing capability, integrates business intelligence in order to improve situational awareness [25]. BORM has proved to be effective in the development and simulation of large and complex business systems such as business intelligence represents [16].

Initiation: Business manager needs to classify a business function by implementing the default recovery case (default classification path.

Action: The activities included in the general classification process no matter the classification path followed[2].

Result: The proposed by the system RTE, IVL values. The result depends on the determined by the business manager (end user) target variable and which of the above delineated decision making rules shall be applied.

The corresponding OR Diagram (see Fig. 5) for the illustration of the BF classification business process has been generated via the recently developed open source promising software platform entitled OpenPonk [26]. The specific tool is a free, open-source, simple to use platform for developing tools for conceptual modeling and involves a user friendly environment for the BORM approach. Moreover, it's an opportunity for experienced developers to extend the existing modelling possibilities of the platform, which is a considerably competitive advantage comparing to other modelling software tools (Fig. 5).

---

[2] Apart from the default classification path, alternative recovery cases are developed by the author. The derivation of the results regarding the statistical tests for the standardization of these paths are still in progress.

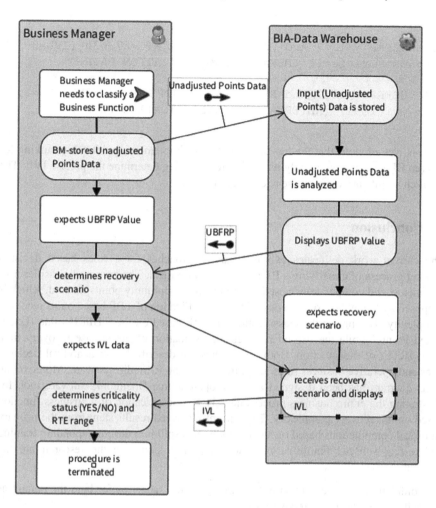

Fig. 5. ORD of the general BF Classification based on the recovery complexity parameters

4 Discussion

The major issue to be discussed concerns mainly the analysis of the term *default recovery case* or *default classification path*. The specific term has been introduced in order to demonstrate the existence of alternative classification procedures. Firstly, the question that rises is "which recovery scenario has to be determined when i.e. UBFRP = 9,9 points?" Another possible question is "will we obtain the same IVL if we follow two different recovery scenarios for the same value?

As we saw in Sect. 3.1 for BFs with i.e. 9 < UBFRP < 15, no specific scenario has been suggested as default. The reason is the prediction of different IVL levels if we follow two or three different recovery scenarios for the same BF. This has been concluded from the most recent testing results. The following example is representative:

```
IF  UBFRP = 13.7 And RS=Simple THEN RTE=67,63h (IVL=3,
BF: Non-Critical) (DEFAULT CLASSIFICATION PATH)

IF  UBFRP = 13.7 And RS=Average THEN RTE=23.63h,(IVL=2,
BF: Critical) (ALTERNATIVE CLASSIFICATION PATH)
```

It is, yet, obvious that the most secure way for implementing criticality ranking for a given BF is to compute firstly its RTE value and then determine the precise IVL. The research results are close to their termination.

5 Conclusion

The current work delineates two important approaches for a rules based decision making process of classifying a BF as critical/non-critical. The proposed classifier uses parameters and computations based on the business continuity points method, which is proposed by the author for the non-arbitrary classification of a BF based on its recovery complexity. The first is the classification of a BF based on the UBFRP value (Unadjusted Points) while the second requires the estimation of the precise recovery time effort (RTE) of the function. Both approaches are described with analytical decision trees and operative business rules [27] inferred via the R-Studio software. Moreover an ORD diagram has been designed with the open source OpenPonk software tool, for illustrating the entire business process namely BF classification of a business function based on its recovery complexity. The currently derived results stem from the primary empirical computations based on a dataset which is split into the corresponding training and testing subsets. Future tasks which remain to complete the research are the following:

- Completion of the computations regarding all the scenarios for both the default as well as the alternative recovery path.
- An ontological model for the proposed business continuity points contribution which will serve as a pattern based crisis management solution. A draft of the semi-formal model including use cases has already been prepared.
- Development of the BIA Data warehouse based on the aforementioned ontology as well as all the involved recovery complexity parameters and calculations. More BIA tasks will be added such as risk assessment and determination of recovery exercise categories.
- Detailed derivation of business rules including all the recovery cases including constrains and rule engines.

References

1. Andreescu, A.I., Mircea, M.: Perspectives on the role of business rules in database design. Database Syst. J. **3**(1), 59–67 (2012)
2. Brás, J., Guerreiro, S.: Designing business continuity processes using DEMO. In: Pergl, R., Molhanec, M., Babkin, E., Fosso Wamba, S. (eds.) EOMAS 2016. LNBIP, vol. 272, pp. 154–171. Springer, Cham (2016). doi:10.1007/978-3-319-49454-8_11
3. Breiman, L., Friedman, J.H., Olshen, R., Stone, C.L.: Classification and Regression Trees. Chapman and Hall, New York (1984)
4. Caelli, W.J., Kwok, L.-F., Longley, D.: A business continuity management simulator. In: Rannenberg, K., Varadharajan, V., Weber, C. (eds.) SEC 2010. IFIP AICT, vol. 330, pp. 9–18. Springer, Heidelberg (2010). doi:10.1007/978-3-642-15257-3_2
5. Chen, G.: Decision-making model of business continuity management. In: Jin, D., Lin, S. (eds.) Advances in Electronic Engineering, Communication and Management Vol.2. LNEE, vol. 140, pp. 285–289. Springer, Heidelberg (2012). doi:10.1007/978-3-642-27296-7_45
6. de Micheaux, P.L., Drouilhet, R., Liquet, B.: The R Software: Fundamentals of Programming and Statistical Analysis. SC, vol. 40. Springer, New York (2013). doi:10.1007/978-1-4614-9020-3
7. Gallagher, M.: Business Continuity Management - How to Protect Your Company from Danger. Prentice Hall, London (2003)
8. Gibson, D.: Managing Risks in Information Systems. Jones & Bartlett Learning, Sudbury (2011)
9. Grąbczewski, K.: Meta-Learning in Decision Tree Induction. Springer, Cham (2014). doi:10.1007/978-3-319-00960-5
10. Hřebík, R., Merunka, V., Kosejková, Z., Kupka, P.: Object-oriented conceptual modeling and simulation of health care processes. In: Barjis, J., Pergl, R., Babkin, E. (eds.) EOMAS 2015. LNBIP, vol. 231, pp. 49–60. Springer, Cham (2015). doi:10.1007/978-3-319-24626-0_4
11. ISO22301: Business Continuity Management. British Standards Institution (2012)
12. Karner, G.: Resource estimation for objectory projects. In: Systems SF AB (1993)
13. Knott, R., Merunka, V., Polak, J.: The BORM method: a third generation object-oriented methodology. In: Liu, L., Roussev, B. (eds.) Management of the Object-Oriented Development Process, pp. 337–360. Idea Group Publishing, Hershey (2006). doi:10.4018/978-1-59140-604-4.ch015, ISBN 978-1-59140-604-4
14. Liu, B.: Supervised learning. Web Data Mining. Data-Centric Systems and Applications, pp. 63–132. Springer, Berlin, Heidelberg (2011). doi:10.1007/978-3-642-19460-3_3
15. Merunka, V.: Instance-level modeling and simulation using lambda-calculus and object-oriented environments. In: Barjis, J., Eldabi, T., Gupta, A. (eds.) EOMAS 2011. LNBIP, vol. 88, pp. 145–158. Springer, Heidelberg (2011). doi:10.1007/978-3-642-24175-8_11
16. Merunka, V., Merunková, I.: Role of OBA approach in object-oriented process modelling and simulation. In: Barjis, J., Gupta, A., Meshkat, A. (eds.) EOMAS 2013. LNBIP, vol. 153, pp. 74–84. Springer, Heidelberg (2013). doi:10.1007/978-3-642-41638-5_5
17. Molhanec, M., Merunka, V.: BORM – Agile Modelling for Business Intelligence. IGI Global, Pennsylvania (2012)
18. Nedvedova, K.: Flood Protection in Historical Towns. Sustainable Development, vol. 168. WIT Press, Southampton (2015)
19. Picka, M., Pergl, R., Šplichal, P.: BORM Model Transformation. Systémová Integrace **18**(2), 112–123 (2011)

20. Podaras, A.: A non-arbitrary method for estimating IT business function recovery complexity via software complexity. In: Aveiro, D., Pergl, R., Valenta, M. (eds.) EEWC 2015. LNBIP, vol. 211, pp. 144–159. Springer, Cham (2015). doi:10.1007/978-3-319-19297-0_10
21. Podaras, A., Antlová, K., Motejlek, J.: Information management tools for implementing an effective enterprise business continuity strategy. E&M Ekonomie Manage. **2016**(1), 165–182 (2016)
22. Podloucký, M., Pergl, R., Kroha, P.: Revisiting the BORM OR diagram composition pattern. In: Barjis, J., Pergl, R., Babkin, E. (eds.) EOMAS 2015. LNBIP, vol. 231, pp. 102–113. Springer, Cham (2015). doi:10.1007/978-3-319-24626-0_8
23. Polák, J., Merunka, V., Carda. A.: Art system design of object-oriented development of information systems by using the original method BORM, Prague, Grada (in Czech) (2003)
24. R-Studio Homepage. https://www.rstudio.com. Accessed 20 Mar 2017
25. Starr, R.: Enterprise Resilience: Managing Risk in the Networked Economy. http://www.boozallen.com/content/dam/boozallen/media/file/Enterprise_Resilience_Report.pdf Accessed 5 Mar 2017
26. Uhnák, P., Pergl, R.: The OpenPonk modeling platform. In: Proceedings of the 11th Edition of the International Workshop on Smalltalk Technologies, pp. 1–12. ACM, New York (2016)
27. Witt, G.: Writing Effective Business Rules. Morgan Kaufmann, Amsterdam (2012)

Conceptual Model of the BIA Data Warehouse

Athanasios Podaras[✉]

Faculty of Economics, Department of Informatics,
Technical University of Liberec, Voroněžská 13, 460 01 Liberec 1, Czech Republic
athanasios.podaras@tul.cz

Abstract. The present article delineates the primary conceptual model of a data warehouse system which is aimed for enterprise business impact analysis. Currently, since the model is in its preliminary stage, only the classification of critical business functions is present in the conceptual schema. Apart from the conceptual model, the specific business impact analysis activity is illustrated using the Business Object Relation Modelling approach, which is ideal for business process requirement analysis. The current conceptual schema will be used as a guide for constructing the future complete meta-model, as well as a logical schema regarding the specific business intelligence solution.

Keywords: Conceptual model · Business impact analysis · Business continuity · BORM · OpenPonk · Ontology · Datawarehouse

1 Introduction

Modern enterprise information systems are developed in order to support highly critical business activities. A major challenge for the current business era is to minimize or eliminate the probability of an unexpected system failover which can have a significantly negative impact for any business entity. Business continuity plan (BCP) ensures the continuity of business processes in catastrophe or disaster situations, building organizational resilience and mitigating risks [1].

Business continuity is a discipline which includes several disciplines such as, business continuity planning, service continuity and crisis management. Multiple researchers and practitioners focus on the provision of new and practical software solutions [2] which will enable organizations face the business continuity challenge. "In practice, when the IT units formulate a business continuity plan they have to prioritize their business objectives. The specific task is performed with the business impact analysis (BIA)" [7]. A recent, interesting and analytical checklist for prioritizing and classifying critical business functions has been proposed by industry experts [6].

Data collection is an important activity throughout the business continuity management (BCM) development process [4]. Furthermore, every resilient organization, through an enhanced sensing capability, integrates business intelligence in order to improve situational awareness [20]. The main goal of the present article is to contribute to the business continuity management domain by introducing a conceptual model of a data warehouse solution which is aimed to assist in the efficient collection of the BIA

R. Pergl et al. (Eds.): EOMAS 2017, LNBIP 298, pp. 125–133, 2017.
DOI: 10.1007/978-3-319-68185-6_9

data in an enterprise. Currently the solution has been designed in order to support the non-arbitrary ranking of critical business functions, which is a crucial and omitted element in currently available business continuity software tools. Finally, the contribution can be utilized as a guide for creating ontological meta-models for the business continuity management domain.

2 Motivation

Databases are the most important components of the modern information systems. The most important database objects in relational databases are called entities and belong to an entity type which, in its turn is a set of real world objects of interest to an application [24]. The relationship between Entities and their information representation has become the forefront of ontologies and information modeling, because conceptual models [3] have become critical in encoding human understanding of information [18].

The Ontological approach to representing the transmission of clear and with low risk of interruption messages in critical and unpredicted events via modern technological infrastructure, is a prominent research topic within the global academic community. In order to ensure clear communication, as well as to facilitate Critical Infrastructure (CI) software interoperability, a common disaster ontology is needed [7]. Ontologies, can be used to share knowledge with incident parameters, and thus effectively increase the communication and countermeasures. Consequently, Ontological models can be used as an effective approach to the formulation of a strategic policy towards unforeseen critical events.

Business intelligence tools, such as data warehouses, can help organizations to deal with enterprise related critical situations, for instance unexpected information system interruptions. The BIA process helps in prioritizing business objectives in order to plan recovery strategies including the rapid restoration of the most critical business activities. However, the BIA task is, unfortunately, based on the business experts' opinions. Some studies indicate that "BIA is an exercise about the ability to home in on the things that are important rather than the 'hobby-horses' of particular managers. Managers will have different perspectives ranging from 'there is no problem here so it doesn't concern me' to 'my function is the most critical in the business, and I need many levels of resilience built in, ready-to-roll recovery arrangements at an alternative site, etc'" [6].

The major challenge of the current contribution is to propose an ontological conceptual schema for ameliorating the IT based communication within an organization in order to prioritize non-arbitrarily their core business objectives. Multiple experts have already proposed conceptual modelling solutions for data warehouses [24] which support the manipulation of multidimensional data.

This can be achieved by estimating and determining proactively the approximate maximum downtime periods of disruptions (MTD) of the core business functions. The parameters involved in the corresponding mathematical computations are stored in the facts and dimensions tables of the DW schemas. Thus, vast volumes of data from various organizational resources can be gathered via IT based collaboration.

3 Methodology

3.1 Ontology Theory

There are various definitions of ontologies, but perhaps the most cited one is "a formal, explicit specification of a shared conceptualization" [23] that provides a common understanding of information [8]. Several methodologies for ontology engineering are proposed to design ontologies [18]. The most complete ones are METHONTOLOGY [5] and On-to-knowledge [21]. Both approaches involve several activities among which the most important are ontology specification, knowledge acquisition, conceptualization, formalization, implementation, evaluation, maintenance and documentation [19]. The current contribution includes the representation of a primary conceptual schema of the target BIA data warehouse solution including the ontology specification of the involved entities. Additionally, the conceptual schema is supported by its corresponding business process model, illustrated by the BORM Object Relation Diagram [15].

The software tool which has been utilized to design the ontological schema is the recently proposed open source and user friendly platform entitled OpenPonk [22]. In its primary state, the conceptual formal expression of our proposed model is performed with the help of the classical UML class diagram, due to the fact that "there is no well-established and universally adopted conceptual model for multidimensional data" [24], and also, "data warehouse design is usually directly performed at the logical level, based on star and/or snowflake schemas leading to schemas that are difficult to understand by a typical user"[24]. More sophisticated approaches for the conceptual representation of an ontology, i.e. OntoUML [25], exist, however they have not been selected for the current model due to the following reasons:

- further investigation of these approaches is required to determine their precise adjustment to the data warehouse case of conceptualization, and
- some experts indicate that the extensions of UML or ER models will not indeed solve the problem of the complex and difficult for end users to understand schemas, as above mentioned, because "ultimately they represent a reflection and visualization of the relational underlying concepts and, in addition, reveal their own problems" [24].

3.2 Object Relation Diagram (BORM Model)

BORM has proved to be effective in the development and simulation of large and complex business systems such as business intelligence represents [15]. The BORM method has been in development since 1993 and has been a considerably effective and popular tool for both users and analysts. BORM [13, 14] was intended to provide seamless support for the building of object oriented software systems based on pure object-oriented languages, databases and distributed environments [8]. Moreover, BORM has been applied to various projects and case studies [16]. The Object Relation Diagram (ORD) which is part of the BORM method, is utilized for depicting the criticality ranking of a core business function based on specific computations.

3.3   The Business Continuity Points Method

This method has been recently introduced by the author [17] as a tool for estimating the recovery complexity of a business function. The method finds its roots in the use case points method [11] used for software complexity estimation. The specific approach permits the non-arbitrary criticality ranking of an individual business function in a simple and objective manner. The analysis of the Business Continuity Points is beyond the scope of the current article. However, a small reference is required in order for the reader to understand the core entities included in the target ontological schema. The main parameters of the business continuity points are the following:

- The **Unadjusted Business Function Recovery Points** (hereinafter *UBFRP* Value).
- The Estimation of the **Technical, Environmental and Unexpected Recovery Factor** (hereinafter *TRF, ERF, URF* values).
- The **Adjusted Business Function Recovery Points** (hereinafter *ABFRP* value).
- The estimation of the **Recovery Time Effort** (hereinafter *RTE* value).

Impact Value Levels: the IVL concept has been proposed by Gibson [9] in order to classify business functions based on their demanded recovery time. The criticality ranking in IVLs is depicted in Table 1.

Table 1. Criticality ranking of business functions [9]

Impact value level	Importance/criticality of BF	RTO[a]	MAO[b]
IVL = 4	BF maybe interrupted for extended period	<168 h	=168 h
IVL = 3	BF maybe interrupted for 1 or more days	<72 h	=72 h
IVL = 2	BF maybe interrupted for a short period	<24 h	=24 h
IVL = 1	BF should be running without interruption	<2 h	=2 h

[a]RTO = Recovery Time Objective, [b]MAO = Maximum Accepted Outage.

4   Results

4.1   Conceptual Model

Ontology Capture and Conceptual Representation
The specific steps include the creation of the core entities which participate in the BIA process. Currently only the entities which are related to the criticality ranking of a business function based on its recovery complexity are demonstrated. The involved entities are the following (see Fig. 1):

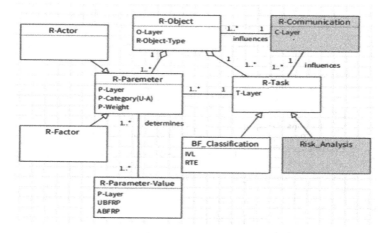

Fig. 1. Model's conceptual representation with UML class diagram (BIA data warehouse)

- **Recovery Object** (R-Object): the specific entity is the highest level ontological object. A recovery object can be, a *business function,* a *business process,* a *business activity* or an *information system.*
- **Recovery Task** (R-Task): the specific entity indicates the most important tasks included in the BIA process. A recovery task is the criticality ranking of a recovery object.
- **Recovery Parameter** (R-Parameter): the specific ontological entity includes Actors and Factors which, according to the Business Continuity Points method, are parameters which help define the Unadjusted Points (UBFRP), Adjusted Points (ABFRP) and the Recovery Time Effort (RTE) values.
- **Recovery Parameter Value** (R-Parameter Value): in this entity the above mentioned values are present as attributes of the specific class.

In the above representation, two objects are highlighted, namely R-Communication and Risk Analysis. Communication is an entity which influences the entire BIA process. The specific entity is inspired by an ontology which includes the "communication package" [12] and which considers "communication" as a critical entity towards social crisis events. The model includes two different ontological layers where communication belongs to the Social Layer. The Physical Layer includes 3 other possible entity groups which are all explained in detail by the author and are the following (see Fig. 2):

- Regions, Cells, Businesses, Wellness, People
- Infrastructures
- Events, Disasters

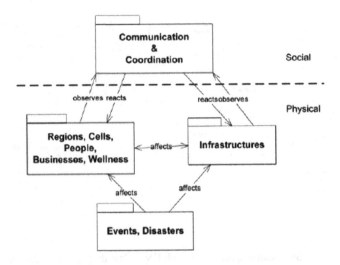

Fig. 2. The four packages of Kruchten's Model [12]

4.2 Business Process Model

The second output of the current paper is the Object Relation Diagram (ORD) (see Fig. 3) which stems from the BORM approach to business process modeling and simulation. The specific diagram includes the following elements:

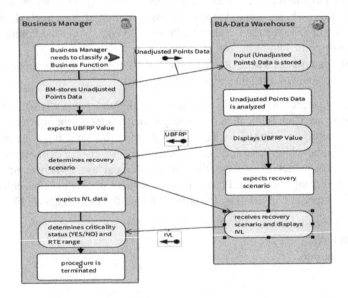

Fig. 3. ORD of the general BF classification process

Participant A: Business Manager. A business manager may be any user who participates in daily operations involved in the business function, a business continuity consultant or any stakeholder who has an active role in the recovery process of any unexpectedly interrupted business function.

Participant B: The BIA Data warehouse. For efficient business continuity management decisions business intelligence tools are ideal. According to business continuity experts the resilient organization, through an enhanced sensing capability, integrates business intelligence in order to improve situational awareness [20]. BORM has proved to be effective in the development and simulation of large and complex business systems such as business intelligence represents [15].

Initiation: A business manager needs to classify a business function.

Action: The activities included in the general classification process.

Result: The proposed by the system RTE, IVL values. The result depends on which of the two values the business manager (end user) will decide to use in order to classify a business function.

5   Discussion

The first issue which should be explained further is the connection between the currently proposed conceptual model and the ontological layers proposed by Kruchten [12]. The current model, as inspired by Kruchten's approach, includes Communication as a separate entity which influences the BIA process. Moreover, the ontological layers in the present model are not limited to social and physical, as in Kruchten's model, but are now expanded to 3 layers, which are depicted as attributes to the designed classes in the conceptual model. For instance, in the Class Communication the attribute *c-layer* is included (c-Layer stands for communication layer). The other two layers are the *o-layer (object layer), and the p-layer* and *t-layer (parameter layer and task layer).*

Moreover, the current conceptual model is not proposed as the final conceptual meta-model, where all the facts and dimensions tables are determined. The present contribution serves as a tool for the initial ontology capture which precedes the design of the conceptual meta-model.

Ontology evaluation is another remaining task in the current research. A detailed evaluation as proposed by ontology experts can be divided into two sections, such as internal evaluation (during the design process) and external evaluation (after designing) [26]. An immediate research concern is the internal evaluation of the current model using a highly sophisticated and recognized software solution for ontology evaluation and validation, which is the Protégé tool [26]. The specific task is implemented throughout the coding stage of the ontology construction and after the integrated conceptual model has been standardized. The second evaluation step is the application of the approach in a realistic case study. User feedback of the proposed business continuity data model, initially at a departmental level as a data mart solution, can be utilized as a driver for its further application to a broader organizational environment. In order for the user's feedback can be obtained, the development of the physical model is an additional prerequisite.

6 Conclusion – Future Work

The currently presented conceptual model includes the preliminary expression of the target BIA data warehouse solution. The current state of the research includes the important entities which participate in the BIA process, as well as an OR Diagram which illustrates the decision making process with respect to a crucial BIA activity, namely criticality ranking of the critical business functions. The work is in progress and the entire solution will include more BIA tasks, i.e. Risk Assessment, Documentation of Recovery Exercises and Decision Making with regard to the MBCO (Minimum Business Continuity Objective).

Moreover, the development of the BIA data warehouse logical schema is still in progress. The logical schema shall include a set of dimensions and facts [24]. The overall mapping between the logical schema and the finalized conceptual model will be the subject of a forthcoming paper. Finally, an important pending research task is the model's testing using data from the industry after the completion of the physical model.

References

1. Brás, J., Guerreiro, S.: Designing business continuity processes using DEMO. In: Pergl, R., Molhanec, M., Babkin, E., Fosso Wamba, S. (eds.) EOMAS 2016. LNBIP, vol. 272, pp. 154–171. Springer, Cham (2016). doi:10.1007/978-3-319-49454-8_11
2. Caelli, W.J., Kwok, L.-F., Longley, D.: A business continuity management simulator. In: Rannenberg, K., Varadharajan, V., Weber, C. (eds.) SEC 2010. IAICT, vol. 330, pp. 9–18. Springer, Heidelberg (2010). doi:10.1007/978-3-642-15257-3_2
3. Ceusters, W., Smith, B.: Foundations for a realist ontology of mental disease. J. Biomed. Semant. 1, 10 (2010)
4. Engemann, K.J., Henderson, D.M.: Business Continuity and Risk Management: Essentials for an Organizational Resilience. Rothstein Associates Inc., Connecticut (2012)
5. Fernández-López, M., Gómez-Pérez, A., Juristo, N.: METHONTOLOGY: from ontological art towards ontological engineering. In: Spring Symposium on Ontological Engineering of AAAI, pp. 33–40. Stanford University, California (1997)
6. Gallagher, A.J.: Critical business functions checklist (2014). https://www.ajg.com/media/1329771/Critical-Business-Functions.pdf
7. Gallagher, M.: Business Continuity Management - How to Protect Your Company from Danger. Prentice Hall, London (2003)
8. Grolinger, K., Brown, K.P., Carpetz, M.A.M.: From glossaries to ontologies: disaster management domain. Electrical and Computer Engineering Publications, Paper 31 (2011). http://ir.lib.uwo.ca/electricalpub/31
9. Gibson, D.: Managing Risks in Information Systems. Jones & Bartlett Learning, Sudbury (2011)
10. Hřebík, R., Merunka, V., Kosejková, Z., Kupka, P.: Object-oriented conceptual modeling and simulation of health care processes. In: Barjis, J., Pergl, R., Babkin, E. (eds.) EOMAS 2015. LNBIP, vol. 231, pp. 49–60. Springer, Cham (2015). doi:10.1007/978-3-319-24626-0_4

11. Karner, G.: 'Resource estimation for objectory projects,' systems SF AB (1993). http://www.bfpug.com.br/Artigos/UCP/Karner%20-%20Resource%20Estimation%20for%20Objectory%20Projects.doc. Accessed 20 April 2013

12. Kruchten, P., Woo, C., Monu, K., Sotoodeh, M.: A human-centered conceptual model of disasters affecting critical infrastructures. In: Paper presented at the Intelligent Human Computer Systems for Crisis Response and Management, Netherlands (2007)

13. Merunka, V.: Instance-level modeling and simulation using lambda-calculus and object-oriented environments. In: Barjis, J., Eldabi, T., Gupta, A. (eds.) EOMAS 2011. LNBIP, vol. 88, pp. 145–158. Springer, Heidelberg (2011). doi:10.1007/978-3-642-24175-8_11

14. Merunka, V., Nouza, O., Brožek, J.: Automated model transformations using the C.C language. In: Dietz, Jan L.G., Albani, A., Barjis, J. (eds.) CIAO!/EOMAS -2008. LNBIP, vol. 10, pp. 137–151. Springer, Heidelberg (2008). doi:10.1007/978-3-540-68644-6_10

15. Molhanec, M., Merunka, V.: BORM – Agile Modelling for Business Intelligence. IGI Global, Pennsylvania (2012)

16. Nedvedova, K.: Flood protection in historical towns. In: Sustainable development, vol. 168. WIT Press, Southampton (2015)

17. Podaras, A.: A non-arbitrary method for estimating IT business function recovery complexity via software complexity. In: Aveiro, D., Pergl, R., Valenta, M. (eds.) EEWC 2015. LNBIP, vol. 211, pp. 144–159. Springer, Cham (2015). doi:10.1007/978-3-319-19297-0_10

18. Roussey, C., Pinet, F., Kang, M.A., Corcho, O.: Ontologies in urban development projects. In: Falquet, G., et al. (eds.) Advanced Information and Knowledge Processing, vol. 1, pp. 9–38. Springer, London (2011). doi:10.1007/978-0-85729-724-2

19. Smith, B., Kusnierczyk, W., Schober, D., Ceusters, W.: Towards a reference terminology for ontology research and development in the biomedical domain. In: Proceedings of KR-MED Citeseer, pp. 57–65 (2006)

20. Starr, R.: Enterprise resilience: managing risk in the networked economy (2003). http://www.boozallen.com/content/dam/boozallen/media/file/Enterprise_Resilience_Report.pdf

21. Sure, Y., Staab, S., Studer, R.: On-to-knowledge methodology (OTKM). In: Staab, S., Studer, R. (eds.) Handbook on Ontologies. International Handbooks on Information Systems, pp. 117–132. Springer, Heidelberg (2004). doi:10.1007/978-3-540-24750-0_6

22. Uhnák, P., Pergl, R.: The OpenPonk modeling platform. In: Proceedings of the 11th Edition of the International Workshop on Smalltalk Technologies, pp. 1–12. ACM, New York (2016)

23. Studer, R., Benjamins, R., Fensel, D.: Knowledge engineering: principles and methods. Data Knowl. Eng. 25(1-2), 161–197 (1998)

24. Vaisman, A., Zimányi, E.: Data Warehouse Systems: Design and Implementation. Data-Centric Systems and Applications. Springer, Heidelberg (2014). doi:10.1007/978-3-642-54655-6

25. Walisadeera, A.I., Ginige, A., Wikramanayake, G.N.: Ontology evaluation approaches: a case study from agriculture domain. In: Gervasi, O., et al. (eds.) ICCSA 2016. LNCS, vol. 9789, pp. 318–333. Springer, Cham (2016). doi:10.1007/978-3-319-42089-9_23

26. Rybola, Z., Pergl, R.: Towards OntoUML for software engineering: introduction to the transformation of OntoUML into relational databases. In: Pergl, R., Molhanec, M., Babkin, E., Fosso Wamba, S. (eds.) EOMAS 2016. LNBIP, vol. 272, pp. 67–83. Springer, Cham (2016). doi:10.1007/978-3-319-49454-8_5

The Business Process Model Quality Metrics

Josef Pavlicek[1(✉)], Radek Hronza[2], Petra Pavlickova[3], and Klara Jelinkova[3]

[1] Faculty of Economics and Management, Department of Information Engineering,
Czech University of Life Sciences, Kamycka 959, 165 00 Prague, Czech Republic
pavlicek@pef.czu.cz
[2] Faculty of Electrical Engineering, CTU, Zikova 4, Prague 6 – Dejvice,
166 27 Prague, Czech Republic
hronzrad@fel.cvut.cz
[3] Faculty of Information Technology, CTU, Zikova 4, Prague 6 – Dejvice,
166 27 Prague, Czech Republic
Petra.Pavlickova@fit.cvut.cz, kjelinkova@post.cz

Abstract. The Business Process Management is considered as a new way of managing the organization. It's based on the principles managing the organization when the processes have the key role. It is managerial discipline that uses the technologies for the process oriented management. The authors discuss the possibilities to measure quality of process models' design and give the answer to the questions: how to measure the BPM quality, if it is possible and, if yes, how to do that. The authors use collaborative usability lab and suggest to implement "pair usability testing" principle for BPM quality evaluation.

Keywords: Business process model · BPMN · Measures of quality of process models

1 Introduction

The Business Process Management is according to [1] considered as a new way of managing organization and it is based on the principles managing the organization when the processes have the key role. According to [2] it is the managerial discipline that uses the technologies for the **process oriented management.** Generally, it is said that Business Process Management is a complex of methods, tools and technologies used for design, approval, analyses and company process management. Thanks to that, it is possible to set customer needs as primary ones, achieving success by what stated in [1].

The Business Process Management brings the change of the view from production oriented (a large number of products at a low price with a goal to meet the needs of the market for the price of surplus products – see consumer industry also so called industry 3.0) to the production targeted at the customer needs fully utilizing opportunities of the organizations. This production, characterized by the product (or service) is not only a tangible object produced according to the defined technological processes. The product is supplemented by a digital dispatch. The digital dispatch carries the identifying target customer, his specific needs (for example color of the product is not determined by heuristic estimate of the future demand of the market – black cars 20%, white 18% and

© Springer International Publishing AG 2017
R. Pergl et al. (Eds.): EOMAS 2017, LNBIP 298, pp. 134–148, 2017.
DOI: 10.1007/978-3-319-68185-6_10

red ones 5%) and also technology procedure needed for the realization of the final product. These are the thoughts of the industry 4.0. These are based on the mechanism of the "Cyber-physical system" [3].

This mode procedure of the management brings synergy effect in terms of customer satisfaction to achieve maximum possible efficiency of the organization (the minimum production to warehouse, accurate production planning etc.). To get the real meaning, it is necessary to bridge a lot of real problems. Among these errors there are ambiguous designation of:

- scope (where direct the process),
- metrics (how to fulfil the individual's goals),
- owner of the process (who is responsible of the business process),
- inputs (what really joins the process),
- outputs (what really stands out of the process),
- limitations (connected to the process).

These questions come out from the Capability Maturity Model [4], that defines following levels of maturity of the project:

1. **level** - there is no process management. The processes and their management within the organization is chaotic and undefined.
2. **level** - initial management of the processes. The processes are realized ad-hoc. The organization's success is based on the individual performance.
3. **level** - repeated project management. The basic processes of the company are identified and their execution complies with the certain discipline.
4. **level** - defining the process management. The basic processes are described, standardized, documented and integrated within all of the organization. The compliance of these processes in the organization is enshrined as a duty.
5. **level** - driven process execution. The processes have defined appropriate indicators, regularly reviewed. Thanks to that it is possible to realize minor changes of the software without measurable loss.
6. **level** - optimized process control. Processes are continuously improved. defining an innovation cycle.

To allow the target improving the level of maturity of processes, the organization should be implemented with the life cycle of the Business Process Management (see Fig. 1).

Thanks to the BPM, life cycle can increase organizational effectiveness, minimize the cost and eliminate increasing the cost and their overwork [1]. Just the first step of the BPM life cycle is a model and designing that it brings following advantages [5, 6] and this is turn brings following advantages:

- visibility of processes – anyone can see the process, measure and simulate different parts of the process, detect the errors in the design,
- transparency of the process – all participants can see the whole of the process and not only a part defined for them.

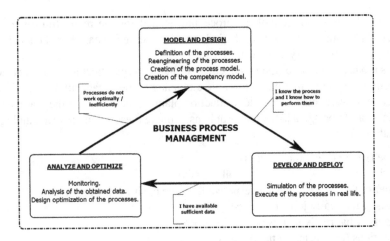

Fig. 1. Business Process Management life cycle.

None of the modelling languages or tool alone are enough to create concise, clear, precise and graphic quality process models. It is necessary to deal with the possible ways of interfering the quality of the process models. Affecting the quality of the process models is possible in several ways. Either during the modelling or retrospectively or after the modelling of the process models. Affecting the quality during the modelling helps methodologies and recommendations how to design the processes. These methodologies include:

- SEQUAL Framework [7, 8].
- The Guidelines of Modelling (GoM).
- Quality Framework for conceptual modelling (ISO 9126 standard for software quality).
- Seven Process Modelling Guidelines (7PMG) [9].
- Process models quality metrics [5].

Disadvantage of using the first four methodologies can be that except some experiences with modelling of the business processes; it can be difficult for the non experienced designer to apply the recommendations in the model because he may misunderstand or apply them wrongly.

Numerous modelling languages exist for the creating of the process models during the model and design phase.

For example:

- Unified Modeling Language (UML) [10].
- Business Process Model & Notation (BPMN) [11, 26].
- Event-driven Process Chain (EPC) [12].
- Petri Nets [13].
- Finite State Machine (FSM) [14].
- Subject Oriented Business Process Management (S-BPM) [15].

- Yet Another Workflow Language (YAWL) [16].
- Business Object Relation Modeling (BORM) [17].

Outputs of the modelling languages is possible generally understanding it as a graphs. Sometimes the process is possible to write down in structured form. We are able to work with the graph using familiar mathematical procedures. Most of the applied metrics for quality measurement is based on the graph analysis. The most widely used measures are:

- The number of elements.
- The complexity of the flow control.
- The immersion of the depth decision.
- The degree of clarity.
- The complexity of interconnections.

Each of the measures focus on one area of the process model and ignores other areas. The measure can mark the model as a correct modelled one according to one specific area. The model can be incomprehensible for the reader of the model. According to [6] *"It does not exist one general measure that can affect the process model from all the areas and determine if it is clear and "understable""* (Fig. 2).

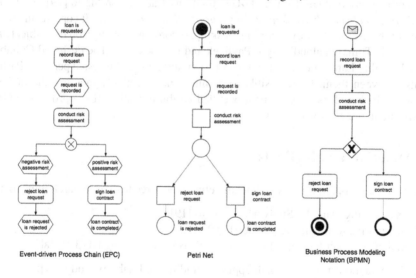

Fig. 2. Business Process Models common notations

Here we define the factors that influence "usability" of the process model. These are:

1. Graph elements (symbols for the nodes and arches, limitation of the logic blocks of the process, option and view of the nesting node).
2. Possibility due to the notation of the graph to affect modelled reality. If we try to generalize the process steps, we will lose part of the modelled reality. Or if we choose the approach similar to BORM (i.e. we are trying to write down the streams and we are creating the model with a lot of the elements).

3. The ability of the process designer to convey the reality.
4. The ability of the reader to understand the process reality.

We are calling these attributes 4F4U BPM … which stands for Four factors For Usability BPM.

2 Research Questions

The research team focused just on factors 4F4U BPM and provided following research questions:

- Have the size and model structure influence to the intelligibility of the process model?
- From what number of elements does it make sense starting the process model hierarchically divided?

The team decided for these questions to process the feasibility study in the Collaborative Usability Lab in the context of 4F4U. The modelled language for the process models design was chosen from the BPMN [11, 18] and Camunda Modeler tool was chosen for the modelling.

The right environment for the 4F4U is Usability Lab. According to [19] "*Usability Lab Allows to effectively track user interaction with the computer.*" It consists in observation of the user activity by recording desktop, recording responses on the subject and call record "Thinking aloud". By J. Pavlicek and R. Bock [25]: The designed Collaborative Usability Lab complements interaction to interaction of the tested persons (Participants) between them. It is possible to monitor and effectively measure the defined factors in the lab. This measurement is called Usability testing of the process models (Therefore in the context of 4F4U).

3 Materials and Methods

Based on the [5, 6, 20] the research team defined the three testing research methods:

- Classic testing using UI Study according to [19].
- Collaborative testing using the lab HUBRU [25].
- Collaborative pair testing J. Pavlicek and R. Bock [25] using HUBRU lab.

All the methods used as default approach traditional Usability study [19]:

- definition of the users (Personifications),
- qualitative test,
- test scenarios (cognitive or heuristic),
- screen records,
- Think aloud record,
- Moderator leading,
- Post interview.

Furthermore, it was completed by new approaches J. Pavlicek and R. Bock [25]:

- monitoring by the eye camera,
- collaborative testing (by the collaborative studies),
- pair testing (by the pair studies).

3.1 Classic Testing

Classical usability test approach

During this test the participant tries to achieve everything from defined goals Fig. 3. During his/her work the usability researcher records his/her behaviour by the behaviour camcorder and records the computer desktop. The participant has to think aloud. It means, he/she has to comment his/her activity. His/her ideas are recorded too. Finally, (after the test is finished) the researcher makes the final interview. This interview can expose gaps at the GUI design. These gaps can be (not matter of course) recorded by researched during the study. The researcher tries to recapitulate them. Thanks to this approach the researcher can finally define all usability issues. According to the Jacob Nielsen [19] 8 participants are enough to expose 90 percent of Usability bugs. It means, we should test minimally 8 participants, but for example twice more (16 participants) is ineffective yet. It consumes more resources (time, money) and the results are not significantly different.

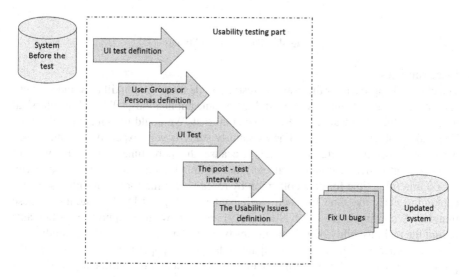

Fig. 3. Usability study approach

We call this approach l "classical" of "common" according to the J. Pavlicek and R. Bock [25].

Advantages

The main advantage for the classical usability study (Fig. 3) is the deeply known methodology, how to lead it, how to gain data from it. The Jacob Nielsen team [19] developed huge amount of technics and UI Lab used for this purposes (Fig. 4). In the world there are teams that perform these studies and get business result from them.

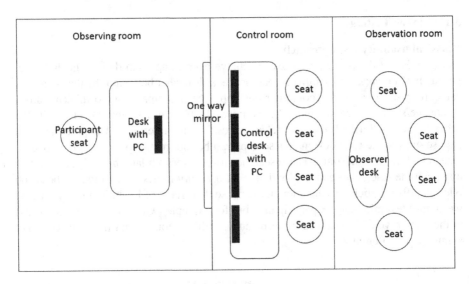

Fig. 4. Classical usability lab

Disadvantages

The classical approach for the usability testing is "de facto" etalon till now and it's very hard to classify disadvantages. We didn't gain some publications, talking about classical usability testing disadvantages. But we can do that. We could be – maybe – the first. The main problem is the price. Each Usability study is very expensive, because each participant "occupies" the whole lab. Because the pure time (pure time without researches introduction, coffee break etc.) for common Usability test consumes between 30–60 min (plus time for data collection by researcher, time for the usability scenario explaining etc.), the time for each participant is multiplied by the amount of these minutes. According to the Jacob Nielsen [19] research, we need approx. 8 participants to find the main usability bugs. That means two working days for Usability study.

But another problem is the participant isolation. No paper talks about that, but the problem really exists. By the term isolation we understand: the participant works over the psychical pressure. He/she is recorded by camcorders, eye tracking system, his/her ideas are recorded by "think aloud" mechanism. The participant might spend more time of investigation of some problem, than in the real live. This behaviour really exists and we recorded that during the collaborative usability study. We will be talking about this in this paper.

3.2   Collaborative Testing

The term Collaborative testing approach was defined by J. Pavlicek and R. Bock [25] for the collaborative usability lab (Fig. 5) developed at the CULS Prague as a part of HUBRU lab [25]. This approach follows the authors' experiences gained during their work on the usability labs constructions at the California, Menlo Park USA and the CTU UI lab construction. The Jacob Nielsen usability studies tests only one person/participant during the one session. In some cases, this kind of usability test allows to test two participants. Some specific type is "baby lab". In this case we are testing GUI used for babies. So babies are performing the test at the group. But this study focuses on children's interaction. Pavlicek and Bock defined new lab architecture for the observing room. While the classical usability study tests only one participant, our approach can tests 10 participants together (according to Nielsen 8 is enough for classical study). It's possible thanks to different Usability Lab architectures. In epitome we designed two crescents desks with 5 PC. The whole of the room is controlled by 4 environmental camcorders. Each PC desktop can be recorded and the middle PC's are equipped by Eyes tracking system. So we can record the participant eyes activity during the test. The final interview can be performed at the Usability room or in the meeting room (outside the lab).

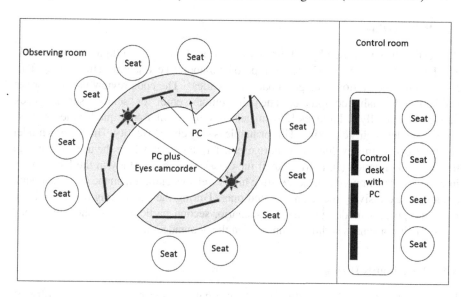

Fig. 5. Collaborative usability lab [25]

Advantages
Main advantage is the price for the study. As the Usability study can be done in one lab with 10 participants simultaneously (Fig. 5), the study time is rapidly decreasing. During this kind of study, we can very quickly expose the design bugs at the GUI. Thanks to the UI Lab architecture, it's possible to test process steps as for example:

- call center,
- service department,
- customer (who needs help).

and we are able to test all mandatory business process steps in real time. This mechanism brings new horizons for GUI testing. Now it's possible to test not only GUI, but the business steps too. Each business process, each kind of business process needs specific GUI expression. And we are able to test all possibilities in real time.

Disadvantages

We have to state [25], we don't expose some fundamental problems during the Usability studies. The collaborative UI Study opponents discussed about the missing "Think aloud" technic. During this study type it is really problematic to be loud because it's disturbing to the others participants. Another criticism is that during the UI study, participants can copy from the others. And another idea is, that during collaborative usability study is not possible to expose all bugs (in comparison with classical) because the UI researcher doesn't have time to do it (because he/she has to control even 10 participants). But nothing about this was detected during our studies.

3.3   Pair Testing

Pair testing was proposed by J. Pavlicek for the K. Jelinkova [6] diploma thesis CTU FIT Prague. It is "de facto" special type of collaborative Usability study. The "Pair testing principle" follows the pair code review ideas. The code review is used for the software code quality compliance. The pair "junior - senior" or "senior – senior" check their code mutually. J. Pavlicek [25] suggested to use similar principle for the business process model quality checking. This principle is very close to reality. The process model is almost every time evaluated by more users. The situation, where the user is alone, in the stressful situation (similarly like at the classical usability study in the lab) is very improbable. The important tasks needing high level concentration on the process model, are almost exclusively the team oriented ones. During the pair testing one participant reads the process model and the test scenario, second participant finishes demanded tasks. Their consensus is thus the answer on the demanded task.

3.4   Participants Hiring

Participants were hired from students of Informatics science or engineers - software developers from business area. The age interval was from 22–38 years old. In the participants group we did not hire experienced BPM designers. The highest participant's level of business modelling was intermediate. This condition was very important. We need to gain answers from the humans, who are close to the process modelling area, but who are not natively doing it. Laymen's are not able to understand the problem context, experienced designers have influent the mental model and their answers are out or reality (respective out of "standard" process model users).

The time for the Usability study was not directly set. But we noticed: If the model consumes more than 10 min, the participant started to be stressed. This stress brakes the main idea of Usability which we intuitively call: "Do not make me feel dumb". It the participant starts to feel dumb, he/she loses enthusiasms to continue the test. In this case we have to expose what happened:

- the Usability of model is bad (it should be improved = Usability bug).
- the test scenario is wrong (the usability researcher prepared wrong test).
- the participant skills are not suitable to finish the task (it means, he/she is wrongly hired and it's generally usability researcher bud – if the participant didn't lie during the hiring questionnaire – unfortunately, sometimes it happens.).

According to these findings we can deduce quality or less quality of designed model.

3.5 Post Review

After the Usability test it is necessary to make participant's final review. This review exposes:

- Likes – what was great (during usability test performance).
- Dislikes – what was wrong.
- Recommendation – that's very often deeply described, what should be better in the design (that is not so sharp Like or Dislike).

4 Results

4.1 The Size and the Structure Affect the Clarity of the Model

The test was conducted on the selected processes of the university study department and selected logical games. These processes are relatively simple and understandable. These processes are easy imaginable for the students (the students formed the main testing group) [6, 21, 22]. The final verification was divided into three groups:

- cognitive Usability testing of the flat process,
- cognitive Usability testing with the hierarchical process with nesting,
- verification participants gained knowledge and gaining feedback.

The test was conducted in 3 groups for 7 participants.

The tested models were in paper form (with possibility also to view it electronically). The study was conducted in collaborative environment. However, there was no collaboration.

The size of the model is very important. It is an expected result. The participants worked the best with the plain model. All the information was readable from one model. The model was worse readable due to its size. It was not clear which process was the main one in the hierarchical model.

The process has the purpose to nest only in the case of the high number of the elements. The result is 4F4U:

1. the used elements are understandable,
2. the BMPN notation enables capture the modelled process with the sufficient fidelity,
3. the designer did not design the model precisely enough,
4. understanding of the model decreases with the number of the nesting and with the model size.

4.2 From What Number of Elements, Does It Make Sense to Start the Process Model Hierarchically Divided

The research team work to answer this question for a long time [5, 6, 20–24]. As it is stated in [6] for the testing in the second phase it was chosen 5 processes from the FEL CVUT portal. The 3 processes were prepared according to the own experience and with the supervisor consultations. She modelled 6 processes for the testing of the number of elements measure and for the depth of the process 2 processes. The methods 7PMG [9] recommends to divide the process into hierarchical with over the 50 elements. The goal was to prove or disprove this claim.

The processes for the measure of number of the elements:

- the tax form (the process contains 27 elements),
- the study termination due to transfer to another faculty (31 elements),
- the study interruption (35 elements),
- the self-employed registration form (40 elements),
- inclusion to the specialization (university) (48 elements),
- Erasmus study (61 elements).

The processes and the set of the questions were presented to the participants. The participants should evaluate the process after the completion of the issues. They were to evaluate, on the scale from 1 to 3, how the process was intelligible, how they could orient in the process, how difficult for them was it to understand the process and how well-arranged was the process.

The values were set as follows:

- intelligibility: 1 (intelligible) - 2 (less intelligible) - 3 (non intelligible),
- process understanding: 1 (easy) - 2 (slightly difficult) - 3 (difficult),
- clarity: 1 (well-arranged) - 2 - (less well-arranged) - 3 (confused).

After every evaluation the participants could stop the study. It was very important to obtain the feedback of the participants (Table 1).

The table shows, that the number of the participants filling the questionnaire decreases with the higher number of the process elements. It is due to difficulty to understand the process model. The process is more complicated and less well- arranged with the higher number of elements. It is very difficult to search in the large processes. The number of errors decreases with the higher number of elements. It is given due to the fact that with the higher number of the elements decreases the number of the participants that evaluated the process. It was given due to the fact that the complex models were able to read only the experienced participants (seniors). This process is unreadable for the beginners.

Table 1. Number of elements measure in classical test

	Process 1	Process 2	Process 3	Process 4	Process 5	Process 6
Number of elements	27	31	35	40	48	61
Participants count	10	10	7	5	4	3
Process understandability percentage (%)	1,7	1,5	1,86	1,6	1,75	1,67
Process clarity percentage (%)	1,7	1,7	1,71	1,6	2	2
Process orientation (%)	1,7	1,6	1,86	1,6	1,75	1,67

That is why we introduce the collaborative test in which all the participants could advise each other and they worked still in pairs (Pair Usability test).

The table shows the significant decrease of the orientation evaluation, clarity and intelligibility. The participants could explain each other different parts of the model. They easily understood the process then.

Notice

We have to expose, that the results contain methodological error. From mathematical point of view, it is not possible to make averages from ordinal values. We should present histograms, mode or median. But none of these discussed show the model dependency strongest quality attributes, like average. And we are sure, if we used one from discussed, the result will be similar (sure - not the same) but the results will be hardly readable. Finally, we decided to make this error and we take example from Function point analysis [27] or Use Case point's analysis [28] (which solves the same problem – averages from the ordinal values. Authors know about this methodological error, but will work with that, because there is not an easier way, nevertheless notice that).

The findings from the results we try to interpret according to [6]:

- The process is more complicated and less well- arranged with the higher number of elements.
- The user has the problem with the orientation in the large process.
- Zooming into the detail the user does not have the view about the whole of the process.
- Optimal number of elements, in which is needed to divide the process into hierarchical, is 35.
- Maximal number of elements, in which is needed to dive the process into hierarchical, is 40.

The collaborative test showed the new result (which should be studied in the future). Time for the finishing of the usability task is limited. Especially for the Business process model probably exists (we should study it in the future) something as maximal time spend for the model comprehension. And this time probably short correlates with the process complexity. As we can read from Table 2, the big size processes are not finished in the Collaborative approach with the Pavlicek's [25] Usability pair testing method. During the post review we gained the participants don't want to perform so big process models.

Table 2. Number of elements measure in collaborative test with the pair testing

	Process 1	Process 2	Process 3	Process 4	Process 5	Process 6
Number of elements	27	31	35	40	48	61
Participants tuples count	6	6	6	2	–	–
Process understandability percentage (%)	1	1,17	1,5	1,5	–	–
Process clarity percentage (%)	1,33	1,33	1,33	1,5	–	–
Process orientation (%)	1,17	1,17	1,5	1,5	–	–

5   Discussion

It is evident, that the size of the process model (number of its elements) affect the itself readability. Of course, the generalization of this problem must be placed into the context. The different evaluation will be by the experienced process model designers, and different for common user (like we described at the Participants hiring chapter). All process models are prepared by our team, and follow these ideas: the model has to be readable by common user, the model must contain the "common" symbols only, the model must follow the BPMN rules, the model must describe common process (as it is for example the course final exam enrolment). The models were focusing for common users as the students, parking system users, some internet shop users ... etc. – briefly normal users who have elementary computer skills. In this context the tests were prepared and in this context it should be interpreted.

The usability pair test showed, the participants don't want to "waste" time to read (and understand) such a big process model. This finding is very important. It says (as we discussed in the chapter "Results") that the process model size has to be in 30–40 intervals. But it shows that the process model reader enthusiasm disappears, if the process model is so complex. This phenomenon is underlined, if work with the process more users and if they can collaborate (as is usual). In this case – could happened, the readers make deal – the process is incomprehensible. And they lose the enthusiasm to try to understand that. This is a big difference between classical usability approach, where the participant tries to finish the task (because he/she feels to be monitored and important to achieve the goal), although he/she stopped it in the real life. The collaborative usability pair test exposes this gap very early. If the process is "incomprehensible", the participants gain the same feeling and stopped the test immediately (one human is alone – he/she can make mistake, but if two have the same opinion? It's probably true).

The problem of elements number at the process model is not the new finding. According to 7PMG [9] is needed with the 50 elements reduce the process by nesting. This statement we propose to state. Already with the number of 30 elements the process began to be complicated for the beginner reader (non experienced). The intermediate reader (designer) begins to have the problems with more of the 40 elements. The problematic of the process nesting is one of the other dimension of the complexity. It is clear that the complex processes should be divided into subprocesses. Our research proves that the process nesting has purpose in the moment when the number of the elements is between 30–40. When the designer decides to nest the process with the less number of the elements, he unnecessarily complicates the readability and usability.

6   Conclusion

The business process model usability is possible to measure and directly influent by the suitable metrics, at the context of our 4F4U factors. The first measure, which describes the model complexity, is the number of used elements in the model. Second measure is the nesting number. Third measure is the process average nesting number. Unfortunately, we cannot define that the process is less usable if the number of nesting is 2 in comparison with number of nesting 1. It's evident that thanks to the digital technology, the problem with number of nesting partially drops out. Especially in the comparison with the printed (hard copy) version. From this point of view, we have to keep in mind, who is the final process consumer. The context is significant here. The student visiting the university web page by the HTTP browser has with the number of nesting smaller usability issues, than the parking guidelines consumer in front of the printed version in the department store garages.

Acknowledgements. This article was supported by the grant the Faculty of Economic and Management Czech University of Life Sciences Prague number: OP OPPR CZ. 07.1.02/0.0/0.0/16_023/0000111

References

1. Hammer, M., Champy, J.: Reengineering the Company - A Manifesto for Business Revolution (2001)
2. Garimella, K., Lees, M., Williams, B.: BPM basics for Dummies, Software A. Wiley, Hoboken (2008)
3. Cyber-physical system (2017). https://en.wikipedia.org/wiki/Cyber-physical_system
4. Kaur, J.: Comparative study of capability maturity model. Int. J. Adv. Res. Comput. Sci. Technol. (2014). https://en.wikipedia.org/wiki/Capability_Maturity_Model
5. Hronza, R., Pavlíček, J., Náplava, P.: Míry kvality procesních modelů vytvořených v notaci BPMN. Acta Inform. Pragensia 4(2), 140–153 (2015)
6. Jelínková, K.: Návrh měr kvality obchodních procesních modelů. Czech Technical University in Prague (2017)
7. Lindland, O.I., Sindre, G., Solvberg, A.: Understanding quality in conceptual modeling. IEEE Softw. 11(2), 42–49 (1994)

8. Krogstie, J., Sindre, G., Jørgensen, H.: Process models representing knowledge for action: a revised quality framework. Eur. J. Inf. Syst. **15**(1), 91–102 (2006)
9. Mendling, J., Reijers, H.A., van der Aalst, W.M.P.: Seven process modeling guidelines (7PMG). Inf. Softw. Technol. **52**(2), 127–136 (2010)
10. OMG, Unified Modeling Language (UML). (2008). http://www.uml.org
11. OMG, Business Process Model & Notation (BPMN) (2016). http://www.omg.org/bpmn/index.htm.Accessed 21 Mar 2017
12. Scheer, A.W., Oliver, T., Otmar, A.: Process modeling using event- driven process chains. Process-Aware Information Systems, pp. 119–146. Wiley, Hoboken (2005)
13. Marsan, M.A., Balbo, G., Conte, G., Donatelli, S., Franceschinis, G.: Modelling with Generalized Stochastic Petri Nets, 1st edn. Wiley, West Sussex (1994)
14. Wright, D.R.: Finite State Machines (2005). http://www4.ncsu.edu/~drwrigh3/docs/courses/csc216/fsm-notes.pdf
15. Fleischmann, A., Schmidt, W., Stary, C., Obermeier, S., Börger, E.: Subject-Oriented Business Process Management. Springer, Heidelberg (2012). doi:10.1007/978-3-642-32392-8
16. Ter Hofstede, A.H.M., Van Der Aalst, W.M.P., Adams, M., Russell, N.: Modern Business Process Automation: YAWL and its Support Environment. Springer, Heidelberg (2010). doi:10.1007/978-3-642-03121-2
17. Merunková, I., Merunka, V.: OBA and BORM approach in the organizational modeling and simulation of local government processes and country planning. Procedia Technol. **8**, 81–89 (2013)
18. Bruce, S.: BPMN Method and Style. Cody-Cassidy Press, Aptos (2011)
19. Nielsen, J.: Why you only need to test with 5 users. Alertbox **19**, 1–4 (2000)
20. Pavlicek, J., Hronza, R., Pavlickova, P.: Educational business process model skills improvement. In: Pergl, R., Molhanec, M., Babkin, E., Fosso Wamba, S. (eds.) EOMAS 2016. LNBIP, vol. 272, pp. 172–184. Springer, Cham (2016). doi:10.1007/978-3-319-49454-8_12
21. Lassaková, M.: Návrh a tvorba měr pro výpočet kvality procesních modelů. Czech Technical University in Prague (2016)
22. Neumann, M.: Míry kvality procesních modelů. Czech Technical University in Prague (2016)
23. Hronza, R., Pavlíček, J., Mach, R., Náplava, P.: Míry kvality v procesním modelování. Acta Inform. Pragensia **4**(1), 18–29 (2015)
24. Mach, R.: Návrh a tvorba nástroje pro optimalizaci procesů na základě analýzy BPM modelů. Czech Technical University in Prague (2015)
25. Pavlicek, J., Bock, R.: Collaborative Usability lab design and methodology to use that, part of HUBRU (2017). hubru.pef.czu.cz
26. Náplava, P., Pergl, R.: Empirical study of applying the DEMO method for improving BPMN process models in academic environment. In: Proceedings of the 17th IEEE Conference on Business Informatics, pp. 18–26. IEEE Operations Center, Piscataway (2015). ISBN 978-1-4673-7340-1
27. Garmus, D., Herron, D.: Function Point Analysis: Measurement Practices for Successful Software Projects. Addison Wesley Professional, Boston (2001). ISBN 0201699443
28. Karner, G.: Metrics for objectory. Diploma thesis, University of Linköping, Sweden. No. LiTHIDA - Ex-9344:21, December 1993

Enterprise Engineering

Pattern-Based Misalignment Symptom Detection with XML Validation: A Case Study

Dóra Őri[✉]

Department of Information Systems, Corvinus University of Budapest, Budapest, Hungary
DOri@informatika.uni-corvinus.hu

Abstract. In this paper, an analytical solution is built to approach the topic of strategic misalignment from an enterprise architecture (EA)-based perspective. The study aims to accomplish an EA-based, systematic analysis of mismatches between business and information systems. The research takes a pattern-based approach to reveal the symptoms of malfunctioning alignment areas. In this study, the analytical potential of pattern generation and rule testing are utilized in complex EA environment. Misalignment symptoms – defined as formal patterns – are detected in the underlying EA models by using XML validation tools. Pattern generation and rule testing are supported by Schematron, a pattern-based XML validation language. The operation, the correctness and the significance of the approach is validated via a compound case study at a road management authority. The proposed research has the potential to extend our understanding on assessing the state of misalignment in a complex EA model structure by applying rule testing and XML validation techniques in EA environment.

Keywords: Strategic alignment · Misalignment symptom detection · Enterprise architecture analysis · Pattern generation · Rule testing

1 Introduction

The study discusses the strategic misalignment between the business dimension and the information systems dimension. The aim of the study is to contribute to the above-mentioned concerns and gaps by introducing a framework that addresses these issues. The study conducts misalignment analysis by proposing a pattern-based framework to detect the typical signs of misalignment in an organization. The proposed framework performs misalignment analysis by taking a symptom-based approach. It aims to accomplish an EA-based, systematic analysis of mismatches between business and information systems.

In recent years growing body of literature has examined alignment evaluation methods [e.g. 5, 11]. Most of the introduced approaches for alignment measurement build on strategic and/or functional level assessment and include top-down construction approach. On the other hand, the minority of the cited approaches deal with the evaluation and correction of alignment, which significantly decreases the applicability of these methods for misalignment assessment. The proposed research will extensively utilize the technique of misalignment detection [3]. The research framework will reflect the

© Springer International Publishing AG 2017
R. Pergl et al. (Eds.): EOMAS 2017, LNBIP 298, pp. 151–158, 2017.
DOI: 10.1007/978-3-319-68185-6_11

recent studies of misalignment models and processes [3, 6, 10]. The proposed misalignment assessment framework will use a symptom-based method. A misalignment symptom catalog will be generated from recent literature on misalignment symptoms [e.g. 3]. Several works have addressed the problem of EA analysis [e.g. 2, 12]. All these works explore the applicability of EA analysis for EA evaluation, however, they do not specialize EA analysis for (mis)alignment assessment. There have been many attempts to investigate reciprocal contributions between strategic (mis)alignment assessment and EA analysis [e.g. 1, 8, 9]. Recently, there has been an increased interest in EA-based alignment assessment, especially in matching EA domains to evaluate the state of alignment in an organization. The problem of enterprise architecture alignment has also been extensively studied in the literature [e.g. 4, 7]. EA alignment methods try to integrate alignment evaluation frameworks, misalignment assessment frameworks and EA analysis techniques to propose EA-based tools for (mis)alignment assessment. However, for the most part, existing approaches have no explicit potential for misalignment symptom detection. None of the proposed techniques can be directly applied to this problem. The contribution of this study extends results on approaching EA-based misalignment symptom detection. The framework proposed in the study can be considered as a precursor step for integrating the concepts and potentials of EA analysis, (mis)alignment assessment and EA alignment.

In this study, a pattern-based misalignment assessment framework will be tested via a case study at a road management authority. The framework is able to reveal the mismatches between the different alignment domains in the underlying EA models. This study is concerned with illustrating the applicability of the proposed framework. Case analysis will demonstrate the operation, correctness, relevance and accuracy of the framework. The empirical validation will contain all the analysis results on pattern-based misalignment assessment.

The rest of the paper is structured as follows. It first establishes the research methodology in Sect. 2. Empirical validation of the proposed framework is presented by a case study in Sect. 3. Results are discussed and implications are presented in Sect. 4. At the end of the paper, conclusions are drawn and future research directions are determined.

2   Research Methodology

This section proposes an overview of the research methodology used in the study. In this part, an analytical solution is built to approach the topic of strategic alignment from an EA-based perspective. The problem of business-IT alignment is translated into the aspects and analytical potential of enterprise architecture. The section has two main parts. First, the conceptual design is given about the research framework. This part is followed by the introduction of the proposed research methodology.

Conceptual Design. The research takes a rule-based approach to reveal the symptoms of malfunctioning alignment areas. The research steps are aggregated into three layers: (1) *Misalignment Layer* is concerned with the construction and formal description of misalignment symptoms. Misalignment symptom construction is based on the matching of the Strategic Alignment Model (SAM) alignment domains [11]. Formal description of misalignment symptoms consists of pattern generation. (2) *EA Model Layer* aims at preparing the underlying enterprise architecture models for the misalignment symptom detection. The phase consists of model transformation, artifact decomposition, and export file generation. (3) *Analysis Layer* is concerned with the implementation details of the proposed research. EA-based misalignment symptom detection will be performed by means of formal rule testing, i.e. the analytical potential of pattern generation and rule testing are exploited. Misalignment symptoms are defined as formal rules. After rule construction, rule testing approaches are introduced.

Proposed Research Methodology. The proposed research methodology builds on the above introduced conceptual design and uses the three-layer approach. The framework has four main parts, which are connected to the corresponding conceptual design layers: (1) *Alignment perspectives* (P.§§) are used to structure the approach of misalignment symptom detection. Alignment perspectives are decomposed into constituent SAM domain matches (C.§§). It refers to the Misalignment Layer. (2) A *misalignment symptom catalog* (S.§§) is composed of symptom collections found in the recent literature on misalignment. It also refers to the Misalignment Layer. (3) An *artifact catalog* (AF.§§) is introduced, which summarizes potential containing EA models. It refers to the EA Model Layer. (4) *EA analysis catalog* (A.§§) describes potential EA analysis types that are suitable for revealing misalignment symptoms in containing EA models. It refers to the Analysis Layer. The proposed research methodology uses an alignment perspective-driven approach. In the first step, traditional alignment perspectives are provided with typical misalignment symptoms. In the second step, relevant artifacts are connected to the misalignment symptoms, which may contain the symptom in question. In the third step, suitable EA analysis types are recommended to the misalignment symptoms. These EA analysis types are able to detect the symptoms in the recommended containing artifacts.

Implementation details of operating the proposed framework are summarized briefly as follows. Queries are written by using the XPath language and the Schematron language. Schematron language is used for making assertions about patterns (i.e. misalignment symptoms) found in the XML exports of the EA models. XPath language serves as a supportive language for defining the context of the queries. Schematron-based queries with embedded XPath expressions are written and later validated in an XML validation tool.

3 Pattern-Based Misalignment Symptom Detection with XML Validation: A Case Study

In order to provide a proof-of-concept evaluation of the proposed approach, a case study was conducted employing a prototype of the research framework in a road management authority. The case study clarifies the operation of the framework by applying it in the context of a real EA model structure. The study was carried out in a fragment of the road management authority's EA model structure. It described a road control initiative, showing the relevant EA models and artifacts to be modified during the progression of the project.

The road management authority is a non-profit government corporation that handles matters relating to road safety, road traffic management, and transportation for around 32000 km national public road network. The scope of activities spans from road operation and road maintenance over professional services to providing road information. In its actual form, the authority was set up in 2006 as a successor of a previous road management government authority. The headquarter and three sites are located in Budapest, and the authority has approx. 170 branches around Hungary. In 2016 the authority employed around 8200 employees. Road control initiative is a pilot project for setting up the EA practice in the authority. The initiative is part of an integrated road network development project which aims to transform the internal operation as well as to optimize processes in order to increase operational efficiency and transparency within the road management authority. As part of the above introduced integrated road network development project, the road control project is concerned with the implementation of a traveling warrant system. The goal of the project was manifold: (1) to achieve real-time road control information forwarding, (2) to deliver up-to-date information and control specifications onboard, (3) to provide exact information retrieval about past activities and coordinates by place and by date, (4) to provide electronic administration about road control, (5) to provide an expandable and integral solution for road control support, (6) to decrease paper administration related to road control tasks.

The general model structure at the road management authority consists of several layers. There are some modeling resources available concerning the Business Architecture, Data Architecture and Application Architecture, but there is no modeling instance for technological, the infrastructural projection of the organization. As for the model structure of the road control initiative, the model structure consists of 4 EA domains: Business Architecture, Data Architecture, Application Architecture, and Technology Architecture. There are both between-layer and within-layer artifact connections in the model structure. The model structure in the road control initiative offers an in-depth analytical potential for EA-based misalignment assessment. The small size and the compact nature of the project ensure minimal but sufficient validation of the proposed framework.

Before commencing misalignment symptom detection at the case organization, preliminary reviews were organized in order to get acquainted with the conditions in the organizational state. Preliminary reviews were conducted by interviewing stakeholders of the initiative. Interviews served as an initial consultation about influential areas to review and the perceived problems concerning business-IT alignment. Interviews revealed several problematic business-IT areas and therefore provided us with preliminary assumptions of alignment problems and possible organizational areas for misalignment investigations. An initial list of problematic business-IT areas is referred to as a prefatory step for operating the proposed framework. In order to prepare for misalignment symptom analysis, perceived malfunctioning areas are translated into misalignment symptoms using the proposed misalignment symptom catalog. Subsequently, an EA layer-based categorization was given about the perceived misalignment symptoms. This categorization has guided the symptom detection and it helped to understand the nature and scope of perceived misalignment symptoms in the case organization. Perceived alignment problems were analyzed according to the following misalignment symptom categorization scheme: *S.C.01*. Symptoms that can be managed and detected in EA scope. *S.C.02*. Symptoms that can be managed in EA scope in reduced extent, i.e. analytical potential only for simplified, incomplete symptom detection. *S.C.03*. Symptoms that cannot be managed and detected solely in EA scope, other information sources are needed for symptom detection. These symptoms will be handled in future work. The analysis formed limitations for framework applicability i.e. detected those symptoms that cannot be handled within EA scope. Thus, misalignment symptoms being under the category of S.C.03 were not analyzed with the proposed research framework.

As part of misalignment symptom detection, Schematron queries were processed against every suitable EA model within the road management initiative. Most of the symptoms used several EA models for detection but there were also examples for sole EA model symptom detection. In the former case there are three alternatives for multi-model usage: (1) Different model variants are analyzed in the query. This means that the symptom is processed in more or every state of the project. (2) Two or more EA models are used in the queries for mostly comparative queries. In this alternative, the queries can be later analyzed according to the changes in model variants over time. (3) Both different model variants and two or more distinctive model types are used in the queries. Similar to the previous alternative, changes in model variants can be analyzed over time as well. Subsequently, the general Schematron queries will be personalized to the suitable EA models. The expressions of rule context and assert or report test were provided with appropriate attributes and values from the EA models under review. Outputs and processing results were interpreted in detail for every misalignment symptom together with indicating constraints and possible extensions.

4   Discussion

The case study was concerned with illustrating the applicability of the proposed research framework. To assess the state of misalignment at the road management authority, the proposed research framework was used. The case study provided considerable insight into the applicability of the proposed research framework. In addition, it has demonstrated the utility and usability of the proposed framework as well. The detection results confirmed the usefulness of the proposed research framework as a misalignment assessment framework

The proposed framework has highlighted significant analytical potential compared to the inbuilt query power of sole EA modeling tools. The relevance of the proposed research framework against the simple and usually limited analytical potential of EA modeling tools was clearly demonstrated by the in-depth analysis in the empirical validation section. In addition, the study provided support for transforming misalignment symptoms into misalignment queries via pattern generation and rule testing techniques.

Misalignment symptom analysis and detection provided insights about query types. Evidence from the case study suggested that there are distinct types of misalignment symptoms that can be detected by the proposed research framework. The case study demonstrated that the proposed research framework is applicable for detecting the following types of misalignment symptoms: (1) Symptoms in which the presence or lack of the certain type of attributes has to be investigated. (2) Symptoms in which the cardinality of certain connection types has to be analyzed. (3) Symptoms in which more models have to be compared. (4) Symptoms in which more model variants have to be analyzed and compared during the progression of the project.

The study has also given an account for symptom validation. In this case study, validation was accomplished by follow-up interviews at the case organization after successfully operating the research framework. The topic of validation raises two concerns which have to be clarified. First, the proposed research framework does not provide the potential for matching the EA models under review with an ideal model. This approach would imply the existence of an ideal, aligned model which can be used for the benchmark. The presence of a fully aligned model base at case organizations would elicit the need for further alignment steps. Thus, this kind of matching cannot be accomplished, and the proposed framework does not deal with the analysis of this kind of ideal alignment model base. Second, the preliminary validation of misalignment symptoms cannot be done due to the specific follow-up interpretations of misalignment phenomena at the test organizations. There is no need for the in vitro testing of misalignment symptoms, i.e. the preliminary interpretation and evaluation of misalignment symptoms. This kind of validation also involves a reference model about the ideal state of the case organization, against that an organization can evaluate the presence of misalignment symptoms in advance. In contrast to the need for in vitro testing, the proposed framework uses a soft, follow-up validation based on post factum interviews and the interpretation of specific organizational characteristics and organizational context.

Based on the experience gathered during framework and empirical validation, the proposed framework has limitations on the following areas: The first is that the framework examines only the model environment, i.e. the details that are modeled. In fact, the real operation of the organizations cannot be investigated, only the part which is presented on modeling level. This observation recalls the need for investigating the state of models and the difference between models and reality in form of further follow-up interviews. Future work will concentrate on solving this issue. The second limitation is the problems of modeling tool lock-in and document format lock-in. The same misalignment symptoms in different modeling tools and in different document formats have to be defined in a different way, which undermines the portability of the proposed framework. This limitation can be solved by an intermediate transformation layer between the layer of documents under review and the layer of misalignment pattern generation. This topic is deferred to future work. Another way to solve the problem of lock-ins is to use XSLT transformation language to filter the relevant analysis details from documents in different formats. This approach would make the models in different document formats comparable for processing detection of the same misalignment symptom. Further work needs to be carried out to implement the standardization of different document formats.

5   Conclusion

The paper dealt with the concept of enterprise architecture-based misalignment analysis. It presented a research approach for EA-based misalignment assessment. The main purpose of the proposed research was to analyze strategic misalignment between the business dimension and the information systems dimension. The research addressed misalignment symptom analysis by introducing an enterprise architecture-based framework to detect the typical signs of misalignment in an organization. The construction and operation of the framework have been discussed and explained in detail in the previous sections. To illustrate the feasibility of the proposed framework in practice as well as to provide guidance on applicability, a case study was performed. Examples of mismatches have been provided in the investigated EA models by using the proposed artifact-based and EA analysis-based approach.

With the conducted case study considerable insight has been gained and significant progress has been made with regard to the applicability of the proposed framework in practice. Nevertheless, there are topics reserved for further examinations. The next research step will be to focus on a tool-independent, automated implementation of the misalignment symptom detection framework. Future work will also focus on the dynamic nature of symptom detection, i.e. to analyze the different states of the EA models as well as the overarching changes in EA models over time.

Acknowledgement.   This paper has been written with the support of the National University of Public Service in the framework of the priority project KÖFOP-2.1.2-VEKOP-15-2016-00001 titled "Public Service Development for Establishing Good Governance" - Ludovika Digital Governance Research Group.

References

1. Bounabat, B.: Enterprise architecture based metrics for assessing IT strategic alignment. In: The European Conference on Information Technology Evaluation, vol. 13, pp. 83–90 (2006)
2. Buckl, S., Matthes, F., Schweda, C.M.: Classifying enterprise architecture analysis approaches. In: Poler, R., van Sinderen, M., Sanchis, R. (eds.) IWEI 2009. LNBIP, vol. 38, pp. 66–79. Springer, Heidelberg (2009). doi:10.1007/978-3-642-04750-3_6
3. Carvalho, G., Sousa, P.: Business and information systems misalignment model (BISMAM): an holistic model leveraged on misalignment and medical sciences approaches. In: Proceedings of the Third International Workshop on Business/IT Alignment and Interoperability (BUSITAL 2008), CEUR, vol. 336, CEUR-WS, Aachen, pp. 104–119 (2008)
4. Castellanos, C., Correal, D.: KALCAS: a framework for semi-automatic alignment of data and business processes architectures. In: Morzy, T., Härder, T., Wrembel, R. (eds.) ADBIS 2012. LNCS, vol. 7503, pp. 111–124. Springer, Heidelberg (2012). doi:10.1007/978-3-642-33074-2_9
5. Chan, Y.E., Reich, B.H.: State of the art. IT alignment: what have we learned? J. Inf. Technol. **22**(4), 297–315 (2007). doi:10.1057/palgrave.jit.2000109
6. Chen, H.M., Kazman, R., Garg, A.: BITAM: an engineering-principled method for managing misalignments between business and IT architectures. Sci. Comput. Program. **57**(1), 5–26 (2005). doi:10.1016/j.scico.2004.10.002

7. Clark, T., Barn, B.S., Oussena, S.: A method for enterprise architecture alignment. In: Proper, E., Gaaloul, K., Harmsen, F., Wrycza, S. (eds.) PRET 2012. LNBIP, vol. 120, pp. 48–76. Springer, Heidelberg (2012). doi:10.1007/978-3-642-31134-5_3

8. Dahalin, Z.M., Razak, R.A., Ibrahim, H., Yusop, N.I., Kasiran, M.K.: An enterprise architecture methodology for business-IT alignment: adopter and developer perspectives. Commun. IBIMA **2011**, 1–15 (2011). doi:10.5171/2011.222028

9. Elhari, K., Bounabat, B.: Platform for assessing strategic alignment using enterprise architecture: application to e-government process assessment. IJCSI Int. J. Comput. Sci. Issues **8**(1), 257–264 (2011)

10. Fritscher, B., Pigneur, Y.: Business IT alignment from business model to enterprise architecture. In: Salinesi, C., Pastor, O. (eds.) CAiSE 2011. LNBIP, vol. 83, pp. 4–15. Springer, Heidelberg (2011). doi:10.1007/978-3-642-22056-2_2

11. Henderson, J.C., Venkatraman, N.: Strategic alignment: leveraging information technology for transforming organizations. IBM Syst. J. **32**(1), 4–16 (1993). doi:10.1147/sj.1999.5387096

12. Niemann, K.D.: From Enterprise Architecture to IT Governance: Elements of Effective IT Management. Friedr. Vieweg & Sohn Verlag, Wiesbaden (2006)

An Enterprise Architecture-Based Approach to the IT-Business Alignment: An Integration of SAM and TOGAF Framework

Pavel Malyzhenkov[✉] and Marina Ivanova

Department of Information Systems and Technologies, National Research University Higher School of Economics, Bol. Pecherskaya 25, 603155 Nizhny Novgorod, Russia
pmalyzhenkov@hse.ru, miivanova_1@edu.hse.ru

Abstract. Information technologies have evolved from its traditional back office role to a strategic resource role able not only to support but also to shape business strategies. For over a decade IT-business alignment has been ranked as a top-priority management concern and is widely covered in literature. However, conceptual studies dominate the field, while there is little research on practical ways to achieve the alignment. Enterprise Architecture development is a methodological approach to design of mutually aligned business and IT architectures. Most of the existing EA approaches do not distinguish between diverse IT-business alignment perspectives. Thus, the paper aims to attempt at providing a practical guidance for IT-business alignment as well as a strategic guidance for EA development by integrating traditional Strategic Alignment Model and The TOGAF framework.

Keywords: IT-business alignment · Enterprise architecture · SAM · TOGAF

1 Introduction

In the context of today's dynamic, highly competitive business environment, it is crucial for a company's survival to acquire high level of strategic flexibility, which, in turn, requires agile organizational structure and processes, and, therefore, flexible underlying information systems architecture.

Information technology and information systems have evolved from its traditional use as an organization's operations automation tool to a critical strategic resource influencing the business value created by the company.

The strategic alignment of business and information systems has consistently been reported as one of the key concerns of business and IT managers across different industries. From this point of view it represents an important issue on the field of organizational modeling of enterprise. According to the research on international IT management trends [29] the alignment issue has held its position in the top-three key concerns of IT managers since 2000 along with business agility, productivity and cost reduction (Fig. 1).

© Springer International Publishing AG 2017
R. Pergl et al. (Eds.): EOMAS 2017, LNBIP 298, pp. 159–173, 2017.
DOI: 10.1007/978-3-319-68185-6_12

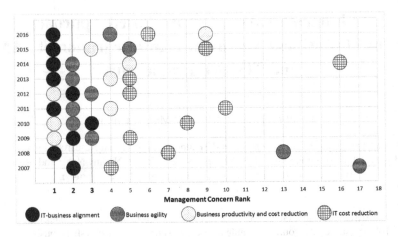

Fig. 1. Top IT management concerns (based on the data provided in [29])

The trend is caused by benefits alignment may provide as well as risks entailed by misalignment. IT-business alignment enables organization to enhance its flexibility and maximize return on IT investments, which, in turn, leads to increased profitability and sustainable competitive advantage. Thus, failure in leveraging IT may have a considerable negative effect on a firm's performance and viability [6, 8, 9, 11, 15].

Conceptual studies on the nature of the IT-business alignment dominate the literature, but there is still little research on the practical appliance of the alignment concept and ways to achieve it.

Enterprise Architecture development is a comprehensive approach which implicitly ensures the achievement of a specific level of alignment. However, existing EA design models usually follow a predefined pattern and do not distinguish between diverse IT-business alignment perspectives.

Most of the existing research focuses on the alignment assessment using questionnaire methods based on the subjective judgement of IT and business executives. Moreover, little studies [16] provide the guidance on the alignment assessment results interpretation and further misalignment elimination. So, the aim of the paper is to attempt at fulfilling the gap in a practical guidance for IT-business alignment as well as in a strategic guidance for EA development, by proposing an integration of a conceptual alignment model described in [11] and EA framework (The Open Group Architecture Framework [30]).

The rest of the paper is organized as follows. Section 2 summarizes the theoretical background relevant for the approach proposed. Section 3 presents the linkage between the main components of SAM and TOGAF framework. Finally, in the Sect. 4 conclusions are drawn and the future research directions are identified.

2 Theoretical Background

To place the present contribution in a proper context this section outlines some related work and important concepts.

There is an extensive research conducted on the nature of the IT-business alignment, criteria for its evaluation and approaches to address the issue. IT-business alignment can be determined as "the extent to which the IS strategy supports and is supported by the business strategy" [20] or as "the degree to which the IT mission, objectives and plans support and are supported by business mission, objectives and plans" [23].

However, many researchers consider alignment to be not a static state that can be measured at a single point in time but rather a continuous process of adjustment of business and IT domains [4, 5, 11, 21].

Two dimensions of the IT-business alignment, intellectual and social, are distinguished [23]. Intellectual dimension is concerned with the consistency, interrelation and validity of IT and business plans. Social dimension is related to the mutual understanding and commitment between business and IT managers with respect to each other's missions, objectives and plans.

There are multiple reasons causing misalignment within organization. Most commonly mentioned ones derived from the literature review are listed in Table 1. It is important to notice that misalignment reasons pertaining to the social dimension of alignment dominate the literature: shared knowledge domain, mutual understanding and efficient communication between business and IT executives are perceived as the key antecedents to alignment.

Table 1. Causes of misalignment

	Reason of misalignment	Alignment dimension
1	Undefined business strategy: most of alignment models presuppose the existence of corporate strategy to which IT should be aligned	Intellectual
2	IT managers do not take part in the formulation of the corporate strategy and, thus, have a poor understanding of business strategy and objectives; and vice versa, business managers are not involved in the formulation of IT strategy and therefore have a low comprehension of IT strategy and objectives	Social
3	Poor understanding and lack of effective communication channels between business and IT managers	Social
4	"Back office" status of IT department within organization	Social
5	Most of the benefits brought by IT are intangible and/or can only be seen in a long-term which causes difficulty in measuring the return on IT investments. Thus, business managers do not have an accurate perception of the value added by IT to the corporate competitive advantage	Intellectual/ Social
6	Time lag between business and IT planning processes: business and IT external environments change so quickly that previously aligned plans become obsolete	Intellectual

Mostly the researches focus on the intellectual dimension of alignment and contribute to the study of its social dimension by examining the cognitive basis of shared understanding between business and IT executives – the similarities and differences of their mental models, assumptions, expectations, values and beliefs. The results indicate that cognitive commonality between business and IT managers ensures their efficient communication having a positive impact on the alignment [28].

As any other problem, the lack of alignment is characterized by different symptoms. The most evident one is a negative return on investment in information technologies. Others include inefficient business processes and decision making, inability to quickly react to market changes and opportunities, decline in operational productivity and performance [6–9, 11, 15].

In order to manage the alignment, it should be first assessed. The literature provides multiple approaches to the alignment evaluation, most of them are questionnaire-based.

For example, in [14] a questionnaire-based method representing 12-item measurement scale is developed: six items were scored on a 7-point Linkert scale to evaluate the alignment of IT plan with business plan, and the other six items were rated the same way to measure the alignment of business plan with IT plan. Another questionnaire-based approach was proposed in [18]. The Strategy Alignment Maturity model (SAMM) allows to identify which of the five alignment maturity levels organization is at by evaluating six alignment criteria:

1. *Communications Maturity*: ensuring efficient information exchange and knowledge sharing and mutual understanding between IT and business departments.
2. *Competency/Value Measurements Maturity*: ensuring the development of business and IT performance metrics allowing to measure the contribution of information technologies to the company's value chain.
3. *Governance Maturity*: ensuring formal identification of decision-making authorities among business and IT managers responsible for priorities reviewing and IT resource allocation.
4. *Partnership Maturity*: ensuring IT and business functions have an equal role in defining corporate strategy, share common vision, risks and rewards.
5. *Technology Scope Maturity*: ensuring flexible IT architecture able to support organizational infrastructure and processes, leverage emerging technologies effectively, enable and drive changes in business processes and strategies.
6. *Skills Maturity*: ensuring efficient IT human resource management – hiring, firing, training, encouraging innovation, leveraging ideas.

SAMM provides different attributes (or practices) to be assessed within each of the six maturity criteria. For example, under Communication Maturity criterion there is a practice "Understanding of IT by business".

These practices are being evaluated by the assessment team consisting of IT and business executives using a five-point Linkert scale. After each practice within each maturity criterion is assessed by all members of the assessment team, an average score for each practice and then for each of the six maturity criteria is calculated. The evaluation team then uses these scores to derive an overall estimation of the corporate's IT-business alignment maturity level. The next higher level of maturity is then used as a roadmap to identify the set of actions needed to improve alignment.

There are five alignment maturity levels that may be assigned to a company according to the SAMM:

1. No Alignment Processes
2. Beginning Alignment Processes
3. Establishing Alignment Processes
4. Improved Alignment Processes
5. Optimized Alignment Processes.

At the first level of maturity alignment processes are ad-hoc in nature or nonexistent, communication channels are ineffective and IT and business functions have no mutual contribution. The fifth level is characterized by an ongoing process of IT-business alignment, efficient communication and mutual understanding between IT and business departments, leveraging IT to attain and sustain competitive advantage.

After the current IT-business alignment level is identified it is essential to define the range of strategic choices needed to be made in order to achieve a desirable level of alignment.

One of the most fundamental and well-recognized alignment frameworks is the Strategy Alignment Model (SAM) [11, 31]. Figure 2 is a schematic representation of the SAM illustrating an integration of business domain, consisting of business strategy and organizational infrastructure and processes, and IT domain represented by IT strategy and IS infrastructure and processes. The authors distinguish between two types of domains integration:

1. *Strategic integration (of external business and IT domains)*: the link between business and IT strategies reflecting the capability to leverage IT strategy to both shape and support business strategy.
2. *Operational integration (of internal business and IT domains)*: the link between organizational infrastructure and processes and IS infrastructure and processes reflecting coherence between internal customer requirements and expectations and the delivery capability within the IS function.

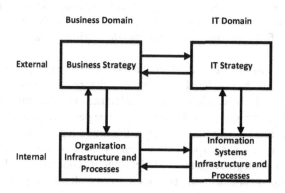

Fig. 2. Strategic alignment model (adapted from [31])

In order to ensure the right balance between the choices made across all four domains it is vital to review multivariate cross-domain relationships. SAM distinguishes between four dominant cross-domain relationships (called alignment perspectives) based on the premise that strategic alignment can only be attained when three of the four domains are in alignment. Therefore, changes in one domain affect at least two of the three remaining domains.

Four alignment perspectives may be divided into two groups based on what kind of a strategy (business or IT) is considered as a driving force.

1. *Perspective One: Strategy Execution.* Business strategy is the driver of both organization and information systems design choices. Strategy is formulated by the top management and executed by the IS management.
2. *Perspective Two: Competitive Potential.* Business strategy drives the development of supporting IT strategy and corresponding IS infrastructure and processes. Business managers seek to identify the best possible IT competencies to support the business strategy. IT managers are responsible for efficient design and implementation of the IS architecture consistent with the IT strategy chosen.
3. *Perspective Three: Technology Transformation.* IT strategy is the driving force of new products and services fostering business strategy and organizational infrastructure and processes modifications. IS management identifies and interprets trends existing in the IT environment that may be considered as opportunities to gain competitive advantage or as a threat to the company's market position. Business executives are up to articulate how to leverage emerging IT capabilities to transform business strategy.
4. *Perspective Four: Service Level.* IT strategy drives the development of IS infrastructure and processes with corresponding implications for the organizational infrastructure and processes. IT executives seeks to provide the best possible service to the internal client by developing and implementing the appropriate basis for the IS architecture redesign. Business managers are responsible for IT resource allocation and project prioritization.

After alternative strategic choices within four dominant alignment perspectives have been analyzed and evaluated, one or more perspectives should be selected and adopted as the driving force of organizational transformation towards strategic alignment (Fig. 3).

It is important to stress that all alignment perspectives are equally useful and should be chosen based on the continual assessment of the trends across four business and IT domains mentioned above. Thus, strategic alignment is a dynamic process rather than a static procedure. It requires evolvement from one perspective to another based on the shifts in the business environment to allow the firm's repositioning and internal infrastructure rearrangement in respond to the market changes, threats and opportunities.

The original Strategic Alignment Model is purely conceptual and does not offer any tools for misalignment detection nor does it capture alignment processes needed to be established within each of the four alignment perspectives. Therefore, the model extensions were later proposed. So, in [20] the original SAM was reviewed in a more practical perspective identifying the major enablers and inhibitors of IT-business alignment but the model itself was not elaborated. The SAM was also expanded with additional domain components related to the information and knowledge management [22] and then

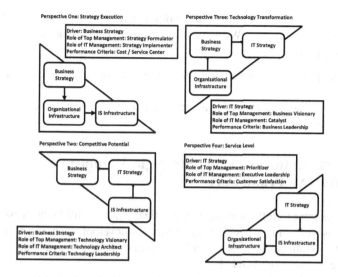

Fig. 3. Alignment perspectives (adapted from [31])

combined with the integrated architecture framework (IAM) in order to enhance practical applicability of the alignment concept.

However, there is still little literature covering activities that should be applied within each SAM domain to enhance the level of alignment as well as the literature on practical application of the model.

As stated above SAM suggests the alignment of four domains: business strategy and organization infrastructure and processes, IT strategy and IS infrastructure and processes. Unfortunately, in practice, enterprises lack formal definition of business strategy [24]. IT strategy is often not even present or is restricted by internally-oriented view [11]. Moreover, the organization structure is rarely stable in many organizations and the ever-increasing complexity of IT applications and infrastructure is referred to by CIO's as a major concern. Therefore, there is a need for an instrument providing a holistic enterprise view [27, 32].

This need is fulfilled by a concept of Enterprise Architecture which is defined as a set of models and definitions describing the structure of an enterprise, its subsystems and the relationships between them, terminology to employ and guiding principles for design and future evolution [1]. EA development is a continuous iterative process which may be approached using EA frameworks including tools, techniques, process model, artefacts descriptions and guidance for EA design.

EA frameworks implicitly ensure the achievement of a specific IT-business alignment level. However, they do not distinguish between different alignment perspectives: most of approaches claim that EA development must start with the business strategy and structure definition followed by supporting IT infrastructure and application portfolio design. Whereas diverse misalignment situations require different design approaches. And IT may and should be used in an innovative way as an enabler for renewed or even completely new business strategies, products and services, organization forms and processes.

An integration of EA framework with traditional SAM may contribute to the solution of the problems mentioned. We believe that although different in scope they may complement each other:

1. EA design process may incorporate diverse alignment perspectives when guided by SAM
2. SAM may be operationalized using methodologies, tools and techniques provided by EA framework.

3   Towards an Integration of Strategic Alignment Model and TOGAF Framework

Thus, as an attempt to fulfill the gap in a practical guidance for IT-business alignment using SAM as well as in a strategic guidance for EA development using EA framework, we propose to combine Henderson and Venkatraman's SAM with The Open Group Architecture Framework (TOGAF).

The framework supports four architecture domains that are commonly accepted as subsets of an overall enterprise architecture (Fig. 4):

1. *Business Architecture*: business strategy, organization structure and processes, business governance.
2. *Information Systems Architecture:*
    2.1. *Data Architecture*: structure of organization's data assets and data management resources.
    2.2. *Application Architecture*: application portfolio.
3. *Technology Architecture*: software and hardware capabilities including IT infrastructure, networks, communications, standards, etc.

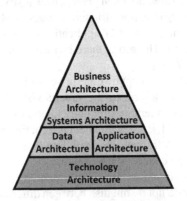

Fig. 4. Enterprise Architecture

TOGAF is based on an iterative process model called Architecture Development Method (ADM), consisting of the following phases each provided with its own objectives, approaches, inputs, steps (activities) and outputs:

1. *Preliminary Phase.* Preparation and initiation activities required for an enterprise architecture design including customization of TOGAF and definition of Architecture Principles.
2. *Phase A: Architecture Vision.* Development of a high-level vision of the capabilities and business value to be delivered as a result of the proposed enterprise architecture.
3. *Phase B: Business Architecture.* Development of a Business Architecture supporting the approved Architecture Vision; namely, description of the product/service strategy, organizational, process, information and geographical aspects of the business environment.
4. *Phase C: Information Systems Architecture.* Development of the Information Systems (Data and Applications) Architecture supporting the agreed Business Architecture and Architecture Vision.
5. *Phase D: Technology Architecture.* Development of the Technology Architecture supporting the chosen Information Systems Data and Application Architectures as well as Business Architecture and Architecture Vision.
6. *Phase E: Opportunities & Solutions.* Identification of projects, programs and/or portfolios that effectively deliver the Target Architectures identified in previous phases.
7. *Phase F: Migration Planning.* Planning the transition from the Baseline to the Target Architectures by finalizing a detailed Implementation and Migration Plan.
8. *Phase G: Implementation Governance.* Development of the implementation architectural oversight.
9. *Phase H: Architecture Change Management.* Establishment of architecture change management procedures.

It is important to note that the framework has a strong documentation support: each of the ADM phase is provided with a set of templates (catalogs, matrices, diagrams, deliverables). For example, the first phase may take advantage of the "Business Principles, Goals, Drivers" and "Architecture Vision" templates; the second may employ "Architecture Definition" and "Architecture Requirements Specification" templates.

Table 2 represents the linkage between the main components of SAM (four integration domains) and TOGAF framework (architecture domains, ADM phases and artifacts).

External and internal business domains of SAM correspond to the TOGAF's Business Architecture domain. SAM's internal IT domain matches TOGAF's Application, Data and Technology Architecture domains. Finally, SAM's external IT domain does not seem to have a clear match because TOGAF does not explicitly determine the IT strategy or its essential components such as IT vision, goals and objectives, justification of IT investments etc. However, it is reasonable to assume that the IT strategy is formulated and implemented as part of the overall TOGAF's Information Systems Architecture domain.

In our proposal each TOGAF's architecture domain is covered by some ADM phases: A, B, C (Data), C (Application) and D are used to develop baseline and target Business/Data/Application/Technology Architectures and analyze the gap between them.

Table 2. Linking the main components of the SAM and TOGAF framework

SAM integration domains		Business domains		IT domains			
		Business strategy	Organizational infrastructure and processes	IT strategy	IS infrastructure and processes		
TOGAF	**Architecture domains**	Business architecture		IS architecture	Application architecture	Data architecture	Technology architecture
	ADM phases	Phase A	Phase B	Phase C	Phase C (Applications)	Phase C (Data)	Phase D
	Artifacts	• Stakeholder map matrix • Value chain diagram • Driver/Goal/Objective catalog	• Driver/Goal/Objective catalog • Role catalog • Business service/Function catalog • Process/Event/Control/Product catalog • Contract/Measure catalog • Business interaction matrix • Business footprint diagram • Functional decomposition diagram • Goal/Objective/Service diagram • Business use-case diagram • Organization decomposition diagram • process flow diagram	• IT Strategy	• Application portfolio catalog • Application/Function matrix • Application interaction matrix • application use-case diagram • Process/Application realization diagram • Software distribution diagram	• Data Entity/Data component catalog • Data Entity/Business function matrix • Application/Data matrix	• Technology standards catalog • Technology portfolio catalog • Application/Technology matrix • Platform Decomposition diagram • Processing diagram

Thus, ADM phases A-B may be used to detect the misalignment between SAM's business and IT domains and identify the target aligned architectures. Then, the next ADM phase E allows to identify ways of misalignment elimination by determining projects, programs and/or portfolios that effectively deliver the target aligned architectures. Finally, ADM phases F-H guide the alignment implementation (the transition from the baseline to the target architectures).

It is worth noting that TOGAF framework is not limited to a fixed set of methods and tools. It allows adaptation to the needs of particular organization. Thus, the ADM phase order as well as the corresponding set of inputs, steps and outputs may be tailored to fit a specific alignment perspective.

According to the Strategic Alignment Model there are two alignment perspectives having the IT strategy as the driving force. One of them is the "Technology Transformation" perspective where the change in the external IT environment enables the development of new products and/or services fostering business strategy and organizational infrastructure and processes modifications. When approaching "Technology Transformation" alignment perspective, the ADM phases A-B should be implemented not before but after the phase C.

As it was previously mentioned, TOGAF does not explicitly determine the IT strategy and there is no artifact able to replace it. Thus, in order to fully implement the application of alignment perspectives to the EA development, the IT strategy artifact should be introduced.

Unfortunately, there is no commonly accepted formal structure of the IT strategy document. Overall, accordingly to the literature research, IT strategy is a plan that covers all facets related to the use of information systems and technologies within an organization as part of the overall corporate strategy. So, the IT strategy document may have the following outline.

1. Title page
2. Revision history
3. Table of contents
4. Executive summary
5. Introductionss
   a. The background
   b. The project's purpose and scope
   c. The relationship to the overall business strategy
6. IT strategy vision, goals and objectives
7. Internal IT capabilities
   a. IT components: IT project portfolio, Application portfolio, IT infrastructure
   b. IT organization structure and governance: IT organization roles and responsibilities, IT resources, IT governance
8. External forces
   a. Business and IT market changes
   b. Strategic business requirements
   c. Business service requirements
9. IT problems, issues and threats
10. IT opportunities
    a. List of cost reduction/efficiency increase opportunities
    b. Justification of IT investments
11. IT strategy implementation roadmap: list of projects, activities, milestones, deliverables, measures, resource allocation, budgeting etc.
12. Appendices

Thus, the IT strategy artifact may take advantage of some other artifacts delivered by the ADM phases such as "Application Portfolio Catalog" created by phase C (Application), "Driver/Goal/Objective Catalog" created by preliminary phase, refined by phase A and validated by phase B, or "Contract/Measure Catalog" delivered by phase B.

So, the proposed framework may be used to measure the alignment by identifying interrelationships and establishing correspondence between artifacts delivered by ADM phases in different SAM's integration domains. Figure 5 illustrates the application of SAM's "Strategy Execution" alignment perspective to the TOGAF framework for misalignment detection.

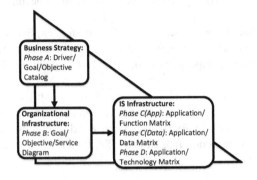

Fig. 5. SAM "Strategy Execution" alignment perspective and TOGAF

Business external and internal domains are considered aligned if every goal and objective identified by the ADM phase A's "Driver/Goal/Objective Catalog" is covered with some services in the ADM phase B's "Goal/Objective/Service Diagram".

Then, internal business and IT domains are considered aligned if these services are covered by some applications defined by the ADM phase C's "Application/Function Matrix". Which in turn should operate the data from the ADM phase C's "Application/Data Matrix" and be based on the technologies identified by the ADM phase D's "Application/Technology Matrix".

If, for example, "Driver/Goal/Objective Catalog" contains some goals which are not covered by the "Goal/Objective/Service Diagram" then some new business processes should be introduced in order to implement the business strategy. Or, if the "Application/Function Matrix" contains more/less services than indicated by the "Goal/Objective/Service Diagram", then the company's application portfolio is probably excessive/insufficient.

Moreover, the proposed framework may be used to create new strategies, structures and processes already aligned across business and IT domains. Figure 6 illustrates the application of SAM's "Technology Transformation" alignment perspective to the TOGAF framework for creating new business capabilities by leveraging IT opportunities.

Assume that the "IT Strategy" defined by the ADM phase C identifies the opportunity to transform the way the company produces or distributes its products and services with the use of new technologies introduced on the IT market. If these technologies are to be employed, then the company's value chain should be modified (the ADM phase A's "Value Chain Diagram"). If, for example, some production operation is automated then there will be process changes which should be reflected in the ADM phase B's "Process/Event/Control/Product Catalog" and "Process Flow Diagram". Moreover, the

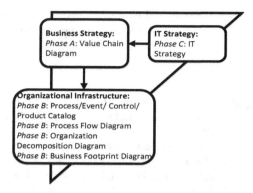

Fig. 6. SAM "Technology Transformation" alignment perspective and TOGAF

organizational structure may change: the department manually performing the operation which is to be automated may be disbanded; this should be reflected by the ADM phase B's "Organization Decomposition Diagram". Overall, these changes may be summarized in the ADM phase B's "Business Footprint Diagram" which describes the linkage between business goals, organizational units, business functions and services, and maps these functions to the technical components delivering the required capability.

4   Conclusions

The paper addresses the issue of IT-business alignment, a top-priority concern of business and IT executives in the last two decades. The integration of Strategic Alignment Model and TOGAF was proposed as an attempt to create a practical guidance for IT-business alignment and a strategic one for EA development.

Although different in scope these frameworks complement each other: SAM is a conceptual managerial approach enabling an appropriate IT-business alignment strategy, while TOGAF is a practical methodology for development of mutually aligned business and IT architectures.

In this paper, we establish formal criteria for IT-business alignment by integrating Strategic Alignment Model with EA framework. The presented approach, unlike some previous studies (e.g. [16]) allows us to consider the alignment of IT and business components of EA within different alignment perspectives where the driving force is either the business strategy affecting organizational and IT design choices, or the IT strategy fostering business strategy and organizational changes. The latter requires the definition of the IT strategy document which has no commonly accepted formal structure. The present research contributes to the problem suggesting the possible outline of the IT strategy document which is essential to the IT-business alignment.

Further research activities follow but are not limited to the following branches:

1. specification of each ADM phases' inputs and outputs for each SAM's alignment perspectives
2. formalization of the alignment assessment model for the resulting EA evaluation

3. practical application of the proposed framework taking into account such business factors as industry sector, organizational size and type of strategic positioning.

References

1. Alaeddini, M., Asgari, H., Gharibi, A., Rashidi Rad, M.: Leveraging business-IT alignment through enterprise architecture – an empirical study to estimate the extents. Inf. Technol. Manage. **18**(1), 55–82 (2016)
2. Alzayed, A., Alraggas, B.: The alignment of information technology and business strategy in the Kuwaiti companies. Int. J. Comput. Appl. **101**(7), 39–45 (2014)
3. Azevedo, C.L.B., van Sinderen, M., Pires, L.F., Almeida, J.P.A.: Aligning enterprise architecture with strategic planning. In: Advanced Information Systems Engineering Workshops, pp. 426–437 (2015)
4. Baets, W.: Aligning information systems with business strategy. J. Strateg. Inf. Syst. **1**(4), 205–213 (1992)
5. Broadbent, M., Weill, P.: Improving business and information strategy alignment: Learning from the banking industry. IBM Syst. J. **32**(1), 162–179 (1993)
6. Byrd, A., Lewis, B.R., Bryan, R.W.: The leveraging influence of strategic alignment on IT investment: an empirical examination. Inf. Manag. **43**(3), 308–321 (2006)
7. Coltman, T., Tallon, P., Sharma, R., Queiroz, M.: Strategic IT alignment: twenty-five years on. J. Inf. Technol. **30**, 91–100 (2015)
8. Chan, Y.E., Sabherwal, R., Thatcher, J.B.: Antecedents and outcomes of strategic IS alignment: an empirical investigation. IEEE Trans. Eng. Manage. **53**(1), 27–47 (2006)
9. Gerow, J.E., Grover, V., Thatcher, J.B., Roth, P.L.: Looking toward the future of IT-business strategic alignment through the past: a meta-analysis. MIS Q. **38**(4), 1059–1085 (2014)
10. Gleeson, M.: The link between business strategy and information systems. Dublin Institute of Technology, School of Computing Research Paper (ITSM), Ireland (2004)
11. Henderson, J.C., Venkatraman, N.: Strategic alignment: leveraging information technology for transforming organizations. IBM Syst. J. **38**(1), 4–16 (1993)
12. Kajalo, S., Rajala, R., Westerlund, M.: Approaches to strategic alignment of business and information systems: a study on application service acquisitions. J. Syst. Inf. Technol. **9**(2), 155–166 (2007)
13. Kearns, G.S., Lederer, A.L.: A resource-based view of strategic IT alignment: how knowledge sharing creates competitive advantage. Decis. Sci. **34**(1), 1–29 (2003)
14. Kearns, G.S., Lederer, A.L.: The effect of strategic alignment on the use of IS-based resources for competitive advantage. J. Strateg. Inf. Syst. **9**(4), 265–293 (2000)
15. Kearns, G.S., Sabherwal, R.: Strategic alignment between Business and Information Technology: a knowledge-based view of behaviors, outcome, and consequences. J. Manage. Inf. Syst. **23**(3), 129–162 (2007)
16. Kurniawan, N.B., Suhardi: Enterprise architecture design for ensuring strategic business IT alignment (integrating SAMM with TOGAF 9.1). In: Joint International Conference on Rural Information & Communication Technology and Electric-Vehicle Technology (2013)
17. Lederer, A.L., Mendelow, A.L.: Coordination of information systems plans with business plans. J. Manage. Inf. Syst. **6**(2), 5–19 (1989)
18. Luftman, J.N.: Assessing IT/business alignment. Inf. Syst. Manage. **20**(4), 9–15 (2003)
19. Luftman, J.N., Derksen, B., Dwivedi, R., Santana, M., Zadeh, H.S., Rigoni, E.H.: Influential IT management trends: an international study. J. Inf. Technol. **30**, 293–305 (2015)

20. Luftman, J.N., Lewis, P.R., Oldach, S.H.: Transforming the enterprise: the alignment of business and information technology strategies. IBM Syst. J. **32**(1), 198–221 (1993)
21. Luftman, J.N., Papp, R., Brier, T.: Achieving and Sustaining Business-IT alignment. Calif. Manag. Rev. **42**(1), 109–122 (1999)
22. Maes, R., Rijsenbrij, D., Truijens, O., Goedvolk, H.: Redefining Business-IT Alignment through a unified framework. Primevera Working Paper Series – University of Amsterdam (2000)
23. Reich, B.H., Benbasat, I.: Measuring the linkage between business and information technology objectives. MIS Q. **20**(1), 55–81 (1996)
24. Reich, B.H., Benbasat, I.: Factors that influence the social dimension of alignment between business and IT objectives. MIS Q. **24**(1), 81–113 (2000)
25. Sabherwal, R., Chan, Y.E.: Alignment between business and IS strategies: a study of prospectors, analyzers, and defenders. Inf. Syst. Res. **12**(1), 11–33 (2001)
26. Sabherwal, R., King, W.: Towards a theory of strategic use of information resources. Inf. Manag. **20**, 191–212 (1991)
27. Schmidt, R., Möhring, M., Härting, R.C., Reichstein, C., Zimmermann, A., Luceri, S.: Benefits of enterprise architecture management – insights from european experts. In: Proceedings of Practice of Enterprise Modelling (PoEM), vol. 235, pp. 223–236 (2015)
28. Tan, F.B., Gallupe, R.B.: Aligning business and information systems thinking: a cognitive approach. IEEE Trans. Eng. Manage. **53**(2), 223–237 (2006)
29. The Global IT Trends Survey (2016). http://www.globaliim.com/
30. The Open Group Architecture Framework (TOGAF Version 9.1). http://www.opengroup.org/
31. Venkatraman, N., Henderson, J.C., Oldach, S.: Continuous strategic alignment: Exploiting information technology capabilities for competitive success. Eur. Manag. J. **11**(2), 139–149 (1993)
32. Wang, X., Zhou, X., Jiang, L.: A method of business and IT alignment based on enterprise architecture. In: Proceedings of IEEE International Conference on Service Operations, Logistics and Informatics, vol. 1, pp. 740–745 (2008)

Author Index